The Art of Designing Behaviour

T0293680

You are what you do.
Not what you say you'll do.
– Carl Jung

ASTRID GROENEWEGEN

THE ART OF
DESIGNING
BEHAVIOUR

Mastering a practical method
to influence decisions and
shape desired behaviours

Boom

Graphic design and cover: Douwe Hoendervanger

Illustrations: Demmy Onink

Editor: Joost den Haan & Rolandt Tweehuysen

ISBN 9789024451777

ISBN e-book 9789024451784

NUR 801

www.boommanagement.nl

www.suebehaviouraldesign.com/the-art-of-designing-behaviour

© 2022 Astrid Groenewegen & Boom uitgevers Amsterdam

CONTENTS

Step II Intervention

Step III Impact

Step IV Implement

How to turn ideas into a success
SUE | Behavioural Design Method©

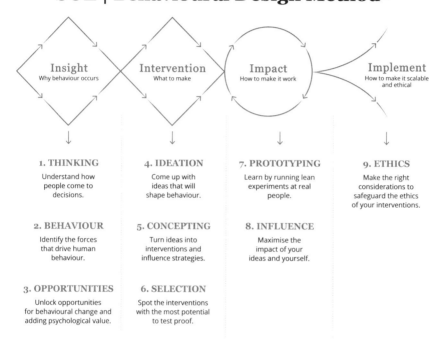

Insight
Why behaviour occurs

Intervention
What to make

Impact
How to make it work

Implement
How to make it scalable
and ethical

1. THINKING

Understand how
people come to
decisions.

4. IDEATION

Come up with
ideas that will
shape behaviour.

7. PROTOTYPING

Learn by running lean
experiments at real
people.

9. ETHICS

Make the right
considerations to
safeguard the ethics
of your interventions.

2. BEHAVIOUR

Identify the forces
that drive human
behaviour.

5. CONCEPTING

Turn ideas into
interventions and
influence strategies.

8. INFLUENCE

Maximise the
impact of your
ideas and yourself.

3. OPPORTUNITIES

Unlock opportunities
for behavioural change and
adding psychological value.

6. SELECTION

Spot the interventions
with the most potential
to test proof.

INTRODUCTION

Introduction

Let me guess. At this point, you have probably read the book blurb and have quickly flipped through the pages to scan whether this is a book worth buying and reading - which means I have only a few paragraphs left to convince you to do so. Let me cut to the chase then, as the selling pitch of this book boils down to one simple thing. We all want to experience success in our lives. It could be that you want to raise your children to become great human beings. Or it could be that you desire to get your business to expand. Or perhaps you will experience success when people embrace your ideas, plans or policies. Triumph to you might be if your company teams perform far above average. Victoriously transforming an organisation could also be your definition of success. Yet it may also be more personal. Perhaps you want to stick to some sporting activity or healthy eating habit. Perhaps it's even more 'philanthropic', and you would like to contribute to a better world.

The bottom line is that all of these things have to do with behaviour. Just think about it for a minute. If you want your children to be the best versions of themselves. They need to behave politely, do their homework, be explorers, show curiosity. If you want your business to thrive, then people will have to buy your products, recommend you, and come back for repeat sales. If you want your plans to happen, then you need someone to approve or back them up. If you're going to set up successful teams, you will need your talent to develop more innovative ideas or act more agile. If you want to bring organisational change to a successful end, you need people to stop resisting and start moving in the right direction. If you're going to live more healthily, you will need to start exercising and buy different food. If you want to make the world just a bit more beautiful, you need people to recycle, eat less meat and make donations.

The key to success is understanding how behaviour is shaped (or isn't)

I am not saying behavioural change is easy. In fact, it is very hard. There's no magical recipe to change people's opinions or behaviours overnight with one formula. We, as humans, are far too complex for that. But the fact is also that we have potentially far more influence on successful outcomes than we realise. The key is to grasp some basic (but fundamental) science on how our brain works. How we as people make decisions. How we are triggered to do things, or what the things are that hold us back. Suppose we start to understand how human psychology and human decision-making works. In that case, we can begin to understand what interventions we have to develop, or what techniques or mechanisms we can implement in order to influence behaviour successfully. With that, you gain a far stronger position to make both your personal and business goals a success. The powerful realisation is that behaviour can be designed, and this book will teach you a method to do so based on behavioural science. Or, as I like to call it: *the science of influence*.

The Missing Layer: Why even brilliant ideas fail

Although there isn't one clear-cut formula that applies to everyone, the science of influence provides a clear insight into how humans arrive at decisions, and how you can influence their minds to shape desired behaviours. The know-how is out there, but not many people have mastered it. When you think of it, this is crazy: we all spend so much time, energy, money, and shed sweat – and sometimes tears (and I hope not too much blood) as to our ideas, without very little know-how about human decision-making. This is crucial knowledge if you want to turn your ideas into a success. You need to know how you can make people choose for you. You need to understand how you can move people in the direction in which you want them to move. You need to know how to get people to start (or stop) doing things. Or to get yourself to do so.

The truth is, we all roll the dice and hope that things will turn out for the best. I don't mean this in a demeaning way. Most of us simply weren't taught how human decision-making works, or how behaviour is shaped. Behavioural economics wasn't part of our education, or integrated into our daily work practice. Some of us may have read or heard about the theory, but it got lost in the practical translation. And there we are: we all tend to put our expertise and experience into everything we do, but we haven't got the one crucial – though so essential! – part of the puzzle that will help us to make better decisions: *behavioural science*. This book adds a 'Missing Layer' to your existing expertise. It will provide you with an extra tool in your mental toolbox. It is all about giving you the method to uncover that hidden, irrational logic in human decision-making which is the key to moving people into the right direction. And it will show you the evidence-based principles from behavioural science to reinforce your ideas. This book is your guide to help you unlock the power of the science of influencing, which is crucial in getting more control over your successful outcomes.

It is all about influence

I know that some of you are immediately put off by the word *influence*. However, this is a book about influence. But think about it for a moment. Influence is not a bad word or verb. Or influencing behaviour isn't evil. Influencing is something that we as people are constantly doing. We are trying to shape people's behaviour all the time. If you have kids, you try to teach them socially accepted behaviours. If you want your manager to sign a budget, you are trying to influence his or her approval behaviour. If the government puts recycling containers in your street, then they are trying to influence your recycling behaviour. If you get flirty with that nice-looking person at the other side of the bar, you are trying to influence someone with a sweet *Barry White*-style love-making act. The way supermarkets position the products upon their shelves, is an attempt to influence your buying behaviour. When you give someone a gift or a compliment, you influence his or her 'liking behaviour'. Well, you get my point. Influence isn't a bad thing; it is a natural human condition. Every request we have, every cooperation or connection we seek, requires influencing someone's behaviour. Even if you want to invite a friend to a movie, or want friends to come over to your dinner party. Influencing behaviour is everywhere. We are just not that good at it. Or to put it better: we are not very well-equipped for it.

Although influencing behaviour is our daily mechanism to cope, learn, progress and connect in life, we have a blind spot for how influence works

'Why is not everybody using it right now, then?', I can almost hear you think. Well, there is more than one answer to that. First of all, more people and organisations are already using behavioural science on you, than you might realise. Therefore, it is intriguing and relevant to know more about Behavioural Design, as we are all continuously surrounded and influenced by it. Most of the time, we don't realise it. We all tend to think that we make our own decisions based on our own free will every day. However, most of our behaviour is thoughtfully triggered, and our choices are carefully designed.

Do you check your phone or email when you see the red notification light up? Do you go for the mid-priced wine on a restaurant menu? Do you follow the route in an Ikea store? Eat a whole bag of potato chips, instead of having just a few crisps? Buy something while you didn't have the budget for it? The way you buy, vote, walk, eat, work, interact, shop, react, look, is often discreetly designed and carefully crafted, using the science of influence. You might think you are calling the shots, but you usually have less control over your own decisions and behaviour than you assume. In this book, I will give you examples, so you'll see it happening in the future, and so that you'll come prepared then. Therefore, knowing more about behavioural science will be a very important eye-opener. Next to that, many people are fascinated by behavioural psychology. Many are reading about it, but few have adopted it in practice. This is your chance to become a frontrunner in this field and outsmart the competition, whether that is your competitor, boss, colleague (or your significant 'other half').

Behavioural science made practical

However, a lot of the knowledge from behavioural science is quite theoretical, and is arrived at in academic research settings. That doesn't make it very easy to apply for us 'hands-on mortals'. We have a strategic innovation company called SUE | Behavioural Design, which specialises in using behavioural science to influence minds and shape desired behaviours. It took its name from the Johnny Cash-song *A boy named SUE*.[1] We started out as a creative agency; however, we noticed that the most exciting progress wasn't in creative industry but in behavioural science. We also noticed that in Silicon Valley, the winning companies were those that took humans and their behaviour as a starting point. At that

time, there were a lot of fascinating insights about human behaviour and decision-making, but they felt like pieces of a puzzle that didn't fall into place. There
was no easy method to apply them in practice, yet this was what we desperately
needed. We, as SUE, had clients looking for ways to develop next-generation,
people-centred products, services, campaigns, or policies that people would
embrace. We needed a way to leverage all the exciting know-how on human
behaviour and the psychology of decision-making in practice.

We've studied the academic books and articles that gave us the latest insights
into human psychology and behavioural science over the last few years. We've
read hundreds of research papers, submerged ourselves in psychological experiments, visited conferences and talked to experts – all this with one goal:
to make that powerful know-how actionable, helping our clients solve complex
challenges with tangible results. That's why (and how) we developed our *SUE |
Behavioural Design Method©*. It is built upon the groundbreaking insights from behavioural science that are most frequently replicated and acknowledged. These
insights have been translated into a method with three easy-to-apply steps. The
word *method* is essential. It's not magic; it's not alchemy, it's a structured process revealing how people (often unawarely) arrive at decisions, and turn this
deep human understanding into validated ideas that will trigger behaviour. It's
a method that you can master. This book will take you through all these steps of
the Behavioural Design Method· and will help you to apply the method yourself.

Principles of persuasion alone won't do the trick, aka 'what this book is not'

Before you decide to read on, you need to understand what this book is not.
There is a common misunderstanding that Behavioural Design is about applying a set of persuasion principles.[2] You probably know the principles from
hotel-booking websites, such as *social proof* ('this room was already booked 235
times, and had an 8.7 rating') and *scarcity* ('only three bedrooms left'). These are
powerful principles, but sometimes they are mere 'tricks' up a designer's sleeve
in order to boost sales. If you want to be successful, you need to realise that just
adding some principles won't do the trick of turning your ideas into a success.
You first need to know *why* people do things, and why they don't. Successful

influence begins with a deep understanding of the human decision-making that shapes behaviours.

Every behaviour starts with a decision. People must make the decision to start or to stop doing things

Just let me give you an example. I am a Berlin lover. And I regularly go there (as a matter of fact, I am writing these words in Berlin as we speak). I flew in here. But I must admit that, from an ecological perspective, I feel rather guilty about taking the plane. There is a train going from Amsterdam to Berlin – the ICE. You can throw social proof, scarcity and authority at me. Telling me that it runs 90% on time, transports 2,000 happy passengers a day, including many business travellers who give it a 9.7 rating. But I just won't get onto that train. As long as you don't dispel my irrational beliefs that the train will be crowded with noisy travellers, the Wi-Fi will suck, and that I won't have a decent place to work during the seven hours of having to sit on that train. Every idea or intervention will simply bounce off me. To get me on the ICE, you need to understand my (irrational) decision-making, and understand which forces hold me back from or move me onto the train. And then you can start coming up with ideas. So, if we are talking about Behavioural Design, we are talking about understanding what people genuinely need, and what is going to help them to progress in life. For this, you need to have three elements:

1. Insight into the psychology of human decision-making
2. Understanding the forces that shape people's behaviour
3. The ability to turn deep human understanding into the ideas and strategies that can shape the desired behaviours

The SUE | Behavioural Design Method

The question remains: How does one do this? How do you influence decisions and shape desired behaviours? Scientific knowledge can be overwhelming, and difficult to translate into daily life. It often lacks all creativity, making it hard to fit it in with your brand or personality. The good news is: you are holding the answer. This isn't just a book; it's a masterclass with an extensive toolbox. It's a 'very hands-on', practical guide that will help you to start using Behavioural Design right away – to develop strategies and ideas that are going to change your behaviour. It will help you to *power up* your existing ideas with the science of influence step-by-step, from start to finish. In order to make this book work for you, it isn't packed with fancy, complicated theories or eloquent wording. It consists of short, easy to read chapters, with examples, tools and tips for you to skip through, and to use as a quick reference. You don't need to have a sales, marketing or advertising background. You don't need any technological skills. You'll be just okay if you want to learn how to influence people positively, and if you are a curious, forward thinker. This book will show you how to apply behavioural science systematically and pragmatically. You'll learn the SUE | Behavioural Design Method that will help you to influence minds and shape behaviour predictably. So, Lady Luck can take a break. Or at least you don't need to depend too much on her anymore – though she's always welcome to the party, of course.

The beauty of it is: the SUE | Behavioural Design Method works! It is not just a concept I manufactured for this book. At our Behavioural Design-consultancy,[3] we have been applying this method for over ten years now, in order to help national and international organisations to improve their design choices, and to aid them in shaping positive behaviours. The Behavioural Design Method has allowed us to develop validated solutions for financial institutions, NGOs, start-ups, FMCGs, healthcare organisations, public governments, service providers, retailers, hotels, and leadership teams. The method has been applied to a wide range of challenges. To give you some examples: We have helped youngsters to get out of debt and banks like ABN Amro and ING to make sure that people take steps now to secure financial safety for the future. People drive more safely by not using their phones in traffic. People with diabetes use the new medical technology of Medtronic to help them live a more carefree life. Mortgage owners are aided to avoid future financial problems. UNHCR to gain more support and donations for refugees. We have helped a Dutch political party design as to voting behaviour, in order to fight the rise of the extreme right. And have aided nurses in developing their ambitions within their present workplace. We have helped to build strong company cultures that attract talent and retain it. And co-workers to accept organisational change. We have assisted organisations, such as eBay, Roche and Orange, to transform their teams in order to

THE ART OF DESIGNING BEHAVIOUR

become genuinely human-centred, and helped them to embrace the habits of high-performance teams. We have helped SportCity to aid people in creating a lasting exercise regime. Dutch municipalities to boost the recycling behaviour of citizens, and Heineken to design for sustainability by developing behaviours that result in zero plastic waste at festivals. Besides assisting multi-disciplinary teams to become more creative, and organisations to create future proof positioning and propositions – to name but a few things.

We have taught exactly the same Behavioural Design Method to over 1,500 people from more than 45 countries by way of our *SUE | Behavioural Design Academy* – an officially accredited educational institution. In short, what you'll read and learn in this book has been test-proofed in practice on real cases. Our work has helped us to test, validate and optimise the Behavioural Design Method in real-life situations. You might ask yourself: 'What kind of people use the SUE | Behavioural Design Method?' So far, we have worked with leadership teams, politicians, business owners, marketeers, policymakers, innovation managers, UX-designers, architects, hotel owners, HR consultants, physical fitness-trainers, health care-professionals, CMOs, researchers, copywriters, fundraisers, finance experts, innovators, product owners, strategic planners, CEOs, and many more. So, your motivation to pick up this book could be to learn what your competitors may already be using, or in order to stay ahead in the game. But to put it simply: if you want to know more about human decision-making, and learn the skills to influence minds and change behaviour positively, you're holding the right book.

This isn't so much a book, as a masterclass and a toolbox

This book comes with downloads and videos to further boost your ability to apply behavioural science. It comes with easy-to-use tools, cheat sheets, and my guidance. To give you hands-on directions and instructions in order to apply what you've learnt right away. This isn't so much a book – as a masterclass and toolbox that will help you to start practising Behavioural Design. Therefore, by purchasing this book you are actually not buying just a book but a genuine learning experience. That will give you a 24/7-online access to an exclusive website, where you can find downloads and videos which you may use at will.

18

From a Behavioural Design perspective, this was not just a cute gimmick or add-on to this book – it has been essential. In psychology, there's a well-known phenomenon called the *use-it-or-lose-it* principle. One thing that happens in all of our brains is called *pruning*.[4] Our brain clears out the grey matter we do not use, which simply gets eliminated. That sounds scary, but it is hopeful. Whereas we used to think that we all face the decline of our cognitive ability as we age, that is in fact not always the case.[5] If you keep using your brain, it can stay in good health for a long time. And learning new things makes for a perfect brain training. However, if you want the learnings from this book to stick, you must keep using them in order to avoid getting pruned. But that is again great news from a Behavioural Design-perspective: If you do things repeatedly, it turns them into habit through automatic behaviour, in other words: by using the tools and templates from this book, you not only keep your brain healthy, but you will also turn using this newly acquired know-how into a habit – helping you to apply Behavioural Design effortlessly. So, how's that for a pitch in order to use the downloads and tools in this book?

I therefore sincerely hope that this book will become your guide to the fascinating world of applied behavioural science. Earmark your pages, highlight your sentences, scribble your findings on the side-lines, and instead of reading it from beginning to end, occasionally skip ahead or come back to read some parts again. I hope you will put in 'sticky notes' to add your cases and learnings. Making it not just another book on your bookshelf, but your own *Behavioural Design-playbook* that will be your trusted companion in designing for behavioural change. So, there you go. If you're looking to gain more control as to successful outcomes by unlocking the power of Behavioural Design in practice, this book and everything that comes with it is a definite 'keeper'.

Astrid Groenewegen

PS.: Did I use Behavioural Design on you in this introduction? Yes, I most certainly did. I have connected with your job-to-be-done. I have highlighted pains, taken away anxieties, and used authority and other persuasive principles. Do you want to know what all this means and how it works? Please, read on, and you'll find out soon enough.

FOUNDATION

Introduction

How come parents in serious debt still buy expensive toys for their kids? Why do even the most highly motivated people drop out of exercise routines? How come organ donation compliance is 99% in some countries, and in others only 4%? How come patients are more inclined to honour doctor's visits if the doctor's assistant does not write down their appointments? Why doesn't giving your talent a raise in salary make them more loyal? Why do people with far too high mortgages still book expensive holidays? Why do people with higher social security numbers make higher bids at auctions than people with lower social security numbers? How come sales volumes often go up instead of down when products are actually made more expensive instead of cheaper?

These were all questions that I couldn't answer, until I came across behavioural science and it all started to make sense. The science of influence, behavioural economics, or behavioural psychology, is the study of how people make decisions that lead to various behaviours. Unravelling the subconscious mind has proven essential in trying to understand behaviour. Behaviour change isn't a one-dimensional game, and doesn't happen overnight. The human mind is fickle; however, it does follow specific rules. This book aims to help you unravel human decision-making in order to make better decisions and design more positive behaviours. By the end of this chapter, you will understand how people make decisions, and how you can influence those decisions. It will provide you with some essential background information, the science essentials that are going to make you well-grounded in the world of this innovative know-how. All answers to the questions mentioned above will become apparent to you throughout this book.

The first ingredient of successful Behavioural Design may hurt a bit. If you want to design behaviour, it isn't about you or your product, brand or plan. Well, at least not in the first place. It's also all about the people you are trying to influence. Most of the time, marketeers, business owners, executives or policymakers are thinking inside-out – they look at their brand, product, service or policy, and wonder how they might convince people to embrace it. They come up with brand positioning, unique selling points and (product) benefits. In this book I would like to propose the opposite approach: outside-in thinking. Outside-in thinking takes the humans behind the customer, citizen, employee as a starting point, and tries to gain a deep understanding of their goals, needs, barriers and hopes. These are often not logical but psychological.

The secret of designing behaviour: Thinking outside-in

Therefore, the starting point of outside-in thinking is the psychology of your target group. Based on their decision-making and the subconscious forces that keep them within a behaviour, or might move them to a new behaviour, you can shape the strategy of your brand, product, service, business, or policy. And not the other way round. Yes, of course, your brand does comes in too. You can flavour these behavioural insights with a distinctive brand personality or organisation culture, but you don't take this as a starting point.

If you want to move people into the direction you need them to move in, you first have to understand what it is that moves people

This makes perfect sense with the latest insights on how behaviour is formed. The classical models, as have been (or perhaps still are) taught primarily in marketing and communication sciences, were built on the assumption that if you give someone information or knowledge (cognition), he or she will adapt his attitude (feelings or affection). And that will drive behaviour (action). The models explain this as taking sequential and linear steps. And one of the most well-known models that you've perhaps been taught is the AIDA-model (attention, interest, desire, action).[6]

The thing is that the latest research in psychology and social sciences on how behaviour works, completely opposes this thinking. Multiple studies have shown that attitude can follow behaviour. This has to do with a powerful psychological phenomenon from which we all, I wouldn't say 'suffer from', but which operates in all of our brains. It is called *the commitment or consistency principle.*[7] This refers to our psychological need to be consistent with our prior/former actions or statements. For example, suppose I can trigger you into separating your waste. In that case, you will regard yourself as someone who contributes to sustainability, and you will start to see yourself as being (more) environmentally concerned. Our brain strongly dislikes it when things get messy; it causes us cognitive overload. An easy way to fix this is to be consistent with what we said or did previously. Robert Cialdini and his team have researched this psychological principle extensively, as published in his book *Influence*[8] – one of the ground-breaking works in behavioural science. The exciting notion from this is that:

You can change attitudes by changing behaviour first

To illustrate this: if I want you to separate your waste, I could start by giving you information on how this behaviour would contribute to a better living environment. I could give you accurate 'stats' on how much CO_2-emission this will save, and how your waste will be transformed into new products that also can be useful to you, and hoping this will change your attitude to recycling. However, I could also trigger you into separating your garbage by making this extremely easy for you. We know from research that if you have acted in a certain way – in this case by recycling – your mind adapts how you see yourself. If you separate your waste, you are likely to say 'yes' if someone asks you if you consider yourself 'environmentally involved'. Your attitude will match your behaviour. This is often a more effective strategy than the other way round.

I'll get back to this principle in the Intervention chapter, and look at how to use it in order to change behaviour. For now, it is important to realise that if you want people to embrace your plans and ideas (getting a positive attitude towards them), you don't need to start off by giving them information, and will have to win the battle for their attention within this era of information overload. You have an ace in your hands if you start by changing their behaviour. So, that's why it's so essential that your starting point is to understand human behaviour, and not your product or brand. A Behavioural Designer is brilliant at *back engineering*. If there is one thing I want you to remember from this paragraph, it is that.

Behavioural Design is all about thinking outside-in instead of inside-out

Behavioural Design: What is it?

Suppose you start using Behavioural Design, or start talking about it. In that case, I bet you'll come across the first question everyone asked me when I began to get interested in Behavioural Design. The ever returning and legitimate question is: What is Behavioural Design? First, Behavioural Design is not about design as a form. The design part often starts people off on the wrong foot. It opens a world of associations with aesthetics. Is it about creativity then? Is it about interior or exterior design? Is it about furniture? There are a lot of things that are designed. That nice chair you might be sitting on is designed. Also, the way this book has been laid out and the typeface that has been chosen is design. The building you're in right now (or perhaps the park you're sitting in) is design. The interface of your cell phone or computer is design. The way people are directed through a train station or airport is design too. The way a lobby of a hotel or an office is decorated is design. Or the way the customer service of a company answers your call or email is also design.

Behavioural Design is all about creating a context based on deep human understanding, that triggers people to make a decision or take action towards their goals

On a high level, Behavioural Design is about combining the way designers solve problems with the science of influence. It can be used to nudge people towards a desired behaviour, or help people to abandon an undesired behaviour – and thus aid them in shaping 'an autopilot routine' also known as a *habit*. Behavioural Design is where the world of creativity and science collide, creating a magical and potent mix. It's like a marriage of perfect partners you enviously observe. That's what Behavioural Design in fact is: an ideal match. On the one hand, you have this one partner with a crafty personality. Who brings creativity, innovation power, the ability to develop tangible solutions, as well as a creative problem solving from the world of design to the 'spousal table'. And the other partner is the nerdy one. the psychologist who was awarded a Nobel Prize in economics, and introduced the science of behavioural psychology during the dinner conversation. It's not a typical partner combo just yet – but, when it works, you will see that they'll make the most beautiful babies ever.

What a Behavioural Designer takes from the world of design is how designers look at problems in the world

Design thinking: A new approach to innovation and problem solving

That's where *design thinking* comes in. You may have heard of design thinking before. Design thinking comes from innovation and is a new approach, or process if you like, to solve problems taking the user as a focusing point. The method has been described as far back as 1969 by Nobel laureate Herbert Simon,[9] but it took a lift-off when the d.school of Stanford University[10] came up with a five-step approach to design thinking – which was given a boost by Tim Brown of IDEO,[11] and explained in his bestselling book *Change by Design*.[12] I will briefly describe their approach, as it is mainly used nowadays. Design thinking revolves around a deep interest in developing a profound human understanding of the people for whom you are designing these products or services. It helps you to question, and it enables you to resist acting upon (often wrong) assumptions. Design thinking is extremely useful in tackling unclear or complex problems by re-framing the question in human-centric ways. And design thinking is so successful because it focuses on the needs of the actual user – understanding culture and context through observation, and qualitative research by diagnosing the right problem.

Okay, that sounds nice and all. But why do we need this? In order to briefly phrase things, we all think in patterns. We all have ways in which we are used to doing something – our habits, what we get taught in school, by our parents, and in our business place. This is okay, as it can help us deal with everyday situations – we are able to rely on such thought patterns. There's one downside to this patterned thinking: It makes it very difficult for us humans to challenge our assumptions of common knowledge. Especially when one expects you to be a paid expert, it can be tough to start questioning your own experience. So, when we run into a problem that we haven't faced before or that requires a new innovative solution, we often get stuck or come up with the old answers that aren't always the best. This difference between repetitive patterned thinking and innovative thinking (also commonly referred to as 'out-of-the-box thinking' or 'outside-of-the-box thinking') is often illustrated by the truck example. Maybe you've already heard of it. And if not, here's the short version of the story.

Some years ago, a truck driver made a bad judgment and tried to pass under a low bridge that turned out to be too low for his truck. His truck got so firmly jammed under the bridge, that he couldn't manoeuvre the truck through it anymore, but also couldn't reverse his vehicle. Traffic came to a halt behind and in front of him, so there was a problem. The story goes that the fire department, other truck drivers, road assistance, and various experts came along to discuss how to tackle this problem. Everyone was debating whether it was a good idea to dismantle parts of the truck, or else to dismantle the bridge parts. Everyone came up with a solution that fitted into their respective expertise. This went on for some time. A boy walked by, looked at the truck and then suggested, 'Why not just let the air out of the tires?' which took all the specialists and experts by surprise, who had been debating for hours in trying to solve the problem. When they tested the solution, the truck was able to drive through quick enough. This story symbolises that the most obvious answers are often the hardest to come by, due to the thought patterns we all have within us. And it summarised what design thinking helps you to realise: that thinking about design enables you to change how you tackle problems. It encourages you to explore new alternatives, creating options that didn't exist before.

Another advantage of design thinking is that it spurs us to take an integrative approach to developing new strategies or ideas. Whereas in many ideation processes, the research department passes on insights to strategic planners who then hand over a briefing to the 'creatives'. Subsequently, the ideas are handed over to production. Design thinking regards understanding, exploring and development as the three overlapping 'cycles'.

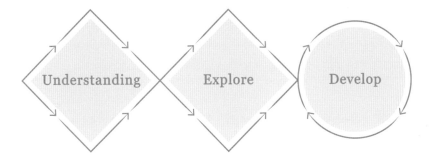

Design thinkers do not follow these three cycles in a strictly linear way. One might very well be able to pass through every cycle more than once. You might for instance have an idea, but after prototyping your idea vis-à-vis the actual users, you may learn that they do not understand it, or have not done what you hoped they would do. Then you will need to adapt your ideas. So, you go back to the drawing board. If you are willing to accept that strategy is nothing more than a hypothesis that you can quickly test. So that you are able to learn from it, upon which you can allow yourself to optimise it before your money or time runs out. Or as Alex Osterwalder[13] puts it:

'If you don't experiment and fail to learn – well, you're simply maximizing your risk to fail big'

I believe that the best strategy is developed through ideation and prototyping. Sometimes the feedback you get in prototyping gives you extra insight into the consumer's decision-making process. You have to make a perception switch, and come to a new understanding that will reshape your strategy. I like to call this 'a process of inclusion and being open to human psychology': so: *the concept of strategy development* instead of the more inside-out *concept of strategic planning*, which is a finished process after the strategy has been set.

The task of a design thinker is to bring all the phases together in one unified solution. Fascinating – I think – is that when you have the design thinker's mindset you will break through silos. Whereas the researchers, the creatives, and the strategic thinkers often work in different departments, you can now go through all of the cycles yourself, with your multidisciplinary team. This makes your work more exciting, and it ensures that many valuable insights are not lost when handing over things to the following stage. Design thinking is an integrative approach that adds value and fun – and it is a springboard towards innovative, visionary thinking which puts human beings first.

The SUE | Behavioural Design Method: Powering up design thinking

Okay, so now you know more about the design part. But what about the behaviour part? You've read the definition of Behavioural Design: creating a context based on a deep human understanding, which triggers people to come to a decision or take action towards their goals. When you combine the process of design thinking with behavioural science, you are creating a method to do so. You get to the 'how to'. So, this is where the SUE | Behavioural Design Method comes in.

Behavioural Design Thinking is the process of design thinking powered by behavioural science

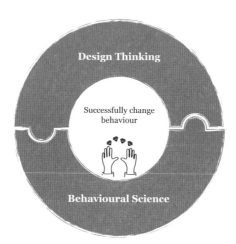

By placing behavioural science within the stage of understanding design thinking, you'll get much stronger insights that will help you to reveal the subconscious powers shaping behaviour. By adding behavioural science to the

explorative phase, you're not simply developing creative ideas but by ideas that will change behaviour. By applying behavioural science at the developing phase, you'll make your final concepts far more effective (mainly through becoming aware of your own psychological biases). In short, what we learn from design thinking is to put humans first within an integrative learning approach, but this we supercharge by adding behavioural science. Thus, we'll be designing behaviour in a very methodological, human-first way. And this is how the SUE | Behavioural Design Method came to be.

The SUE | Behavioural Design Method

So, what does the SUE | Behavioural Design Method look like? As you can see in the visual below, it is firmly based upon the three design-thinking steps, except that we have added a fourth step which is crucial for us. And we've renamed the steps in order to shift them away from the process labels to what these steps should deliver: Insight, Intervention and Impact.

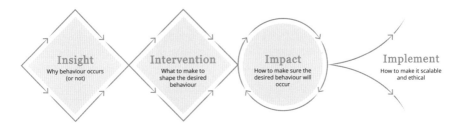

We've also added a fourth step, which is: Implement. Perhaps as a brief explanation of adding the fourth step, as this is not part of the design thinking process. We want to make sure that – whatever intervention we develop– it will have scale. You need scale to make a genuine impact. Furthermore, we aim to include Behavioural Design ethics, ensuring that our interventions are based on the proper ethical considerations. And the scalability and ethical considerations are safeguarded by the 'implement' step. Let's conclude this paragraph with a straightforward definition of the Behavioural Design Method:

The SUE | Behavioural Design Method is a structured creative process that positively influences minds, and shapes human behaviour on the basis of a deep human understanding

And what this methodological approach helps us is create what we call Behavioural Design. This brings us to the definition of Behavioural Design:

Behavioural Design is designing a context in which it is easier for people to make decisions or engage in behaviours that will help them improve their work, private life or living environment

A radically human-centred approach

We have used the process of design thinking as the basis of our method because this process in itself is radically human-centred. It starts with humans (empathy), and it ends with humans (prototyping and testing). When you are trying to influence behaviour, the word *human* isn't a detail. I don't know whether you work for an organisation with the mantra or mission of being (becoming) 'client-focused' or 'customer-centric'? Or alternatively, you may be sincerely committed to putting your clients first? This probably comes from a very noble intention. Still, if you want to become a star Behavioural Designer, I urge you to drop the client-and-customer-part and strive to be radically human-focused or human-centred. Yes, it's all semantics, but sometimes words can make a big difference. There are in this case two main reasons for embracing the human part. First of all, if you start with the customer or client (or target group) in mind, you automatically think about selling a product or service (or policy). Yet, this will limit your thinking. Or to put it bluntly:

Human-centred thinkers are looking for problems to solve; customer-centred thinkers are looking to find a better way of selling their solutions

And this is potentially a serious pitfall. The main reason is best described by Eric Ries in his book *The Lean Start-Up.*[14] He explains that most start-ups don't make it to the finish because they offer a solution in search of a problem, instead of finding a solution to an existing problem. However, a small sidestep: you perhaps have heard of the saying 'scratching your own itch', a mantra for start-up success in Silicon Valley – which means that many successful start-ups, products or services arise from their founders' pain or problem. Starting from a problem can be good advice, as long as you make sure that the pain you remedy is not only yours. Otherwise, you're building a business, product or plan just for yourself. Which literally can be risky businesswise. I want to make the point that we can get so enthusiastic about our products, services, policies or ideas, that we tend to ignore that they do not solve any actual human pain. We are not fulfilling any human need. Eric Ries calls this the *reality distortion field*.[15] What great Behavioural Designers can do is open up to exciting problems.

If you want to become a prime Behavioural Designer, you need to fall in love with the problem

This isn't a detail. I once attended a keynote of Julie Zhuo, VP Product Design of Facebook. She explained that at Facebook the difference between a great team and an average team is precisely this. The great teams fall in love with the problem. If a solution doesn't work, they are still fascinated by the problem, and keep on developing new solutions. The teams captivated by their solution are entirely at odds and demotivated when it fails.

The second reason to substitute 'customer' or 'client' for 'human', is that great Behavioural Designers are intrigued by humans. They aim to unravel the (often subconscious) forces that shape human behaviour. Customer-centred teams are constantly obsessed by 'personas' – those representative samples of their target groups. Okay, I have to admit that I am strongly negatively opinionated as to personas. I have sat in at so many sessions where I had to listen to those 'picture-perfect' people. Vera, a mother of two, works as a consultant. She loves to spend her spare time with her girlfriends drinking wine. She studies Chinese, finishes her part-time MBA, and enjoys travelling with her family. She volunteers at her kids' school to help underprivileged children with reading. She is currently training four times a week for the New York City marathon, as she loves to set herself challenges. She prepares a home-cooked meal every night, twice vegetarian – except for weekends when she orders pizza. She believes fresh food is vital to good health, and believes one should enjoy life. So, pizza and wine are not 'guilty pleasures', but simply pleasures. Her husband, David, whom she met at university, has his own successful company. Once a month, they have a 'date night' in order to spend time together; not everything revolves around the kids. And yes, she does bake *killer-themed* birthday cakes. You can see them on her blog. Does this sound familiar? Does it all ring a bell? Perhaps it reminds you of one of the 'personas' you have come across yourself? Apart from the fact that Vera is irritatingly perfect, it doesn't say much nor gives us any valuable information as to her behaviour. Yes, one could make an advertising campaign based on a persona, but it's no use if you want to design Vera's behaviour by adding human value.

As a Behavioural Designer, you have one aim: Getting to know the human being behind your customer

You always start out with people. You will want to become familiar with their world, emotions, and what drives them. A human-centred focus can help you to emerge yourself into the world of your target group. You will learn what types of lives people desire, and what they do on a daily basis – i.e. their experiences and feelings. You will learn to understand their struggles, fears, pains, hardships in reaching goals, their brave or failing attempts at making something of their lives, their struggle to get rid of their bad habits, and so on. You will not be interested in the big picture. You're interested in the particularities, quirky rituals, and the irrational behaviours. Not in perfection or normalities. You're looking for the things that are not on the surface, but tend to be harder to find – yet are essential in unravelling behaviour if you want to shape this. The better you learn to understand this, the easier it gets to look at your strategy or creative concept as a solution to a real human problem. You'll start to design products, services, policies or spaces, in order to improve people's lives. Therefore, I would like to urge you, should you intend to influence minds and shape behaviour, to forget about any traditional personas, but to start thinking in behavioural patterns instead.

To make the difference clearer between a persona and a behavioural pattern, let me take myself as an example. A persona description of me for, let's say, coffee would be: 'Woman, aged between 40 and 50, married with a child, university education, full-time working, higher income, is a foodie, loves to go out to dinner or cook for friends. She is busy all day; her coffee moments are at the beginning and end of the day. And these moments need to be good. She has invested in a fully automatic coffee machine that grinds coffee beans freshly. She starts with a good espresso in the morning to get her going, and finishes her dinner at night with a high-quality espresso. She believes she deserves good coffee; she can afford it and really appreciates a high-quality brand.' This would put me in the espresso category. But now look at my behavioural pattern: 'Woman, aged 40–50, married with a child, university education, full-time working, higher income, is a foodie, loves to go out to dinner or cook for friends. And is busy all day. In the morning, it is her rush hour; her primary task is to get her daughter to school, get her dressed, make her lunch box, sit down to breakfast with her. She needs caffeine to start off, but has no time for the hassle of it all. A quick coffee capsule in a machine does the trick (behaviour = getting a caffeine shot quickly). Then she must get to work; and on the way, she scores a latte at the local coffee shop in a take-away cup. So, she can sip her coffee and take care of her first business calls while walking (behaviour = drinking coffee while walking and getting things done). At the office, coffee is served at the central coffee machine and during meetings (behaviour = getting coffee is key to fuelling conversations). After work, it is busy again, but after fetching her daughter from school, cooking dinner, spending some quality family time, getting her teeth brushed, reading a bedtime story, her 'me time' arrives. She will again fix a high-quality espresso in the fully automatic coffee machine she bought, which grinds the coffee beans (behaviour = drinking coffee to wind down).' And perhaps you've noticed two things. Firstly, I cannot be categorised under a single coffee brand in the behavioural pattern. Secondly, if you look at my behaviour, you can spot the moments when I need coffee, but for different reasons. As a brand, you can tap into those deeper lying motivations, and spot the opportunities for shaping the coffee behaviours that I need and value – not just 'pushing' coffee, but catering to my underlying reasons for using coffee. This is just a coffee example, but you can imagine that if you're in the business of raising donations, triggering recycling, getting out of debts, and so on, looking at behaviour can give rise to far more valuable opportunities for being relevant and impactful.

While traditional personas represent one ideal fictional customer to target, behavioural patterns are based on what real people do, how they do it and why[16]

A fundamental concept of a behavioural pattern is that you attempt to capture the underlying motivations and irrational decision-making of the people you're trying to influence. 'Rather than the stereotypical assumptions that come with demographic facts such as age, gender, and occupation.'[17] This doesn't mean you cannot be in the business of commercial revenue. The whole point is to reveal new and unmet valuable opportunities using the focus of Behavioural Design. You will gain relevance if you come up with a solution to a genuine human problem. This is what gets people active, or why they are willing to pay you good money. Next to the commercial upside of this, there is another bonus. Taking on a human-centric approach is your free ticket to be unlimitedly curious, observe people, and ask people all kinds of questions as part of your job. That's what makes thinking about Behavioural Design such fun, and at the same time so rewarding. If you start by understanding the research tested on human decision-making and human behaviour, you can find the generalities in your differentiated target groups. And you can put strategies and ideas into place that make all kinds of people say 'yes – even Vera does this!'

We are all different, but in many ways, our brains react to and prompt to action in the same manner

Why should you care about Behavioural Design?

However, there is more good news. I don't know if you ever worry about the world we're living in. I know I do. The Climate change. The poor living conditions of refugees. Mall nutrition. Obesity. Pollution. Lack of education. Poverty. There are so many problems that I genuinely find heart-breaking or at least problematic. And I honestly want to contribute to helping to solve them but never used to know how. These problems are so big and overwhelming. How can you, as an individual, make a difference? But, what is so intensely fascinating about Behavioural Design is that you are able to create a change.

What Behavioural Designers do is take a big, complex problem, and bring it down to the level of behaviour

Let me give you an example. Think about a global concern that we as earthlings are all facing: the threat towards the earth's sustainability. There are many issues related to this: the 'plastic soup' in the oceans, the CO_2-emission, water scarcity, lack of energy resources, unstable food production, etcetera. The first thing a Behavioural Designer does, is look at the possible solutions already out there – let's pick CO_2-emission. Possible solutions to reduce the carbon footprint could limit air travel, the use of electronic means of transport, eating less meat and locally produced foods, supporting clean energy resources, etcetera. The next thing a Behavioural Designer does is, to look at these solutions from a behavioural perspective. For example, the solution of eating less meat involves human behaviour. For, someone has to stop eating meat, and start eating vegetarian at least occasionally.

A Behavioural Designer knows you can create this behaviour by making it concrete. For instance, triggering someone to eat or cook a vegetarian meal every Monday. This sounds trivial, but it's not. It's easy to understand behaviour. You could develop all kinds of ideas to make this desired behaviour do-able. In fact, a lively and worldwide movement arose from this: the *Meatless Monday*.[18] It provides people with recipes, cookbooks, meat substitutes in supermarkets, vegetarian product-promotions, ready-made meals, food- service programmes for schools and hospitals, and a lot more. Just imagine if everyone would stop eating meat on Monday. Plus, it can trigger trial behaviour in people who might have many prejudices against eating vegetarian food. This is a relatively small step for man, 'but it's a giant leap for mankind' – to quote Neil Armstrong offhand. This behavioural approach potentially significantly impacts a reduction of CO_2, as you bring the solution down to the individual's behaviour. And there are masses of individuals. Do you see how working with human behaviour can genuinely help one to find answers to 'wicked problems'? And how you can make a significant change using Behavioural Design. How cool is that then? Pretty cool. And essential too, if not lifesaving.

Everything is Behavioural Design

Now that you know all about the possible impact of Behavioural Design, you might also start feeling that there must be Behavioural Design challenges all over the place. And there indeed are. Almost everything is a Behavioural Design challenge.

You will recognise how Behavioural Design is used on you, and you will start to see a Behavioural Design challenge in almost everything

Your life will never be the same again – but in the best possible way. The fact that there are Behavioural Design challenges everywhere is a good thing. It means that you can also have a helpful say in almost anything. As a Behavioural Designer, your workfield can expand if you acquire this new know-how of Behavioural Design. You can cross the borders of industries, and be rightfully involved in exciting and rewarding projects. This book will give you a taste of the 'bandwidth' of Behavioural Design and its impact. Throughout the book, you'll find practical examples showing that everything is in fact Behavioural Design.

For instance: the route you take in an Ikea. The way you pick a wine on a menu. How your decision to vote for someone is shaped within your subconscious brain. The different impact words can have on your behaviour. How you spontaneously decide within five minutes whether you want to hire someone. How you navigate through a train station. Why it is so hard to keep up an exercise discipline (and why motivation is often a myth) – and so on. You'll read about examples of Behavioural Design that have turned out very well (and its working mechanisms could be an inspiration to you). But I'll also show you some examples of Behavioural Design that went terribly wrong (thus protecting you from the pitfalls others have stepped into), which might even be more valuable to discover. And throughout the book, I've included our experiences from our behaviour-change consultancy practice. We do not just teach Behavioural Design, but we also apply it. And it's mainly the cross-over between the two that brings this usability to the theory.

The final brick in the foundation: the scientific backbone of this book

Before we're ready to dive into the Behavioural Design Method, there's just one more thing I need to do. And that's to add some credibility. It is very valid to question how we know so much about human behaviour. And why is Behavioural Design popping up more massively at present, and didn't do so years ago? In fact, the science of influence and human behaviour has already been studied for decades. The short answer consists of two words: Silicon Valley. The business model of Silicon Valley is to get you hooked to interfaces: To the interface of your phone, the interface of your desktop or laptop. The more time you spend on the interface, the more money comes in. This fascinating article published in *Techcrunch*[19] a few years back summarises it all. It states that the interface is the battle for the customer. A lot of money is involved in it. When you take a closer look at the new billion-dollar companies, like Facebook, Airbnb, Uber, and Alibaba, there's something fascinating going on. According to Tom Goodwin, author of the article, these companies have one thing in common. These firms are just thin interface layers – on top of supply (where the costs are) and demand (where the people are). Airbnb, the world's largest accommodation provider, doesn't have any hotel rooms. Facebook, the world's largest media company, creates no content. Uber, the world's biggest taxi company, doesn't own any cars. Alibaba, the world's greatest retailer, doesn't hold any stock. They own the interface. Their business model is getting people hooked to it, and then providing the supply, content and services. So, the only relevant business question to those new-generation companies is: how do we get people onto our interface, and how do we get them to stay there? And how does one exploit it all, once they are there?

That's where Behavioural Design comes in (and sometimes even evil Behavioural Design). On the one hand, the Internet and Internet-based companies have provided us with ease, entertainment and have opened up our world. But it has also created mobile-phone addiction, unwanted social behaviour, and micro-interruptions that attack our focus constantly. There's been a lot of funding in recent years from that high-tech part of the world, in order to support research in behavioural psychology. Renowned educational institutions and universities – like Stanford, Harvard Business School, Princeton and Berkeley – have done ground-breaking research on human behaviour. And this research is available to us all. Don't get me wrong – not all research is conducted to fill the investors' pockets. There's been a genuine interest in understanding more of human decision-making and human action, and how it can be used to nudge people to make better choices and engage in a more positive behaviour. This knowledge can be found in books like *Thinking Fast and Slow'* by Daniel Kahneman,[20] the first psychologist to win the Nobel Prize for economics. *Nudge* by Richard Thaler,[21] was the second Nobel Prize-winner. But also, the work of Cialdini, who published the books *Influence*[22] and *Presuasion*[23] has laid the basic foundations for what we now know about designing human behaviour. Dan Ariely has written fascinating works on human irrationality, such as *Predictably Irrational*[24] and *The Upside of Irrationality,*[25] to name a few. To summarise – there is a lot of knowledge out there: scientific and empirical knowledge as to human nature.

It's truly fascinating to read and study these books and concepts, but you don't have to. In the Behavioural Design Method, we've integrated the most important findings, and condensed them so as to make them easy for you to use in practice. There's a great quote from Millard Fuller: 'It is easier to act yourself into a new way of thinking, than it is to think yourself into a new way of acting.' Thus, after reading this book, you'll have mastered the Behavioural Design Method – and you can start acting yourself into this new way of thinking, and the rest will follow. So, without any further ado, let's move on to the Behavioural Design Method itself.

Recap Behavioural Design

What is Behavioural Design?	Behavioural Design is all about creating a context based on deep human understanding that triggers people to make a decision or take action towards their goals.
What is important to remember about Behavioural Design?	The key to becoming a great Behavioural Designer is to think outside in. Become genuinely human-centred instead of customer-centric.
How does Behavioural Design differ from design thinking?	Behavioural Design Thinking is the process of design thinking - which main characteristic is putting the human first - powered up with principles from behavioural science. It is design thinking on steriods.
Why is it so important to learn about Behavioural Design?	Behavioural Design is everywhere; we are influenced on a day-to-day basis ourselves. We can use this know-how to help people make better decisions and shape positive behaviours. It can help solve complex challenges by bringing a problem down to the level of behaviour.

SUE | BEHAVIOURAL DESIGN METHOD

Introduction

Perhaps it's interesting to know that, in developing the Behavioural Design Method, we were inspired by one of our heroes. You might have heard of him – but if not, you have most probably heard about his business partner: the billionaire Warren Buffett. I am talking about the 95-year-old Charlie Munger, who's been the business associate of Buffett from the early days on. We're such fans of Munger because he has a fascinating take on decision-making. He argues that most people in business, everyday life and in investing, approach problems through a single mental model. If you work in branding, everything looks like a branding problem; if you work in business consulting, everything sounds like a transformation problem. If you are an economist, everything looks like a marketing problem. One of his most famous quotes to illustrate this point is: 'To a man with a hammer, every problem looks like a nail.' Munger and Buffett pride themselves on locking themselves up most of the day, reading books. What they are looking for is elementary, worldly wisdom. They are obsessed with learning interesting 'mental models'.

Mental models are concepts from all kinds of sciences that offer the world elegant explanations. To quote Munger: 'What is elementary worldly wisdom? The first rule is that you can't know anything if you remember isolated facts, and try and bang them back. If the facts don't hang together on a latticework of theory, you don't have them in a usable form. You've got to have models in your head. And you've got to array your vicarious and direct experiences onto this latticework of models. You may have noticed students who try to remember and pound back what is remembered. Well, they fail in school and in life. You've got to hang experience on a latticework of models in your head.'[26] We had Munger's mental model-theory in mind when designing our Behavioural Design Method. It consists of some very powerful and easy to remember mental models for finding human insights and coming up with intelligent interventions for behaviour change. If you hang onto them, you'll have your latticework of solving a behavioural challenge. And so to nail your problems you won't only have a hammer in your toolbox.

A quick introduction to the SUE | Behavioural Design Method

The SUE | Behavioural Design Method is a four-step process. Step I is 'Insight': gaining a deep human understanding of how people make decisions. Why do they do the things they do? Or why won't they show specific behaviour, even if they know it's for their own good? What forces drive behaviour or inertia? How can you get to people's more profound levels of motivation? What exciting opportunities can we unlock from unique behavioural insights? I'll introduce you to the **SUE | Influence Framework**©, a very easy-to-use model that answers all these questions, and will help you to make choices on what opportunities to move ahead on. For, it's the heart of understanding and designing influence.

In step I 'Insight' you will learn the following:

1. THINKING: Understand how people arrive at decisions
2. BEHAVIOUR: Identify the forces that drive human behaviour
3. OPPORTUNITIES: Unlock opportunities for behaviour change

Step II of the method, 'Intervention', is all about turning behavioural insights into tangible strategies and ideas, that will have the power to influence choice or shape behaviour. These ideas are powered by principles from behavioural psychology, or sometimes completely spring from a persuasion principle. I will introduce you to the **SUE | SWAC Tool**©,[27] which we power up through the principles of influence, from amongst others professor Robert Cialdini.[28] In step two, you'll also learn some creative techniques in order to come up with as many solutions as possible – even if you're not a creative or have no creative background.

In step II, 'Intervention', you will learn the following:

4. IDEATION: Come up with ideas that will change behaviour
5. CONCEPTING: Turn ideas into interventions and influence strategies
6. SELECTION: Spot the interventions with the most potential to test proof

Step III of the method, 'Impact', is all about gathering feedback and learning. You'll be amazed at what you will find out in prototyping. Things you were convinced would be a killer feature, might be neglected. The actual words people use can be the key to convincing someone, and you will learn about small details that can make a massive impact upon the success you didn't see coming. If you have found a working solution or idea in prototyping, you still must get it to the right people, and you will have to convince people to go along with your plans. You can use behavioural psychology to do so with greater success. I will show you how to use Behavioural Design techniques in order to convince someone step-by-step of your idea. And to put a cherry on the top, I'll give you some pointers on how you can be more persuasive as a person.

In step III, 'Impact', you will learn the following:

7. PROTOTYPING: Learn by running lean experiments at real people
8. INFLUENCE: Maximise the impact of your ideas and yourself

Step IV, 'Implement', is the last step of the SUE | Behavioural Design Method. I will introduce you to the **SUE | 4C Influence Flow**©, an easy-to-use tool that helps you set up an influence strategy. Last but certainly not least, we will move into the final step of our method, which is all about Behavioural Design Ethics. The know-how of behavioural psychology can be a powerful tool in order to shape choices and behaviour. Therefore, in Behavioural Design, thinking about ethics and acting upon them is not just relevant – it is indispensable. Through this step, I will show you how you can integrate Behavioural Design ethics on an organisational, project- and personal level. It will shed light on how we incorporate ethics in our work. It will also provide you with practical tools to help you pinpoint the considerations you need to make in order to safeguard your Behavioural Design ethics.

In the 'Implement' step, you will learn the following:

9. ETHICS: Make the right considerations to safeguard the ethics of your interventions

Using the SUE | Behavioural Design Method

For every step of the SUE | Behavioural Design Method, I have developed an easy-to-use tool that will help you turn theory into practice right away:

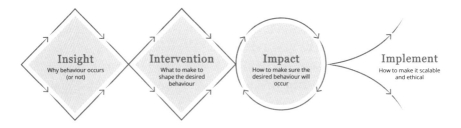

Insight: SUE | Influence Framework
Intervention: SUE | SWAC Tool
Impact: SUE | 4C Influence Flow

Don't worry if it may seem like a lot. In the following chapters, I will guide you through it. My job is to make things simple for you. So, we'll take it step by step, and I will give you the easy tools and templates as we go along. Trust the process.

The shape of the Behavioural Design Method matters. It's not a shape we've developed. It is known as the 'double diamond of design thinking'. The shape of the diamond indicates that you first come up with as many ideas (going wide) as you can, and, after that, come to a decision (narrowing down). So, in the Insight step, you first come up with as many insights as possible, and then narrow them down to a few opportunities (first diamond). In the Intervention step, you first come up with as many solutions as possible, and then narrow them down into a selection to test proof (double diamond). In the Impact step, you test proof the ideas, and go back to the drawing board if you still need to optimise them. You discover, define, develop, deliver[29] until you find a solution that triggers the desired behaviour (represented as an endless circle). If you have found an impactful solution, you make sure that it spreads in the implement step (illustrated as: take off into the open).

Which pains can the Behavioural Design Method help you to solve?

We didn't simply want to create just another method; we wanted it to solve *real* problems. We definitely scratched our own itches, when designing the Behavioural Design Method – but we also talked to our clients, friends, and family, in order to ensure the itch had spread beyond our offices. It helped us to identify several pains you might recognise:

- You have great ideas, but you cannot always convince people of them. It could take place at work, but also in your private life.
- You need to sell more, but you cannot always persuade people to buy more.
- You truly want to put your clients, users, or citizens first, but don't understand what they want, what they need, and how they see the world.
- You need your policy, product, business, or plan to be a success. But you want more certainty that it will lift off before you pour your heart and soul or money into them.
- You want, or even need, people to behave in a certain way, but don't know how to get them to act accordingly.
- You feel you've got little to no control over people's decisions. It could be your co-workers, your partner, your family, or even yourself. Sometimes you feel everything is 'driven by chance'.
- You need to put things in motion, but bump into people that would rather not move, and you don't know how to break this inertia without forcing someone.
- You have wasted time & money on an idea that people said they liked or would buy, but it didn't result in any actual behaviour contributing to your goals. The money wasn't put where the mouth was.
- You want to give people support in living a better life, but you don't know how to help people make better choices for themselves.
- You have or are working in a 'scrum team' now, but while the scum process is in place, the output hasn't changed yet. They are not yet creative, agile, or human-centred.
- You've started a personal goal more than once with a lot of motivation, but you still haven't managed to achieve them or make your resolutions stick, making them to a habit.

Luckily, we potentially have far more control over all these matters than we tend to realise right now. The secret ingredient is mastering a few essential parts of behavioural science and choice psychology, that explain how the brain works, how people make decisions, and why people behave the way we do. Once you understand which forces shape our behaviour, which deeper lying emotions drive our decisions, and how our choice psychology affects our actions, perceptions and feelings, you start to realise that you're no longer at the mercy of chance by grasping this essential knowledge, but that you can predictably design behaviour. The Behavioural Design Method is precisely developed to do this. It helps you not only to master, but foremost to systematically apply this essential know-how in order to help you regain a grip on the outcomes, and puts you in a far stronger position for turning your ideas into a success.

In the following chapters, I will take you through the Behavioural Design Method in a very structured way. Which is the way you should be applying it to practice also. Following each step after the other, and perhaps going into the same loop again if the testing phase gives you insights in order to optimise your strategies or ideas. By building, measuring, learning, you will find the working solution(s) that will influence the behaviour or choices you are pursuing. Then you can move into the final part of the method, making sure you have the impact you want to make as to your validated ideas. This is where you can sense the first smell of success. And oh, is that a pleasant, addictive smell! I realise that bringing a smell into your pitch to use the Behavioural Design Method, might not be the most convincing thing in the workplace. I have made an overview of the gains of using the Behavioural Design Method in a more 'persuading-your-boss-effectively'-way, and it may also provide you with the final arguments to start mastering and using the Behavioural Design Method yourself:

- It integrates research, strategy, ideation, and user testing, instead of having separate agencies working on this, or you having to run and manage multiple projects.
- It dramatically speeds up the solving of your challenge or innovation.
- This makes finding validated solutions much more efficient, and therefore lowers your costs.

- It makes sure no insights are lost when moving into a different phase. It helps to bridge the gap between research and strategy, strategy and ideation.
- It pinpoints precisely which real pain your product, service or plan can solve, so you'll know what to do in order to make it work.
- Before you start spending much budget on genuinely developing a product, service or idea, you can understand what will drive or withhold the behaviour of the people you're trying to influence.
- It forces you to think outside-in, giving you insight into how to add human value – instead of finding a (maybe non-existing) problem to your solution, and being cosmetically customer-centric.
- It helps you to form your opinion in a structured way. It exposes the why of your problem. Making it much easier to explain to your team/management what the job is that needs to be done.
- Your strategy or idea is no longer a hypothesis based on gut feeling or a hunch, but is formed upon factual user/consumer input.
- It helps you to get internal support or back-up, as you can counter arguments, not with your own opinions but with the views of the people you're trying to influence.
- It provides a framework and shared language for multidisciplinary teams in order to work more effectively together in becoming more human-centred.
- In short, it brings back a grip upon what to do and how to do it.

Recap Behavioural Design Method

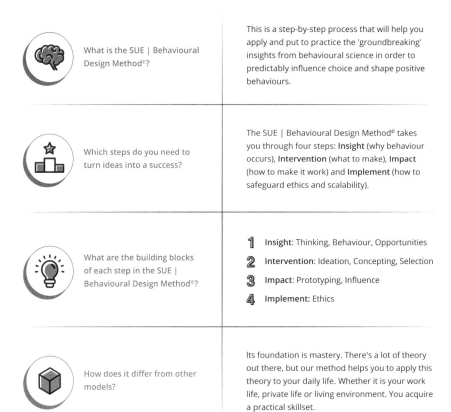

What is the SUE | Behavioural Design Method©?	This is a step-by-step process that will help you apply and put to practice the 'groundbreaking' insights from behavioural science in order to predictably influence choice and shape positive behaviours.
Which steps do you need to turn ideas into a success?	The SUE | Behavioural Design Method© takes you through four steps: **Insight** (why behaviour occurs), **Intervention** (what to make), **Impact** (how to make it work) and **Implement** (how to safeguard ethics and scalability).
What are the building blocks of each step in the SUE | Behavioural Design Method©?	**1** **Insight**: Thinking, Behaviour, Opportunities **2** **Intervention**: Ideation, Concepting, Selection **3** **Impact**: Prototyping, Influence **4** **Implement**: Ethics
How does it differ from other models?	Its foundation is mastery. There's a lot of theory out there, but our method helps you to apply this theory to your daily life. Whether it is your work life, private life or living environment. You acquire a practical skillset.

STEP I

INSIGHT

How to turn ideas into a success
SUE | Behavioural Design Method©

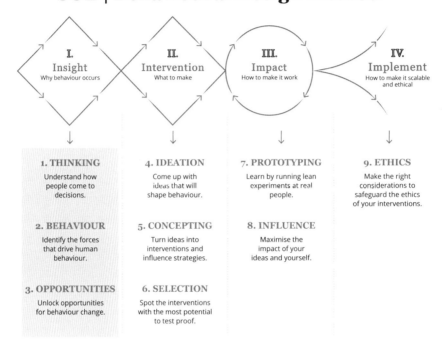

I.
Insight
Why behaviour occurs

II.
Intervention
What to make

III.
Impact
How to make it work

IV.
Implement
How to make it scalable
and ethical

1. THINKING

Understand how
people come to
decisions.

4. IDEATION

Come up with
ideas that will
shape behaviour.

7. PROTOTYPING

Learn by running lean
experiments at real
people.

9. ETHICS

Make the right
considerations to
safeguard the ethics
of your interventions.

2. BEHAVIOUR

Identify the forces
that drive human
behaviour.

5. CONCEPTING

Turn ideas into
interventions and
influence strategies.

8. INFLUENCE

Maximise the
impact of your
ideas and yourself.

3. OPPORTUNITIES

Unlock opportunities
for behaviour change.

6. SELECTION

Spot the interventions
with the most potential
to test proof.

BUILDING
BLOCK 1

THINKING

– Understanding how people think and arrive at decisions

Introduction

To give it to you straight away: if you know how people make decisions, you are able to shape their behaviour. Behaviour is all about decisions. Should I go left or right? Do I decide to buy this or not? Do I act kindly to this person because I've made up my mind that I like him? Do I choose to hire this person or not? Do I decide to eat more healthily, go to the gym, or recycle? Do I choose to vote for the right-wing or rather for the socialists? Do I decide to have my children vaccinated, give them a proper education, or is getting them to eat fresh food the right thing to do? Do I choose to be actively involved in my community or not? Do I decide whether protecting the environment and acting on the climate change are essential or aren't they? Do I choose to admit that I need help with my finances? Do I decide to invest time or money in this new idea or business? Decisions, decisions, decisions – it is estimated that we all must make more than 35,000 decisions per day.[30] Ranging from important decisions to minor ones. How on earth can we manage this?

That's where professor Daniel Kahneman, the Eugene Higgins Professor of Psychology Emeritus at Princeton University, and his long-time collaborator, the late mathematical psychologist Amos Tversky have provided us with profound scientific answers. They did groundbreaking work on human decision-making. They discovered we engage in fast and slow thinking, and revealed the importance of our subconscious mind in making decisions and performing a behaviour. Maybe you've already heard of system 1 and system 2. Or you've heard that Kahneman was the first psychologist to win the Nobel Prize for economics in 2002 (Tversky had already deceased at the time). It might be that you've heard about cognitive biases and heuristics. Enough to be intrigued. Kahneman is one of our heroes, and the godfather of behavioural economics. I'll show you the highlights of Kahneman's and Tversky's thinking that they published in their best-selling book *Thinking Fast and Slow*. It gives you a solid basis to understand human thinking and decision-making.

The two operating systems of our brain: system 1 and system 2

The revolutionary research of Kahneman and Tversky showed that our brain has two operating systems, which they called system 1 and system 2. These are the differences between the two systems of our brain:

• Emotional	• Rational
• Subconscious	• Conscious
• Fast	• Slow
• Automatic	• On-demand
96%	**4%**

Just look at the percentages for a moment. Our conscious brain only makes up 4% of all our thinking. This indicates that a staggering 96% of all our decisions are made completely subconsciously. Discovering not only the two operating systems of our brain, but especially the bandwidth of each system, was what made this research so significant. Some discussion has been raised about the exact percentages. Is it 96%? 98%? Did our rational thinking capacity become worse, now that we're distracted by multiple interfaces and notifications? Another authority in this field, Dr Gazzaniga, professor of psychology at the University of California, tells us in his book *Who's in charge? Free will and the science of the brain*[31] that it is, in fact, a staggering 98%. The truth is, 2% or 4% doesn't matter. Don't start nit-picking the numbers; it is a waste of your energy (unless you want to write a PhD thesis on this subject). We are interested in how we can use breakthrough scientific research in practice. When observing human decision-making in real-life situations, the most respected behavioural researchers and scientists have proven that our decision-making is overwhelmingly influenced by our system 1.

We are not 'lean-mean-rational-thinking-machines' that always make decisions in our best self-interest. You don't even have to be a researcher to know this. You probably have experienced it yourself sometime, or maybe even more than once. When you did or didn't do something merely to fit in with a group of people. Or when you decided to go for instant gratification instead of thinking about future consequences, to be more lazy than healthy, or to spend more money than you knew you should. Maybe that was not rational, perhaps it was not in your best interest either, but it was the choice you made at that given time. And that's okay. That is called 'being human'. And it is because of your system 1. So, if we want to understand how to influence choice and behaviour, what we have to learn from the research of Kahneman and Tversky is that it gave us a breakthrough insight into the power of the subconscious mind. And foremost the fact that:

Behavioural science has revealed the lack of reasoning in human decision-making

How your brain works is what your system 1 is primarily doing: rapidly sifting through information and ideas without you even noticing it. Prioritising whatever seems relevant – and filtering out the rest by taking shortcuts. These shortcuts are also called 'heuristics'. Our system 1 sends suggestions to our system 2. Which then turns them into beliefs. To summarise, you could say that our system 2 is a slave to our system 1.

I'll give you an everyday example that will bring this interaction between the two systems in our brain to life immediately. Think about the first time you met a random person. You instantly liked someone or not: the famous 'first impression'. And you might even feel you are quite a good judge of character, as your first impression often turns out to be correct. What happens in your brain is this. Within milliseconds, your system 1 has decided whether you like a person based on subconscious, automatic short-cuts, like that person's facial expression, the fact that they wear glasses, the colours of their clothes, their walk, their talk and so on. This all happens quickly and without you even being aware of it. What you do knowingly experience is that sensation of a first impression. That's the suggestion your system 1 has sent to your system 2. Your system 2 then actively looks for affirmations of this suggestion, which turns the suggestion into a belief. It becomes true in your mind as you then selectively process all the following information consistent with that first impression. Hence, this evokes your feeling that your first impressions are often so right.

As Kahneman put it: 'Very quickly you form an impression, and then you spend most of your time confirming it instead of collecting evidence. So, if accidentally your impression was in the wrong direction, you're going to confirm it. You don't give yourself a chance to correct it.'[32] I found the following quote of Caroline Webb[33] which I liked, and summed up why system 1- and system 2-thinking is so essential to grasp: 'The startling truth is that we don't experience the world as it is; we're always experiencing an edited, simplified version.' And to add to this, it implies that we don't see an objective version of the world or people: we get to see our version of the world or people. Your personal system 1 decides how you see and judge things. So, the truth isn't only edited and simplified; it is also diversified. Or as Kahneman showed us:

Our two thought systems can arrive at different results even when given the same inputs

I have read about this funny example of how the human brain can interpret information entirely differently, depending on the context. What happened? During the COVID-19 social distancing-restriction, a Hungarian member of parliament was arrested in Brussels when caught breaking lockdown rules at an illegal all-male gay party. Okay, this is not funny yet, I know. This is very irresponsible behaviour. The funny part was when the police entered the party; the partygoers thought these were part of the entertainment of the evening.

In this context, their system 1 picked up those men in uniform as cues for a YMCA-stripper act. It was reported that 30 male guests tried to unzip the police officers' pants, because they didn't realise (at first) that these were genuine officers.[34] It is undeniable that, if those same policemen had stopped the same partygoers during a weekday out on the street for speeding, they would not have shown the same inappropriate behaviour. That would have been another context in which their system 1 would have picked up different cues. Instead of unzipping pants, they would have shown their IDs. This is an exceptional example, but this system 1- and 2-thinking isn't a detail, as it can significantly impact everyday life. Let me build upon that relatively small example of the first impression. It does not seem to be a very big deal. Someone's job can depend on it. Research[35] has shown that, in hiring someone for a new position, roughly 5% of the decisions were made within the first minute of the interview, and nearly 30% within five minutes. The largest block, 52% of interviewers, decides about a candidate within between five and fifteen minutes of the interview. It could be that it's an interview that lasts for an hour, but it's the first five to fifteen minutes that count.

That's why the know-how you're now acquiring about human thinking is essential. If you know how the human brain works, you can be prepared for it. Or you can alter your misconceptions to make sure you take better decisions. This can make a significant difference as to the result or impact of things. Grasping the power of the subconscious mind is a key to human freedom. Or as George Lakoff puts it: 'Cognitive science has something of enormous importance to contribute to human freedom: the ability to learn what our unconscious conceptual systems are like, and how our unconscious cognitive functions. If we do not realise that most of our thought is unconscious and that we think metaphorically, we will indeed be slaves to the cognitive unconscious.'[36] In the case of the job interview, it is said that the best way to handle the interviewer's system 1 is to build rapport. Make sure you arrive early at an interview, and try to create a personal connection (in behavioural psychology, also indicated as activating *the liking principle*) before the interview starts to feed the interviewer's system 1 with positive cues. In the following chapters, I will return to the different techniques for influencing system 1 regarding the people you're trying to influence extensively. Still, you've already got a taste of it. My point is:

Don't underestimate the power of our automatic thinking (system 1)

Although at first sight, it may seem like the less bright sibling it's pretty well a genius. Kahneman has shown us that we as humans are in fact irrational beings. We all tend to think that we make rational decisions based on our experience and know-how, and that we base our behaviour on well-founded choices. However, Kahneman and Tversky showed that we don't. And perhaps this is a concept that is hard to grasp or accept at first. You might be thinking that your percentage balance is a bit different, and that your rationality percentage is reasonably higher. You might argue that you are pretty good at numbers, and are someone who has been depicted in a personality test as being a rational person. You can indeed make great use of your system 2. In fact, for any task you must perform that isn't a routine, you need your system 2 to do your work. It will actively connect to the information or situations in your experience similar to the task at hand, and it will use this to make informed decisions in order to proceed with that task. Let's do a quick experiment to help you to experience how your system 2 works. Think about solving this mathematics question: 'What is 347 – 34 × 67?' Most probably, the answer won't just pop into your head; you cannot depend on a routine to provide you with the answer right away. You have had previous experience in solving equations, and your system 2 will use this to come up with an answer, but it will be slow and it will take effort to come up with the answer. Whereas to the question: 'How much does 2 + 2 add up to?' the outcome 4 will spring to mind right away. That's your system 1. So indeed, you should make serious use of your system 2 in any unfamiliar situation.

Your system 2 you use for something else that's very important: For, your system 2 is also all about your self-control. It regulates your emotions. Emotions are often described as irresistible forces that directly influence behaviour. If we all didn't have a system 2 working for us, we would be blurting out everything we think – and well, let's face it: as grown-up adults, we are all expected to manage our emotions, especially the negative ones like anger, frustration, anxiety or jealousy – in order to make sure these negative thoughts and feelings don't propel our behaviour. And you have a lot to thank your system 2 for, as emotional regulation has also been linked to mental health,[37] psychical health,[38] work performance[39] and relationship satisfaction.[40] However, as said:

The capacity of our deliberate thinking (system 2) is limited

In behavioural science, this is referred to as *bounded rationality*: our rational thinking is bounded as there are limits to our thinking capacity, to the available information and to time.[41] There's something about performing tasks and evaluating information the way your system 2 does. Especially the last years, now that we're in the era of constant connection to everyone and everything, there has been a lot of research on the number of tasks we can perform simultaneously. Whereas we used to think our brain could hold up to seven bits of information at once, research has shown that we are terrible at multitasking[42] – we can't do it if the task requires cognitive effort, i.e. system 2. You can only perform multiple tasks simultaneously if they are routine tasks: system 1. That's why experienced musicians can sing and play the piano simultaneously. This means that our system 2 is continuously switching mode.

We switch from one piece of information to another, from one task to another. And that's pretty tiring on our brain – with the effect that the levels of our motivation, our self-control and rational reasoning drop as we use more of our system 2-cognitive thinking. Research has even shown that, by the end of the day, we tend to lose self-control and motivation more quickly when our cognitive abilities have been used up. Let me illustrate this with a situation you might have found yourself in once or twice. You might be determined to make a day into an 'healthy eating day'. You start right with your freshly blended breakfast smoothie, you hang around there at lunch and eat some vegetable soup or a super green salad with the right kind of protein, while in between you snack on just a handful of nuts or a piece of fruit. But then in the late afternoon, after you've finished a hard day's work, you are also much more likely to convince yourself that you've deserved to have some crisps instead of cucumbers. That's your system 2 being exhausted. So, now you know you are not a spineless human being without self-discipline. You are a normal human being with a human brain.

So yes, to make a long story short: you most definitely can be a system 2-thinker, but your ability to do so is limited. And that's a good thing: it's our survival mechanism. Do you remember when I told you that, on average, we have about 35,000 decisions to make each day? These differ in difficulty and importance. It could be you taking a step to your left or right when talking, or when deciding whether to take the stairs or elevator. But they all hit you on a daily basis. If you had to process all of these decisions consciously, your brain would simply crash.

Your automatic system's primary task is to protect your deliberate system 2

It helps you prevent cognitive overload and enables you to make room in your system 2 for the cognitive thinking you need to do. There are a few ways that our automatic system lightens the load upon our deliberate system. First, it takes care of our more familiar tasks by turning them into autopilot routines, also known as *habits*. But what your system 1 is primarily doing without you noticing is to sift rapidly through the information and ideas. And it prioritises whatever seems relevant and filters out the rest by taking shortcuts. These shortcuts are also called *heuristics*. It's like the triage-system in a hospital emergency room. It is constantly assessing whether information needs a focused system 2-thinking or can be handled by the proven routines of system 1.

Therefore, how our brain operates and handles all the information fired at us is pretty brilliant. So, maybe we shouldn't describe ourselves as irrational. This kind of sounds as if we don't have minds that work, and that we are acting in entirely arbitrary ways. One of the authors of the book Nudge, Cass Sunstein, prefers to call us 'imperfect' instead of 'irrational'.[43] And I catch his drift. The *dual-processing system* in our brains is all about us making (subconscious) mental mistakes, based on system 1 short-cuts and on biases that we can't help making. We focus on today rather than on the long-term, so we don't take action now. We are often overly optimistic in our economic and health situations, so we don't take proper precautions. We find it hard to assess risks, especially when they involve something technical or unfamiliar, so we rely on short-cuts. Behavioural Design is all about understanding how humans behave, by grasping the imperfections in our decision-making, and then figuring out how policies, laws, ideas, and businesses can adapt to that.

See whether you prefer irrationality over imperfection, or the other way round *'tomatos tomatoes, potatoes potatos'*. The most important thing to remember is that you know that the decision-making of humans, these directly desired (and undesired) behaviours, are operated by our automatic (system 1) and the reflective (system 2) thinking processes. And system 1 makes up for most of the bandwidth in your brain. Therefore, you need to grasp the system 1 mental shortcuts and biases that might influence someone's behaviour, or that need to be considered when designing behavioural interventions.

We are only human: Why you should focus on humans and not on econs

And with that, we arrive at Kahneman's last important insight. If you realise that we are all imperfect beings, it becomes clear that we must challenge an existing paradigm about human decision-making. Kahneman makes a clear distinction between econs and humans. Econs are the type of people you find in economics, marketing, and business books. They are smart, make well-informed decisions, do cost-benefit analyses in order to choose what's best for them, make utilitarian decisions, and are thoroughly through-thinking rational decision-makers. And as you might have guessed by now, Kahneman teaches us that these people don't exist. They only live in a world of economic books. In real life, we must deal with humans. Who are biased, impulsive, lazy (we just have to – as we've learnt we can't be actively making every decision ourselves), social animals – and belonging to a group or getting approval of others is critical to us. That's why we sometimes don't make the decisions that aren't objectively the most beneficial for ourselves, but those that help us fit in; we're irrational.

This notion has led to some spicy arguments between economists and psychologists. Who is right here? To prove the point of us being human, and to pull 'long noses' at economists, an experiment was set up by psychologists known as *the ultimatum game*.[44] There have been several varieties of this experiment, but I'd like to briefly tell you about the general set-up, as I think it shows how we humans think and act straightforwardly. Okay, the 'ultimatum game' goes like this. Two people are ushered into a room. One of them receives $100. Then the rules of the game are explained. The one with the dollars has to offer the other player some money; how much is up to them. There's just one crucial second rule: the other person has to accept the deal. If the offer is rejected, both of them will have to walk out of the room with nothing. So, any deal offered to the second person would be a good deal from an economic point of view – right? You come in with nothing, and walk out with some money. That's rational economic reasoning. The truth is that humans don't think that way. If a person was, for instance, offered $10, the second person's human side would kick in: 'You just received a $100, and now you only give me $10? You greedy bastard – you're not getting anything either, for I reject that deal. It went up to $35 before the second person accepted the money offered. To sum things up, you could say that traditional economic theory is based on the concept that people act in their own best interests. Whereas behavioural economics has made a case that:

Human beings do not make rational choices, are greatly influenced by the social norms within their environment, and suffer from biases

As Kahneman himself explained it: 'What gets in the way of clear thinking are those ready-made answers, but we can't help but have them. Emotions get in the way. I would say that independent clear thinking is, for first approximation, impossible, in the sense that we believe in things most of the time, not because we have good reasons to believe them. If you ask me for reasons, I'll always find a reason, but the reasons are not the causes of our beliefs. We have beliefs because mostly we believe in some people, and we trust them, and we adopt their beliefs.'[45] What we've experienced with our clients. and at our SUE | Behavioural Design Academy, is that somehow – after hearing about all this – we can accept our irrationality and the fact that we're human, or at least we can understand it when it is explained to us. But in practice, we keep making the mistake of forgetting that the people we're trying to influence are irrational too. We still so often try to convince somebody with arguments or facts. We love to tell someone about the benefits of our products or services, or ideas. Treating them as econs. This is a recipe for failure, or as we prefer to call it: a design for disappointment. And we're here in order to be more successful, right?

We must accept that our system 2 is a slave to our system 1. And system 1 simply doesn't like facts, arguments or complex information. 'If the facts don't fit one's worldview, one of several things can happen: The fact may be changed to fit your worldview. The fact may be ignored. The fact may be rejected, and possibly ridiculed. Or the facts, if threatening to your worldview, may be attacked.'[46] You may not be in politics, but current politics do influence you. You probably feel right now that this whole concept of grasping this system 1- and 2-thinking might have far more impact than you could imagine. It's vital to grasp it, in order to build your own personal and business success, but it's also crucial to understanding the current events on a global scale that shape the world you live in, – and in which you want yourself, your family or your business to thrive. Why do populists and conservatives rise to power? Because they don't use facts. They use system 1-cues. Fake news? People don't care, or often even can't help themselves ignoring it. Their decision-making brain simply is not receptive to the facts; it's looking for the connection to their values. 'People do not necessarily vote in their self-interest. They vote their identity. They vote their values. They vote for who they identify with.'[47] The things that count are the meanings in people's minds. I think George Lakoff sums it up very nicely: 'What is meaningful are not the words, the mere sound sequences spoken or letter sequences [on a page], but the conceptual content that the words evoke. Meanings are thus in people's minds, not in the words [on the page].'[48] For example, when a Trump supporter sees Donald Trump, he sees a man who hates the liberal elite as much as he himself does. They can identify with this emotion, and therefore identify with Trump.

You now understand that the decision of the person you're trying to convince isn't based on rational information. It's based on their system 1-shortcuts. What is most important to remember as to all this, is that we, human beings, are almost entirely irrational. If you want to influence behaviour, you have to accept this, but you also must design for the mental mistakes which we humans all make.

Make it as easy as possible for someone to perform behaviour without having to think. That's the secret to success

The key is to design a choice in such a way that system 1 can easily bite. If someone's system 1 is convinced of something, then their system 2 will use arguments to confirm their initial action. It will post-rationalise. That's why it can be so important to make sure that someone experiences a system 1-emotion very soon when confronted with your policy, product, service or business. It could be that someone feels welcome, experiences success, or senses that he has superpowers. People who fly business class get champagne served right away when seated – to feed in a system 1-cue of being more special than the other passengers. Forget pre-rationalisation; post-rationalisation is the new influential 'kid on the block'.

Heuristics: The shortcuts our brain uses to make decisions

If you have to design for someone to skip thinking, you're actually designing for someone's system 1. That makes it important to know a bit more about the workings of your automatic brain. As I said earlier, our system 1 uses shortcuts; Kahneman calls these 'heuristics'. If we bring it back to Kahneman's thinking, a heuristics is simply using the shortcut that our automatic (system 1-)brain takes in order to save the mental energy of our deliberate (system 2-)brain. Our survival mechanism is at play. You probably are already familiar with how we describe the experience of heuristics. We sometimes refer to these as our gut feeling, as a guestimate, as common sense or intuition. We use heuristics for any problem-solving that isn't a routine or a habit. The way we 'build' heuristics is by reviewing the information at hand, and by connecting this information to our experience. Heuristics are strategies derived from previous experiences with similar problems. The most common heuristic is the *trial-and-error-heuristic*. And this is trying to solve a problem based on experience instead of on theory.

Another example of a heuristic is the so-called *availability heuristic*. When making a decision, this heuristic provides a mental shortcut that relies on immediate cases that come to a given person's mind. Or, more straightforward, we value information that springs to mind quickly as being more significant. So, when we have to make a decision, we automatically think about related events or situations. As a result, we might judge that such events are more frequent or probable than others. The 'problem' is that we have a greater belief in information. And we tend to overestimate the probability and likelihood of similar things happening in the future. So, when you have just read an article about cancer and have a doctor's appointment the following week, it's more likely that you think you might have a severe problem. This is also related to *the gambler's fallacy*. We believe that the probability of a random event occurring in the future is influenced by previous instances of that type of event. Even trained statisticians get this wrong. The chance that you get ten heads in a row when flipping a coin is 0.00097%. Imagine you get nine heads in a row; how likely is it that the next coin will also land head upwards? The answer is 50%. Given the odds, most people would attribute a much higher probability to tails. But dice don't have a memory, so the chance is 50%. The problem with heuristics is that sometimes they are wrong. They are nothing more than mental shortcuts, that usually involve focusing on one aspect of a complex problem and ignoring others. Therefore, heuristics affect our decision-making, and subsequently our customer's, employee's, citizen's or our own behaviour.

Why we are sometimes so wrong without us even knowing it: Cognitive bias

What Kahneman discovered is truly paradigm shifting, breakthrough thinking that might even hurt egos. We are far less rational and far less correct in our thoughts than we'd like to think or give ourselves credit for. The side-effect of heuristics is that we all suffer from cognitive bias. Individuals create their own 'subjective social reality' from their perception of the input. There are a lot of cognitive biases. There are in fact too many of them to sum them up here (right now there are about 175 of them, all tangled up). To name but a few that you encounter very often. Have you ever heard someone say: 'No, Lois couldn't have done that, she is always so cute.' This is the *Halo bias*. If someone has a positive trait (for instance, being cute) this has a spill-over into their other traits. *Stereotyping* is also a bias: for instance that a man with a pronounced chin is a better leader, or that people wearing glasses are more competent. Your system 1 follows stereotypes blindly. Another one: Have you ever noticed that the more you know, the less confident you are? And that the less you know, the more confident you seem to be? This is known as the *Dunner-Kruger*-effect, a bias that makes overachievers underestimate their performance, and the other way round. Whenever I want to look up a bias, I cannot seem to find it –yet still, there is a saviour: Buster Benson. On his paternity leave (who knew having children could have these great side-effects?) he decided to clean up this tangled mess of biases and organised them. So thank you, Buster! The best thing to do if one wants to know more about cognitive biases is to check out his blog post.[49] It's brilliant. It helps you to get to the right bias much quicker. And simply to give you 'the heads' up', he has grouped the cognitive biases that our brain uses in order to solve four mental problems:

1. *Too much information*

   We are flooded with information! That's why our brain uses cognitive short-cuts to filter out information. Our brain is likely to notice the things that were added to our memory most recently, or that have already been primed in our memory. That's why repetition works: it makes things stick in our memory. And that's also why priming (consciously setting intentions) makes us shift focus to something specific, thus neglecting other information. Or things that stand out like humour, or visually striking things, catching our attention. We are also drawn by details that confirm what we already have experienced, our knowledge or belief. And, finally, we tend to notice negative characteristics in others sooner than we see them in ourselves.

2. *Not enough meaning*

   We get bits and chunks of information that often don't make sense. But our system 1 helps out by making sense of it anyway. Therefore, it tries to see patterns and uses stories to make up for the whole picture. In doing so, system 1 fills in the blanks. We are using things like stereotypes or generalisation. But it also uses shortcuts to form a story about a person. The fact you like someone or just a little something someone does, can create a positive or negative judgment of someone's entire personality or performance. Our brain loves making up stories out of thin air. There are biases deriving from the fact that we think we know what other people are thinking. We are terrible mathematicians (I am happy to learn everyone is, and it wasn't just me); we nibble at calculating probabilities and continuously simplify numbers. Leading up to several cognitive biases. And last but not least, we project our present self onto our past and future self in order to make sense of it all.

3. *Need to act fast*

   Sometimes we need to act fast, even if we do not have all the information. You can imagine biases coming from overconfidence or too much optimism. But we also tend to prefer the things that benefit us right now, rather than in the future. And we have to be smart in acting fast: We tend to complete the things we have already invested in. It could be time, commitment, or money. As humans, we're also risk avoidance. We love keeping the status quo, and prefer decisions that don't rock the boat too much. Especially when your social status is at stake. And if you must act fast, you prefer the simple, easy to follow options – instead of gathering all information and getting complications in the way.

4.   *What should we remember?*
     If we had to remember in detail every piece of information or every experience we have encountered, our brain would simply face a meltdown. Our brain loves generalisations, and isn't so fond of specifics. We tend to step over specifics to form easy-to-remember generalisations. And while we're at it, we rewrite history by editing events and facts. Also, the timing of detail matters: We tend to remember what happened first and last, but the part in the middle gets blurry.

My advice is to make for the blog post of Buster Benson[50] whenever you want to learn more about cognitive bias, or want to see what bias could be at play in the minds of the people you are trying to influence. However, this wouldn't be a proper tool book if I didn't include a little cheat sheet myself, which you can download on the *book download page* you have exclusive access to (see page 351). The biases mentioned there are the most frequent ones you should know. The most important thing to remember is that:

We all base our decisions on heuristics. And we all are influenced by our cognitive biases. By being aware of the most common biases, you can anticipate on them

 TOOL: DOWNLOAD THE COGNITIVE BIAS CHECKLIST

Behavioural Design in practice: How to overcome your biases in hiring people?

Are you ready for some more in-depth elaboration on Daniel Kahneman's work? I just want to show you why being aware of cognitive biases is essential. And the best way to do this is to relate the theory to practice. Human resources are one field of interest in which awareness of cognitive biases is of utmost importance. No, hang on – even if you're not working in HR, this will matter to you. We all want to be surrounded by the best talent, people that we can learn from, people that make our work better, people with whom we want to spend at least eight hours in our day. And we all someday come in the position that we've got to evaluate others. Am I right?

In evaluating talent, whether you are doing a job interview or have to assess a colleague working at your company or organisation, you now know that all are 'suffering' from our cognitive biases in doing so. In people management, some specific cognitive biases come into play. But what can you do with this knowledge? At SUE | Behavioural Design, we all quickly scan the 'HR Bias Form', which is a recap of all the biases that tend to pop up in our judgment of people. Being aware of your biases before you enter a conversation, raises your objectivity. It is a simple habit to learn, it takes five minutes to scan the document before entering the room, and you've done an intervention on your system 1 making mistakes. I have made you a download of the HR Bias Form. It's a handy tool specially developed for you, that you can start using immediately. Oh, and before I forget – if you are being evaluated or going for a job interview, it also comes in handy to know which biases blur the picture people have of you. For example, people see other people as more confident if they make a lot of eye contact. People tend to like people better who remind them of themselves; that's why mimicking behaviours (although limited) works. If you know what might happen, you can anticipate it – raising your chances of success in work. Mr Kahneman is more important to you personally already than you might have imagined before.

  TOOL: DOWNLOAD HR BIAS FORM

Recap Human Decision-Making

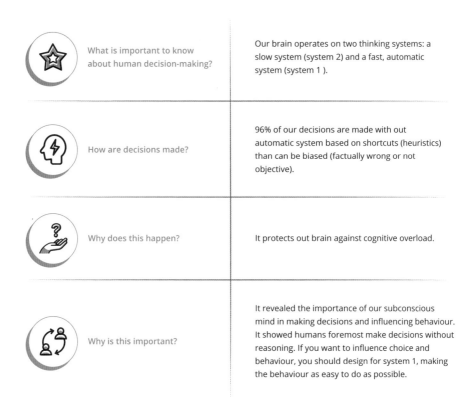

☆	What is important to know about human decision-making?	Our brain operates on two thinking systems: a slow system (system 2) and a fast, automatic system (system 1).
⚡	How are decisions made?	96% of our decisions are made with out automatic system based on shortcuts (heuristics) than can be biased (factually wrong or not objective).
?	Why does this happen?	It protects out brain against cognitive overload.
⟳	Why is this important?	It revealed the importance of our subconscious mind in making decisions and influencing behaviour. It showed humans foremost make decisions without reasoning. If you want to influence choice and behaviour, you should design for system 1, making the behaviour as easy to do as possible.

BEHAVIOUR

– Identifying the forces that drive human behaviour

Introduction

Now that you know how we come to decisions, we can move on to gain more insight into people's behaviour. It's interesting, right? Just look at ourselves: It's hard denying we as humankind are facing serious problems today, and that things need to change. Global warming is happening as we speak; obesity overtakes smoking as the number one cause of death. It isn't that we don't care about these problems regarding most of us. Yet sometimes we care a great deal. Who wasn't shocked after seeing *Before the Flood*,[51] the stunning climate-change documentary starring Leonardo DiCaprio? Who wasn't moved by Jamie Oliver's quest to start a *Food Revolution*,[52] knowing children didn't even recognise real food like an ordinary tomato? And even if you weren't aware of these two specific examples – we all know some serious issues are going on. But the interesting question is, why don't we act? Is it because the problems are too big to comprehend? Or do we feel too powerless to make a difference? It might be because they are – at least if you frame them as a problem for humankind or the world. But if you look at global warming or obesity from a different angle, you realise they have one thing in common: People. You and me. We eat sugar. We don't go to the gym. We save time by buying processed foods in the supermarket. We drive cars. We take flights. We buy loads of packaging and forget to recycle. We love taking long showers and binge-watching Netflix on the couch, while eating crisps. This way, you realise that the significant issues we're facing in the world right now can be brought back to simple daily human behaviour. Things we can comprehend. Things which we could change.

So, why don't we do it? Why don't we cook with fresh fruit and vegetables? Why don't we work out? Why don't we go out and walk more often, for instance to the recycle container? The answer is simple: Because we don't. It's that plain simple. We can play the guilt trip or blame game for much longer, but it isn't relevant and surely doesn't do us any good. Not us as people. Or us as humankind. The only relevant question to ask ourselves is: How can we help people adjust this daily behaviour? How can we nudge people into making better choices on an everyday basis? You have now learnt that most of our decisions are made through shortcuts – such as heuristics and biases – and have nothing to do with a rational or controlled thinking process. As Daniel Kahneman[53] puts it: 'We are very influenced by completely automatic things that we have no control over, and we don't know we're doing it.'[54]

That explains why the blame and guilt trip game isn't beneficial. How can you be blamed or feel guilty if most of the time we're just doing things automatically, without even knowing we're doing it? Dr Kahneman says it even more prosaically: 'We are blind to our blindness. We have very little idea of how little we know. We're not designed to know how little we know.' Is that not good news at the same time? Every time one of your resolutions failed, or you didn't reach a personal goal, you shouldn't take the blame for it. Well, until you have finished reading this book, you won't have any excuse anymore not to persist in performing a behaviour, as you'll be able to design it. But back to behaviour: A crucial part of solving the puzzle of making this world a better, healthier, happier place is the realisation that behavioural psychology challenges a commonly accepted assumption that people who make poor decisions have made a conscious decision to do so. But science has shown us that's not true. Still, millions of euros are invested in campaigns to convince people to act differently, targeting their thinking capacity. Which is just money down the drain. But this does go further than the altruistic desire to make this world a better place. The same goes for your plans, services, products, ideas, business. So, don't hit people with campaigns, information, or benefits. It will paralyse them.

Introducing the SUE | Influence Framework

We immediately start off with the heart of the matter. What is crucial to realise is that:

You don't change behaviour by working at the behaviour itself

Behaviour isn't one-dimensional. You don't go from old to new behaviour in a straight line. There are all kinds of forces that stand between undesired and desired behaviour. And if we are talking about Behavioural Design, we talk about designing interventions that make use of or eradicate those forces. For that, you first need to understand how behaviour arises:

- What forces get someone to maintain current behaviour?
- What forces can drive someone to new behaviour?
- What are the deeper motivations driving behaviour?
- How does someone's decision-psychology thinking process come about, when deciding to do something (or not)?

Only if you know how behaviour is influenced and can be triggered, it is time to head for the 'Insight step' of the SUE | Behavioural Design Method. The good news is we have developed a tool to help you do this more easily. Quite easily even. It's called the *SUE | Influence Framework*. It's the tool that has in practice proved to be the tool people love using the most. It's in fact our *pièce de résistance*. The SUE | Influence Framework consists of four building blocks:

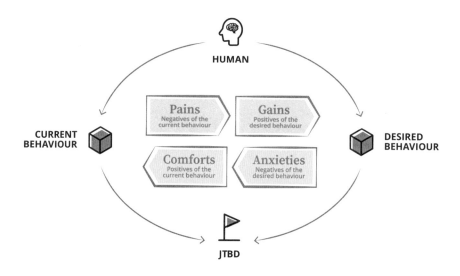

1. The human: the person(s) you are trying to influence
2. The job-to-be-done (JTBD): this person's underlying motivation to show specific behaviour
3. The behaviour: both the current and the desired behaviour
4. The four forces that stand between current and desired behaviour
5. Desired behaviour: a clear definition of what you want someone to do

In this chapter, I will explain the building blocks one by one. Illustrating them with examples from practice, and providing some practical tips so that you can start using the SUE | Influence Framework right away. To really get you started, I'll wrap this chapter up with a bit of advice on how to convince others to let you do behavioural research.

The foundation of behaviour: The job-to-be-done

So, what is the answer here? Understanding how the mind works is just one thing. But how do you translate scientific research into practice? How might it stop me from eating pizza? From buying sneakers for comfort instead of running? From purchasing plastic bottles instead of refilling my own? From people not embracing, buying, recommending, joining, using, eating, drinking, innovating, or doing whatever one needs them to do? How can we apply science to our daily reality and work context? This enigma is solvable as long as you know how to do it. It's like mastering the few movements you have to make with a Rubik's cube to get all the colours to fall into place.

The first move you must make is to understand people's deeper lying motivations. The work that provides us with very valuable answers is the research of professor Clayton Christensen of Harvard Business School. As the writer of the book *The Innovator's Dilemma*,[55] he has been fascinated by revealing why so many innovations fail. The conclusion Christensen draws is that the high hit-and-miss rate of so many companies has to do with correlation. All companies are obsessed with doing research on their (potential) customers. They are collecting demographic and psychographic information, and structure it in a way so that they seem to expose correlations. Or as Christensen puts it: 'The fundamental problem is, most of the masses of customer data companies create is structured to show correlations: This customer looks like that one, *or* 68% of customers say they prefer version A to version B. While it's exciting to find patterns in the numbers, they don't mean that one thing caused another. And though it's no surprise that correlation isn't causality.'[56]

Just let me set myself as an example. I am a woman in my forties; I got married four years ago and have a daughter. Together with my husband, I run my own Behavioural Design Consultancy that I go to on foot, which takes a five-minute walk through Amsterdam. As I walk, I often make my first calls; then, I usually have breakfast in the office: plant-based yoghurt with fresh fruits and grains. I just sip on some tea at home, and prevent my daughter from not smearing jam all over herself. I love to read and have an unexplainable aversion to name tags and lanyards (key cords). Every time I must wear these, I put them in my pocket with the key cord hanging out, so people can still see I didn't crash the event, but I refuse to wear them around my neck. I love flaming red nail polish and watching gymnastics during the Olympic Games. You've got quite some data about me now, but none of them explained why I recently bought expensive headphones.

It could be I need them to focus when I am writing, it could be I am a techno music addict and the bass needs to drop hard, it could be my hearing is damaged, and I need A-quality speakers to hear nuances in music. It could be I love to show off with expensive gadgets. Who could say what holds in this case? The point is you could collect as much demographic or psychological data about me, but you wouldn't have the answer to this question. And there most certainly isn't any correlation. So, if you want to influence behaviour (let's say you wanted to sell me the headphones), you need to get different information above table. It would be best if you tapped into my deeper-lying motivations. That's what Christensen has defined as someone's *job-to-be-done*. Or in his words:

A job-to-be-done is the progress that someone is trying to make in a given circumstance – what someone hopes to accomplish[57]

Christensen says that when you buy a product, you essentially 'hire' it to help us do a job. If the product does the job well, you will hire it again. If you were not satisfied, you'll 'fire' the product and 'hire' a different product next time. You can replace 'product' by any idea or solution; it works the same.

But what are jobs-the-done exactly? They are the underlying motivations of why we do things, the fundaments of our actions. Let me give you an example. Imagine you bought yourself a dog (action). You were not motivated to buy a dog as such. You had a particular job-to-be-done. Could be you wanted a companion, or a reason to go outside; might be you wanted to take care of something or meet new people, or you wanted to feel safer, or consider it to be the ultimate chick magnet (which puppies and babies seem to be, by the way). Or think about drinking a glass of wine. Could be you do this to relax, to reward yourself for hard work, or it's what you do when you hang out with friends; could be it makes it easier to talk to someone, or maybe you are celebrating your anniversary, and so on. Let's end with another example in which we see a lot of failing exercising. Almost no one wants 'to exercise to exercise'. You do it because of a job-to-be-done. Maybe you want to grow old in a healthy way, want to be prepared to run half a marathon, to recover from an injury, or you want to lose weight in order to fit in your wedding dress, or don't want to be ashamed when you take the stairs and start panting for five minutes or more, or have that beach holiday coming up and want to look ravishing, or you need to feel confident in your body as you want to find yourself a date – all valid jobs-to-be-done.

You could have more than one-job-to-be-done at the same time. Jobs-to-be-done can be small (watching a series to relax), be substantial (finding a life partner), some come back all the time (keeping my daughter free from spilling jam over herself each time during breakfast) or arise entirely unexpected (you missed your train and have to kill waiting time). But you can imagine that if you know what someone's job-to-be-done is, you connect to their deeper motivations, and your chances to influence or convince that person increase significantly. A *Harvard Business Review*[58] article by Clayton Christensen describes an example in which this importance becomes very clear. I will give you a quick summary, but it indicates that finding someone's job-to-be-done and connecting with it seems like a detail, yet it never is. It can make a decisive difference in turning something into a success or not. He tells a story about a friend who is a real-estate broker. He was in the business of selling flats to people who wanted to downsize. Before the building started, potential buyers were asked what they thought about the flat's features: the kitchen, the floors, the bedroom, etcetera. They got very positive feedback. People said they liked it. However, when the sales started, they attracted many visitors but no actual buyers. The logical reaction to this is to think if it might be attributed to the quality of the sales team – they added features to the flat like a bay window, or it could be the weather circumstances weren't that great. But instead, Christensen's friend decided to talk to the visitors. And he found out that one subject kept popping up: the living-room table. Often an old, used table, but an essential item that is so much more than a piece of furniture. It is where families get together during Christmas, birthdays, parties, and so on. And the flat wasn't well equipped for putting a dining table in it. As people were downsizing, they didn't need an extra dining room; they wanted the table to fit the living room area. And it didn't. What all of these talks with people revealed was their job-to-be-done. It wasn't moving to a new flat to downsize; it was moving into a new life after retirement. That's something else all right! After that insight, they changed the design of the flat a little, making the second bedroom smaller in order to make the living room space bigger so as to fit the dining table – and they included moving services in the house price. And then sales started taking off.

There are two important things to learn from this example. The first is that finding the right job-to-be-done can be a make-or-break for success. So, if you want your idea to be successful, you must hunt for someone's job-to-be-done and make sure that's what you've got to offer. Whether it is a product, service, policy or idea, it is the best way for someone to hire you, and to fire what he is currently using to get his job done. Secondly, researching before you start your idea, business, product development, policy and so on, is not only very valuable but essential if you want to influence someone. But there's a big but, it won't do you any good if you ask for intentions. Would you like a second bedroom? Yes! Would you like wooden floors? Yes! Would you like to have this granite kitchen counter? We as people are social animals; when asked questions, we are inclined to give people positive or socially acceptable answers. Especially if you're a good sales(wo)man, you know how to get people to like you, and they love being nice to you in return.

Intentions tell us nothing about real behaviour: They don't predict anything

The saying goes: 'The road to hell is paved with good intentions.' That's why when you're looking for someone's job-to-be-done, you ask about their past behaviour. Past behaviour has happened, and therefore is true. So, you ask people to describe how often they get family over in their current house, or to describe one of their favourite moments that took place in their house, how many people were there, and what they did to entertain them. And then suddenly that old, used dining table might pop up when people start talking about memories of the children and grandchildren coming over for Christmas, and them loving to see them all together sitting at the table and eating home-cooked food. And then you know you're on to something. The end of this chapter will extensively explain how to do good behavioural research – but for now, simply remember:

Current behaviours also solve jobs-to-be-done

And the second thing to remember is that jobs-to-be-done solve an existing problem for people. They are probably now using a product, service, way of working, routine that helps them realise their job. It might be that it is not an optimal solution, or sometimes even a no-good solution. Still, if you want to be successful in changing behaviour, you must make sure the solution you're offering solves someone's job-to-be-done better than the solution they are using right now. The success rate of your idea (and I refer to *idea* in the broadest sense of the word) can be far more predictable if you start by identifying the jobs that the people you're targeting are struggling to get done. It could also potentially be far more profitable. So, it feels that now it's an excellent time to teach you how to discover someone's job-to-be-done.

How to find a job-to-be-done

Now that you've got the theory on the job-to-be-done covered, and hopefully have grasped how key it is for your success; it's time to make things tangible. To let you see how to lay down this first building block of the SUE | Influence Framework. In this paragraph, I will show you how you can find a job-to-be-done by asking yourself two questions. Perhaps they may seem still a bit abstract at first, but I'll clarify them with some examples. You know people 'hire' products and services to do something for them, to solve a (big or minor) problem. To remember this, a helpful thing is that you're looking for a verb + objective. The objective is the job-to-be-done. The first question you must ask yourself is: 'What is someone currently trying to accomplish with a product, service or routine?' This question will lead to a verb. The question you then ask is: 'What is the underlying task someone has to do with the verb?' This will lead to the objective. Let me give you some examples to make it more understandable; I have underlined the verbs and objectives:

* Losing weight to be able to actively play with my children
* Overspending my credit card to keep up appearances
* Voting for populist parties to get back at the elite
* Booking a hotel room to explore the world
* Buying a smaller flat to enjoy the last part of our lives
* Drinking water to make me feel I am making an effort to live healthy

- Using my mobile phone in the car to make use of lost time in traffic
- Joining a gym to meet new people
- Eating breakfast at IKEA to fight loneliness
- Invest in stock at a broker to achieve an earlier retirement
- Boycott waffle shops in Amsterdam to feel you're living in your town instead of in a tourist trap

Sometimes the context is also a clarifier. If you think back to the dining table example, the fact that most memorable family meetings took place while eating was a perfect indicator of the job-to-be-done. A third question might also be helpful to ask yourself: 'What, where and when did the job achieve?' Perhaps you have heard of the Milkshake example[59] that Clayton Christensen refers to so often. They worked for a large fast-food chain trying to figure out how to uplift the sales of their milkshakes. They asked people if they wanted the milkshake to be bigger, or wanted a super chocolate one. You know by now that most people said yes, but didn't buy the bigger extra chocolate varieties. They were again asking for intentions. Christensen and his team approached things differently. They started observing the actual behaviour of milkshake customers, and noticed that most of the milkshakes were bought in the morning and taken into the car. After talking to the buyers, they discovered that they all had a long commute to work, and needed something to kill driving time. A doughnut didn't do: too sticky; a bagel: too stale; a Snickers bar: too unhealthy, and a banana: gone in no time. But a milkshake is perfect: it fits the car's cup holder and is nice and thick. So, you have something to occupy yourself with during the whole ride. And so the job-to-be-done was not buying a milkshake to satisfy thirst; it was to kill driving time in the car. And a milkshake got that job done better than the mentioned alternatives. But to get back to the third question, when you're researching, you might be focused on the location where your product is bought, but the fact they found out that the milkshake was used in the car led them to completely different product improvements. Not more chocolate, but making the milkshake even thicker or the straw smaller in order to make sure that people would be entertained during the whole commute. Or framing it as a protein breakfast or campaign at their job-to-be-done. This situational question is most of the times not necessary, but can be a good clue that will direct you to the job-to-be-done.

A last practical tip for finding the job-to-be-done, is searching for the why's behind a problem someone is struggling with. This very often also leads you to the job-to-be-done. For example, an existing problem is 'I am overweight', 'Why do you mind?', 'I cannot move properly', 'Why does that matter?', 'I cannot play with my children like I want to'. I hope these tips help you to find the jobs-to-be-done more easily. If you find an interesting job-to-be-done, it is easier to create interesting creative ideas or offerings. Ideas that are different and, most importantly, are human-centred as they genuinely fulfil a human need. And that's what human-centred thinking is all about (and that's what people are prepared to pay money or get into action for – something that fulfils their needs and solves their problems).

 TOOL: DOWNLOAD JOB-TO-BE-DONE CHEATSHEET

Recap Job-to-be-Done

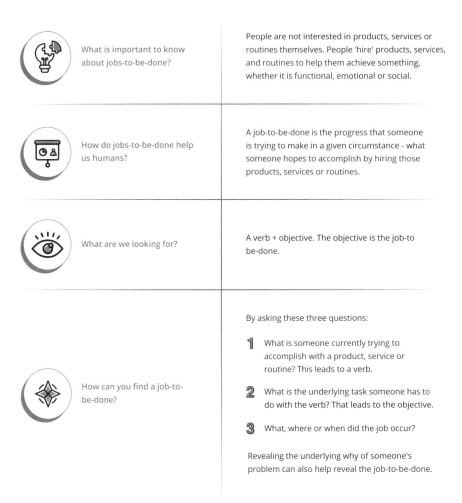

What is important to know about jobs-to-be-done?

People are not interested in products, services or routines themselves. People 'hire' products, services, and routines to help them achieve something, whether it is functional, emotional or social.

How do jobs-to-be-done help us humans?

A job-to-be-done is the progress that someone is trying to make in a given circumstance - what someone hopes to accomplish by hiring those products, services or routines.

What are we looking for?

A verb + objective. The objective is the job-to-be-done.

How can you find a job-to-be-done?

By asking these three questions:

1 What is someone currently trying to accomplish with a product, service or routine? This leads to a verb.

2 What is the underlying task someone has to do with the verb? That leads to the objective.

3 What, where or when did the job occur?

Revealing the underlying why of someone's problem can also help reveal the job-to-be-done.

The forces that stand between current and desired behaviour

If you want someone to engage in new behaviour, you have to ensure that the new behaviour will help him/her realise their job-to-be-done much better than what they are using (current offer) or doing (current behaviour) right now. Tapping into someone's job-to-be-done still isn't a guarantee that people will get in motion or are massively drawn to you. We're all creatures of habit. And doing something new also means we must stop doing what we are doing now. And we don't like that. It's easier to keep on doing what you're used to now, even if it's not the optimal solution.

To break through inertia, you need to be aware of the forces that drive and block behaviour

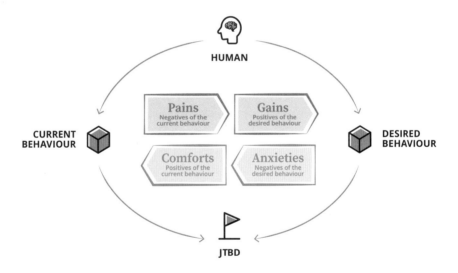

This is where the SUE | Influence Framework comes in. As you can see, it is a straightforward model that helps you to gather deep human understanding. It's about revealing the forces that hold people in a current behaviour, and the forces that can drive people towards a desired behaviour. In this understanding, you can spot unique opportunities to influence someone. Tom, my partner in everything, always has this great metaphor about how we look at the four forces concerning Behavioural Design. He says: 'Influence is far more judo than karate. In karate you try to defend yourself, or to attack someone. In judo, you work with the force of your opponent. You take the force that comes at you, and you try to turn it in a way that will work in your favour.'

Before I explain the SUE | Influence Framework in more detail, I want to give you a little bit more information about the scientific background of our model. The force-field thinking imbibed in our framework is based upon science. It originates from the Force Field Analysis work[60] of Kurt Lewin, a German American psychologist known as one of the modern pioneers of social, organisational and applied psychology in the United States. And who happens to be Kahneman's guru,[61] so that's interesting enough already. The idea behind Force Field Analysis is that situations are maintained (the status quo) by an equilibrium between forces that drive change and others that resist change, as shown in the picture on the next page. The idea behind Force-Field Analysis is that when change isn't moving forward as you would like, there are equally strong restraining forces holding back the driving forces.

Lewin said that: 'To bring about any change, the balance between the forces which maintain the social self-regulation at a given level has to be upset.'[62] So, that's what we will do: we will work with the forces to break through the status quo and move someone into change. I will explain to you how to do this in detail. But before we start, it is also very relevant to keep in mind that Lewin's insight was as well that we are inclined to push someone if we want to move them from A to B. We tend to add force. But there is a far more effective strategy, i.e.: Working on the restraining forces and trying to make them weaker.

We must strengthen the driving forces (pains and gains) and weaken the restricting forces (comforts and anxieties) for change to happen

Force Field Analysis - Kurt Lewin

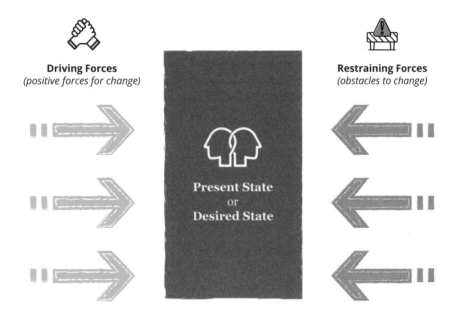

Data source: Lewin (1948)

And that's just something I want to stress again; not only that you don't overlook the mere existence of comforts and anxieties, but that you also work with them in the right way. Truly see them as obstacles you need to move out of the way, while at the same time pains and gains are the building blocks you need to use for a steady foundation. So, in short:

1. Recognise there are four forces at play preventing change to happen (equilibrium)
2. Two forces will help people change; you will make these stronger
3. Two forces that keep people in the status quo; you will weaken these
4. Your job is to identify the forces related to someone's job-to-be-done (JTBD)

Okay, let's get going: what are the four forces, and how do you work with them? I have made a flow chart that will help you understand the forces better.

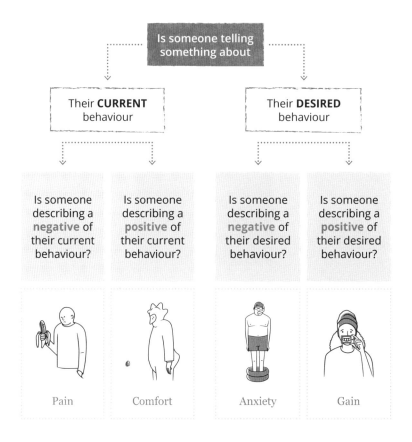

Force 1: Pains (Driving force)

Let me start with the first force (*pains*) that can potentially drive someone towards the desired behaviour. As noted earlier, for people to engage in new behaviour is hard, for it requires switching; they have to stop what they are doing now and start doing something different.

If you want someone to make that switch, it's essential to realise that all change comes from a push

People are geared towards inertia, but it doesn't mean they will put up with anything. Sometimes their current behaviour doesn't do any good and causes them 'pain'. Pain could be physical pain; for example, think about having severe backaches, and knowing that you should start working out in order to strengthen your muscles. But it can also be pain from a social perspective. For example, feeling you aren't seen as a team player, as you never go to the Friday drinks. Pain could also come from a functional perspective. For example, if you are used to reading in bed before going to sleep, but your eyes can't see the letters that clearly anymore when dusk sets in, you might want to start reading on backlit e-readers. It could also be someone experiencing pain from an emotional perspective. Think about feeling down and out, and knowing that going outside for a walk for half an hour every day helps to lift your mood. Pains, in short, are all hindrances that interfere with getting your job-to-be-done good enough – it is all the things that are not working for you.

There is an interesting aspect of this force. You must understand that people can be aware and unaware of their pain. Sometimes someone can tell you what is not working for them in their current behaviour. But it could be they simply don't know what to do otherwise, where to go, which behaviour would be better for them. They just know they should be doing something differently. But sometimes, a pain can be quite profoundly hidden in someone's subconscious, and you need to unlock it and make someone aware of what is not working for them in their current behaviour. However, connecting with someone's pain is a great booster of the willingness for someone to change. I often get asked: 'But isn't stressing pains, stressing a negative?' It's a valid question, but we experience over and over again that it's the people of brands or organisations themselves who fear that stressing a pain is negative communication. Their clients have a completely different reaction towards them. They feel understood. 'Finally, someone says what I am experiencing or feeling.' That's why populists are loved so much: they are masters at highlighting people's pains, which simply makes people feel understood. Finally, someone understands what they are feeling. This resonates much stronger than a system 2-solution. People don't care. They just want to feel that they've been heard. Again system 1 is at play. Rational arguments don't matter; irrational liking does. However, even if someone's pain is (made) more conscious, that still doesn't make someone automatically engage in the desired behaviour.

Working with Pains: Resolve or Highlight

Pains you must resolve or highlight. You can use pains to drive desired behaviour by making someone aware that their current behaviour will result in many negatives, such as frustrations, annoyances, failures, etcetera (highlighting the pains of the current behaviour). Or you could show someone that the desired behaviour takes away the pains they are experiencing right now, with their current behaviour (resolving pains). Both strategies can work to get someone to change their behaviour. Something is interesting in pains. The word itself has negative associations. If you dislike negativity, work for or in an organisation with positive brand values, for enhancing pain seems like an absolute no-go option. But before you discard this option, I must explain more about stressing pains, as it's a potent mechanism to driving behaviour.

Pains are all about understanding the people you are trying to influence, grasping their inner struggles

You might say: why not call them 'needs' then, doesn't that feel a lot more positive? But I must get semantic on you. Needs go straight to the client. What does
a client need, and how can our offering satisfy this? Pains go much deeper
than needs. They are the human feelings and struggles behind the needs. Let
me explain the difference between needs and pains by giving you an example
that I came across a lot in our work with banks and financial institutions. It will
show that it isn't a detail to distinguish between a need and a pain. It could be
the difference between getting clients or not, between delivering actual value
or playing the table-stake game of the market each one of your competitors is
playing already.

If you look at the financial world from a 'need frame', you may come across a customer that wants to be served quickly, wants to be able to consume anywhere
at any time and uses his mobile phone for almost everything. From that need
perspective, banks develop apps, interfaces and services to help their clients
do more transactions faster and more easily. However, this is very inside-out
driven: As a service provider or brand, banks try to figure out which products
or services they can sell to their clients. And the thing is: Every bank is doing it.
If banks would look from a human-centred frame, it gets more interesting. They
would start thinking outside-in: You peel off the layers to find the human behind your client and reveal his pains. You begin to discover that humans have a
highly complex relationship with money. You will see that people are often very
helpless when it comes to managing their finances, and you start to see that a lot
of irrationality is involved in their financial decisions. You discover that most
people really have a hard time budgeting even if they really want to, that people
really feel uncomfortable and insecure when it comes down to numbers, you'll
find out that people are sitting ducks for instant gratification, and think that
they – if they can afford everything *right now* like going on holiday, shopping,
remodelling – they will be able to do that in the future too *(future bias)*, and, have
taken on habits like not saving money but at the same time are dealing with a
constant struggle to manage their daily expenses.

If you look at these human insights, you will develop completely different innovative solutions. You don't create a new, faster app then; you think about how
you can help irrational people, who are (unwillingly) incapable of making the
right financial decisions, to engage in financial behaviour that will help them

create a more secure financial future for themselves. I have one more piece of advice related to pains. It is not only essential to unravel pains, but you must also make them explicit. You need to call them out loud. Why this is important has to do with something you need to constantly remind yourself of when you are trying to get people to change their minds, behaviour or action:

When things aren't terrible, it is harder to get people to move

We as humans are pretty risk-averse, and rather accept our suboptimal situation than move into an unknown direction. In behavioural science, the two potent forces that keep people in their current (even suboptimal) behaviour are the *status quo bias* and *loss aversion*. We are simply afraid of losing what we have right now and take our current state (status quo) as our baseline or reference point for future decisions. Any change from that baseline is perceived as a loss. Inertia is the result. So, no wonder it takes effort to change people. And no surprise that we often see that if something scores average in someone's life, you often see complacency rather than action. Only when things are perceived as painful, will people be open to action. Therefore, stressing pains can be a valuable tactic to break through inertia, and help people move into a better life instead of a mediocre one. So, highlighting pains is the opposite of being negative.

How can you highlight pains? First of all, use the exact words people use to describe the negatives of their current behaviour in your marketing and communication; it can very effectively drive behaviour. You can trust me on this. We have been in so many discussions with our clients on the absolute no-go to do this, coming from their positive brand values. But these are just opinions. Every time I am serious, literally, every time we have prototyped communication materials at real users that highlighted very explicit pains, people loved it. Why? The reactions were unanimous across the products and classes of the population: 'Finally, someone understands me.' They never feel it's negative; they feel understood and appreciated. The second method to use pains is to highlight the costs of doing nothing. Just let me give you a simple example. ConversionXL[63] is a website for people whose job is to grow digital conversions. Their website's main message used to be: 'Your website is leaking money.' If your job is creating revenue through digital conversions, it stresses the costs of doing nothing

(=your website is leaking money). This is smartly combined in a way to resolve this pain: 'Get field-tested, data-driven advice for plugging leaks.' Pain highlighted and resolved.

Force 2: Gains (Driving force)

That brings us to the second force that can push someone to new behaviour: the *gains*. Gains are often mistaken for benefits or USPs (Unique Selling Points). Those are what you see coming back in traditional marketing and communication campaigns. If you want to influence someone's behaviour more effectively and especially more sustainably, highlighting benefits simply is not good enough. You need more. For instance, Nike can tell me as beautifully as possible that 'everybody is an athlete', but the truth is: my Nikes are just an outfit item, and didn't make me go for a run other than catching the green light.

A gain is how the desired behaviour would help someone to progress by better reaching their job-to-be-done. Just as with the pains, someone can be entirely unaware of the potential gains of the desired behaviour. So, your job is again to make them explicit. I'll give you an example: A very effective instrument to make someone aware of gains is called *concretization*. Researchers[64] conducted a study at ING in which employees were asked to enrol in a retirement plan. There used to be a form for that. The researchers added just one item to the form – a question in which the people were asked to answer the following: 'Suppose you decide to save more than you think you should for your retirement. Imagine that, because of this decision, when you retire you can afford a comfortable life, maintaining your lifestyle and not having to worry about financial needs such as paying bills and healthcare expenses, etcetera – how would you feel in this situation?'[65] This question made life very vivid without pains. The result was that there was an increase in enrolment by 20%.

You might say: hey, wait a minute, isn't this asking for intentions? Well, not quite. You're not asking about their intent to enrol in the retirement plan (that would be asking about future behaviour); you ask them to envision a future without obstacles, with gains. From a behavioural psychology perspective, what you're doing is to trigger someone's system 1. Concretization helps ease the workload of your brain to make choices. If we see a clear future, it's easier to follow the staked-out path towards that future. It's a technique you can try for yourself, when you need to unlock gains that may drive the behaviour of the people you're trying to influence. Or in order to steer your own behaviour, of course.

Working with Gains: Enhance

Let me explain how to enhance gains with an example from one of our clients. We discovered a fascinating human insight into the 'gain department' when we worked for a large fitness chain. We got to talk with a somewhat older man. He looked very fit and active, and indeed was one of the regular visitors to the gym. When we asked him about his past behaviour of starting to go to the gym, he revealed something exciting. He told us he began to join the gym when he got retired. My immediate assumption was when he said this that it was because he now had the time to do so but something else arose. He told us he felt so lost after having to quit his job. There is no more reason to get up in the morning, no more talks with someone other than his wife. So, he decided to find a place to go to every day. Our client offers discount gym subscriptions, so initially the low price made him decide to go and check it out. However, what made him decide to keep going is an entirely different gain. It is the fact that he met other pensioned men and women at the gym. They hooked up and now meet each other three times a week at the gym. Working out has become just an excuse to break isolation and gain a newfound life rhythm.

As I was saying, our client is a discount gym chain. At that point, they wanted to economise and remove the coffee machines from the gym lobbies. We found out that these coffee machines were a primary driver to come to the gym for the pensioned (gain). It was at the coffee machine that they met and socialised. Being aware of such a gain can turn a business model around entirely. Or in our client's case: Based on this human gain insight, they have done interventions to attract a whole new target group on different terms. Not to build muscle, but to make sure the social part was integrated into the training.

Force 3: Anxieties (Restricting force)

But clear-cut pains and gains by themselves don't drive behaviour. Someone can still feel incompetent or insecure to engage in the new behaviour. In the SUE | Influence Framework, the forces that prevent someone from doing something new are called *comforts* and *anxieties*. Before I explain both forces in detail, it is vital to address that the misconception between knowing and doing causes many attempts to influence behaviour that have no result.

Knowing is something completely different than doing

For years, it was thought that if you make people aware, giving them the correct information would push them to do the right thing. Recent research[66] has shown a crucial difference between cognitive ability and action ability, also referred to as the 'intention-action gap'. We judge, punish and alienate people because we don't grasp the concept of the intention-action gap. Someone who is overweight and doesn't hold on to a diet – even if the doctor has said there are serious health issues – we judge as undisciplined. Someone not paying their bills, even when debts are running up so high that eviction is close by, we think is irresponsible – someone not looking into his pension plans is being naïve about his future. Or, on a smaller scale, you snacking at 4 pm even if you wanted to be healthy. Not looking for a new job even though you know this present job is making you unhappy. Not putting your children to bed at a decent time even you know that they have school tomorrow. Not stopping yourself from buying that pair of jeans, although you know you have run out of your monthly budget. Stupid? Irresponsible? No self-discipline? Lazy? Could be. But does that conclusion help you to engage in different behaviour in any way? Nope. And is it always true that you were unmotivated or staggeringly undisciplined? No, not at all. No one wants to have debts, be evicted, endanger their health, be trapped in a depressing job or relationship, or wants to break their New Year's resolutions. But we treat people with that oh so familiar 'you should have known better'-judgment. In fact, most governmental policies are set up that way. If you want to influence behaviour successfully, you need to know that:

Making people aware of pains and gains doesn't suffice. The name of the game is removing obstacles

Back to obstacle one: anxieties. Anxieties are crucial to unlocking, if you want to influence behaviour. The word *anxiety* might start you off on the wrong foot. But first, let's get this misconception out of the way: Anxieties are not only fears. Anxieties are much more than fears: they are all the reasons why someone doesn't want to shift to the new behaviour, whether they are valid or invalid. These could be difficulties, uncertainties, prejudgments, doubts, reservations, barriers, insecurities, prejudices, lack of abilities, excuses, lack of money, barriers, etcetera. Anxieties are all the things that block people, and can be both functional and very emotional. They may not objectively be genuine but are truths in people's heads, and they, therefore, hold on to them. Anxieties can come from different places:

1. *From within*: I don't feel confident, it doesn't match my self-image or beliefs, I don't feel secure, I am not a person that does things like that.
2. *From others*: I don't know what people will think of me doing this, the majority doesn't do this, this is not what I was taught to do by others.
3. *From you*: I don't know if I can trust the person who wants me to do something, I don't know whether I like that person, I don't know that person/organisation.
4. *From the desired behaviour*: I don't know if I can do this, I have tried it before, and it failed, I don't believe it will work, I can't afford it.

Without solving the anxieties of people, no one will ever move an inch

So, it's essential to understand the moments when people experience an obstacle. Let me give you a personal example to illustrate the power of anxieties. One of the desired behaviours I would like to perform regularly is exercising. I know it's good for me both physically and mentally. I have all the information that it will truly benefit my health; I know it will bring me muscle power, more energy, happier thoughts. All the gains that would help me to realise my job-to-be-done, being a light-hearted mother who doesn't surround my daughter and husband with negativity and heaviness. And I feel this pain, honestly. I am often so tired that I'm down and out. I get irritated, gloomy, and just don't feel like playing. And still, I don't get my lazy, grumpy butt into the gym. And that's because I have anxieties. This strong force that pushes harder than the pains and gains. I have no time; how can I possibly fit it into my schedule? I don't believe going to the gym will help solve my pains. I feel intimidated by the piercing eyes of experienced fit people. I don't know what to do with the fitness equipment. But mainly, my lack of belief in the results going to the gym can have, keeps me in my inertia. And that leads to me sticking to my daily comfort: rush hour in the mornings totally dedicated to my daughter, working all day, and then again rush hour to get my daughter out of the daycare and spend some quality time with her, after which I splash into the bathtub which comfortably paves the path to my fluffy, comfortable bed.

Working with Anxieties: Resolve

Anxieties you must resolve. An example: Let's say you are a sports-school owner and you want to attract new clients. The current behaviour of your potential client is not doing any sports; the desired behaviour is working out at your gym. We know from research that one significant anxiety for sports schools is what we like to call the 'sports-school sponsorship'. I will go four times, then one time, then never – and then I'll still have to pay for another year. In your marketing, you can stress the pains (being overweight, lack of energy) or stress the gains (being able to run a 10K, and meeting your abs for the first time). But if you don't solve the 'sponsorship' anxiety, someone might not be getting off the couch in the first place.

By solving anxieties, you potentially solve the missing puzzle needed for success

So, when you want to design behaviour, I genuinely hope you will develop the habit of looking at the anxieties and giving them the attention they deserve, as getting rid of anxieties is crucial if you want to change behaviour.

To illustrate this, let me take myself as an example again. Whereas success can be convincing to your manager, in this case success for me was starting to exercise. I had a job-to-be-done that exercise would help me accomplish. I was getting married, and I wanted to look great in my wedding dress. I had a clear insight into my pains at not exercising: I am a skinny chick, but that's it. Skinny. Not toned. I had this pathetic set of arms like kids draw them – sticks. And I wanted my butt to look good: for at that time, it was just a sitting device. Okay, I knew that exercising would provide me with some gains. I would build muscle, my arms would look toned, and my butt would come up at least 5 centimetres. This would make me feel confident and sexy. Easy deal, right? No – I didn't move. Just, like you need to tackle the anxieties of other people you have to convince, you must also take a close look at your own anxieties if you want to change your behaviour. I had so many anxieties. I was tired, and I didn't sleep because of my then one-year-old kid. I had no time, as I'm running my own business. I don't know what to do – for how do I know how fitness equipment works? I feel like a fool in the gym with all those fit people. And to top it all: I do not believe it will have any effect any time soon. All anxieties – things that withheld me from exercising (remember the direction of the anxiety arrow in the SUE | Influence Framework, pointing towards current behaviour). It was only when I tackled these anxieties I finally got moving. Oh...you want to know how I did that, right? I decided to hire a Personal Trainer for three months and have her come to my house right after work. The excuse that I was tired or didn't have time didn't work anymore; she was just there. It was just her and me, and no intimidating fit girls or machines. And she convinced me she would get results. And she did.

Another example of the importance of tackling anxieties is Airbnb. Now one of the world's largest accommodation providers – but at one time just a small start-up under the wings of Y-combinator.[67] The fact is that Airbnb wasn't an overnight success. Basically, they almost ran out of investor money, and were heading towards oblivion. When they started, they listed a few New York City apartments. Quite lovely apartments, but nobody booked them. What happened? Again, an anxiety was to blame what we call *the stranger-danger bias* in behavioural psychology. At that time, people were used to booking a hotel; you go to the reception, you register, and get your keys. What if you booked an Airbnb and the guy with the keys didn't show up? Or showed up stealing your belongings? Or worse? Airbnb felt too gritty, even though the apartments were quite nice. That's why someone suggested them to take their last investment money, fly over to NYC, hire a photographer and have him take some nice photographs of the apartments. The effect was that they saw bookings gradually taking off. It simply felt more like a hotel experience now, and people felt less anxious.

To wrap it up: anxieties are all the obstacles that need to be removed before behaviour can happen. These obstacles can be business-related, but can also be essential in order to experience personal success. If you must convince your manager or your partner to give the go-ahead for a plan you initiated, you need to see if there are any anxieties this person might have in approving your plan. Their current behaviour is saying 'no' to you. The desired behaviour is getting 'a yes'. What could be reasons to hold back on your project? What would seem like risks to them, and makes it easy to say no? Could they think it will take a lot of extra work and money? You should already address that in your plan. Does someone believe it won't get any back-up within the rest of the organisation? Make sure that you already include the people who loved the idea within the organisation in your presentation. Get ahead of the game by tackling anxieties. Address anxieties, and your chances of success will rise.

Anxieties are often forgotten, but they're always very painfully present

Force 4: Comforts (Restricting force)

Now we come to the second force that keeps people in their current behaviour: comforts. Maybe the most potent force to fight, as these are the positives of the current behaviour. People may know there are better alternatives out there, but sometimes only the thought of change is enough to make them stick to what they are doing right now. It's like your 'once a year opportunity' to change your insurance or your energy company. You can do it, and you probably know it will save you some money if you make an effort to compare energy companies, or check if your insurance policies still comply with your living condition. But the thought alone of having to dive into the energy comparison websites, or to check out the small print of different insurance products is a direct line to inertia.

We choose comfort over effort

The same goes for voting for a political party. You could make an effort to take a deep dive into the political programmes of various parties, and measure them up against your beliefs. Or you could simply stick to the party you voted for in recent years, which frees you from any further thinking activity. Comforts are the breeding ground of system 1-decisions. Comforts are all the gains we experience due to sticking to our old behaviour. And they can come in many shapes and forms:

- You could stick to your old behaviour because it has become *a routine.* Habits are perfect examples of 'comfort behaviour' – you don't have to think about them anymore, you just do it. People can have very persistent routines that keep them in the old behaviour. You may have bumped into such a comfortable routine whenever you hear someone say: 'I always' or 'I usually'.

- But *reward and evaluation systems/incentives* could also be a breeding ground for comforts. And when you look at the recent COVID-19 crisis, this becomes very clear. Most of us have been forced to work from home (new behaviour) instead of the office (old behaviour). And many of us have experienced the gains of working from home (e.g.: no more traffic) and have seen the pains resolve (e.g.: no more multiple interruptions due to meetings and colleagues). Still, chances are that people will go back to working at the office. Why? Current employee evaluation-systems are driven by hours in seat, instead of by output. In other words, if you are seen at the office, and people notice you working, you are appreciated and rewarded for it. This is an excellent example of a human insight that might derive from the Influence Framework. If you want people to work more from home, you need to replace the current comfort system, aka the 'reward system'.
- *Personal beliefs* can also be powerful drivers of comfort. Whenever you hear a person say, 'I am just someone who likes [old behaviour]', then you know you are dealing with a 'belief system'. Some people have evident beliefs about who they are as to the old behaviour. 'I am not someone who works out', 'I can eat whatever I want' or 'I don't gain weight, so eating more healthy foods is not something that goes for me' are typical personal beliefs that fit the old behaviour like a glove.
- *Social norms* can also be the reason why someone is more comfortable staying put in the old behaviour. If someone has the feeling 'everyone' does what they are doing now, the current behaviour is regarded as the social norm, and so they are going to stick to it.
- *Experience of advantages* are comforts. If you experience a deep sense of relaxation at having a glass of wine after work instead of going to the gym, that's a comfort. Suppose you like talking to your colleagues about their weekend or latest dating adventures. In that case, you experience the advantage of working in an office, even if you might also experience constant disruptions.

In short: our brain prefers to make decisions that don't distort the current equilibrium or status quo. Also when you know this, it can work in your favour. Anxieties and comforts can be hidden sometimes, or can even be things you didn't see coming. Think back at the example I gave you about the apartments meant for people wanting to downscale. They found out it was all about the dining table not fitting in their new place. The human insight underneath this, the stranger-danger bias, is that the perhaps old-looking, scratched dining table didn't seem valuable, but was something that had built up quite an emotional 'bank account'. The families they talked to told them they had offered the table to their children. Yet these all had gotten their own place, with their own (taste in) furniture, and they turned the offer down. But the alternative to give the table to the thrift shop was just not an option – for they'd spent so many important occasions at that particular table, they couldn't just give it away to some stranger. So, the underlying anxiety was: 'I don't know what to do with my dining table.' Maybe not as evident as my 'I don't know what to do with all that fitness equipment', but it's the same. It's what keeps us back from engaging in desired behaviour: In the one case, buying a new apartment; in my case, going to the gym.

Working with Comforts: Replace or Piggyback

The thing with comforts is that they are sticky. An anxiety can be an excuse or a worry that pops up occasionally, but comforts have staying power. Especially when dealing with a habit, they are autopilot routines that people repeatedly perform without even thinking about them anymore. A habit is a settled or a regular tendency or practise that is hard to give up.[68] In other words, they are the processes operating in the subconscious background of our lives. It could be that your daily habit is to sink onto the couch in order to rewind for half an hour after work, before you do anything else (I do!). It could be that you turn all the lights on in the morning, or let the water run while you're brushing your teeth. It could be you're always throwing all your garbage into one garbage can, instead of separating it. It could be you always go for the tenderloin steak when eating out. Or you check your phone the second you have a spare moment. It's going to the bathroom first thing in the morning. You don't think about it; you just do it (Nike will be proud of you). Therefore, the tricky thing about habits is that they are often entirely automatic and subconscious. We have to reprogramme our brains in order to install new behaviour.

But comforts are more than just habits alone; they are all the positives of the current behaviour – and, therefore, hard to change. You can apply two strategies here. You could try to replace comfort. Let's take the COVID-19 crisis as an example again. We did a lot of research on the behaviour of working people during the lockdown. A comfort that surfaced time and again was that people truly liked working at home (they experienced a lot of gains), though they indicated genuinely missing the social chatter. Although office meetings were a great annoyance ('pains') because of their time-consuming nature, people told us that the meetings in Zoom became too efficient for their liking. The informal chat at the coffee machine, the stories about families, dates or weekends were missed. These are the comforts of being in an office: colleagues are close, and the coffee machine is just a brief stroll away. As a Behavioural Designer, you then try to replace that comfort. You start asking yourself: 'How might we turn the social element of working back into distant working?' I've heard of companies that send their employees a BBQ or lunch box once a month. Basecamp, an organisation promoting 'remote working', has deliberately created online channels which allow people to share their hobbies, crazy stories and small talk. And this is all thinking about replacing comforts.

Another strategy is to piggyback on comforts. As they are very rigid, sometimes they can be tough to replace. So, a method is to link the new behaviour to a comfort. Let's say someone is used to taking out the trash on Tuesdays and Thursdays. You can come up with an intervention that combines this with the recycling behaviour. We worked for a Dutch municipality on a Behavioural Design challenge to make the recycling behaviour as to paper more manageable. We found out that people were for instance more than willing to recycle paper, but were frustrated when they came to the recycling containers that their carton boxes didn't fit. Resulting in the undesirable behaviour of leaving carton boxes next to the recycling containers, or of stuffing them into the paper among the regular trash. So, a comfort is to put your garbage into your trash bin at home. We provided a free, good-looking recycling bin to replace their standard trash bin with. But we also provided people with a doormat that had a template for measuring the openings of the public recycling containers. This way, someone could easily measure what would fit into the recycle containers, and people could fold up their paper at home instead of in the rain outside. By piggybacking on the normal 'I throw away my trash-behaviour and take it outside', the municipality reported less paper trash next to the public containers and more paper volume inside of them.

Some tips using the SUE | Influence Framework

To plot your insights at the right spot in the SUE | Influence Framework, always check the direction of the arrows. They'll guide you to where something belongs. Pains and gains point towards the desired behaviour: and they both push someone towards this desired behaviour. A pain is a negative of the current behaviour. A gain is a positive of the desired behaviour. Comforts and anxieties point towards the current behaviour: for, they both hold someone within the current behaviour. A comfort is a positive of the current behaviour, and an anxiety is a negative of the desired behaviour. Using the previous flow chart is an excellent tool for plotting your insights.

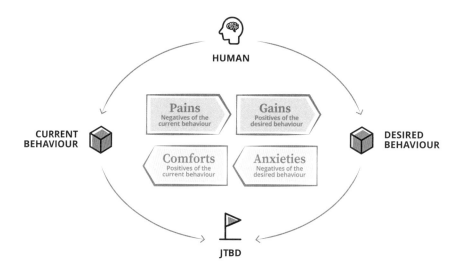

Often, people find it hard to distinguish pains from anxieties. A tip is to listen to whether they are talking about the current or the desired behaviour. Suppose someone is talking about negatives in the current behaviour. In that case, you'll know you're dealing with a pain. If someone is describing the negatives of the desired behaviour, you are dealing with an anxiety. Often is also hard to distinguish a gain and JTBD.

Therefore, a final tip to decide whether something is a job-to-be-done is. Let's take the desired behaviour of exercising again as an example. When you talk to people and try to discover why someone would be willing to exercise, you most probably will first encounter 'pains'. You will hear things like 'I am overweight', 'My back hurts', 'I need to build muscle' or 'I feel tired all the time'. The gains of exercising will also often reveal themselves quite quickly. They will start mentioning things like: 'I'm going to lose weight', 'It would enable me to walk the stairs without panting', 'And I would meet people'. The pains and gains are often exposed more at the surface. But these aren't the jobs-to-be-done. A job-to-be-done is not the losing of weight, but the 'why' behind it. Why does somebody want to lose weight? For example, in order to be able to play with their kids, or to look good in a wedding outfit. Find out the why behind a pain (or the gain for that matter), and nine out of ten, you'll hit upon someone's true job-to-be-done. So, jobs-to-be-done always go one level deeper than a pain or gain, and that's how you can differentiate them from one another.

And last but certainly not least, the job-to-done is the foundation of designing behaviour. Finding opportunities to help someone progress in achieving their job-to-be-done can be challenging, but not if you keep the following questions in mind during the interview:

1. What makes getting the job-to-be-done hard/ time-consuming/inefficient/ unpredictable/inconvenient? = *pinpointing desired outcomes.*
2. When achieving this job-to-be-done, how does someone want to be seen by others? How does that person want to feel? What does that person want to avoid feeling? What wouldn't they like others to think of them? = *unlocking the emotional jobs-to-be-done.*
3. What else does someone do to achieve their job-to-be-done? What was the last time they had to realise their job-to-be-done? What product or service did they use? = *revealing the correct competition.*

 TOOL: DOWNLOAD THE SUE | INFLUENCE FRAMEWORK CHEAT SHEET

Building an Influence Framework: Getting in the exposure hours

When it comes to unlocking behavioural insights, I must give it to you right away: you have to do the work yourself and get up close to and personal with your target group. Quantitative research at this stage won't do you any good. 'Most people think they know what they want – and companies think they know what their customers want, too. But that's not the whole story. Limited by fill-in-the-blank or multiple choice questions, customers give information that reveals their attitudes (how they think they should behave) rather than behaviors (how they actually make decisions).'[69] I've read about a real-life case of Virgin Atlantic that illustrates this mismatch between attitudes and behaviour. VA had to boost the sales of their flight tickets, but they couldn't pinpoint what might cause a lift-off. They decided to do behavioural research by one-on-one interviews. This revealed a huge difference in what clients had reported they wanted to experience when travelling, and what they truly valued in reality. They said travel should bring them things like 'adventure', 'excitement', 'discovery'. They booked tickets at companies that felt 'stress-free', 'responsive' and 'helpful'. Whether people had a great experience was not measured by the amount of fun they had, but by the comfort they experienced. Was the air hostess quick as to problem-solving? Were the seats clean? Was the time-table reliable? By overturning assumptions and pinpointing the behaviours that mattered most, Virgin Atlantic was able to optimise its customer experience. And clients came flying back in (sorry, this was a pun I just couldn't resist). VA announced a £1 million profit after these changes, compared to the same period in the previous three years. It was the most successful reframing exercise Virgin Atlantic had ever undertaken.[70]

There genuinely is no better way to understand what people's fears, ambitions, hopes, desires, prejudices, barriers, dreams, anxieties, or drivers are, than hearing it from themselves. No research report can beat this. You need to be genuinely interested in people to be able to make them do what you want them to do. You need to want to get to know them, and their peculiar wishes, hopes and dreams.

Creating a working idea isn't about what you want; it is working out what the people you're trying to influence want

The assumptions we make as professionals are something that's quite strong. We combine our past experiences, add some 'logical' thinking, and we make up our minds about people. I came across this example that illustrates how quick we are to assume something or to draw conclusions. What if I told you that it is much harder to get a taxi when there is a large conference in New York City or on rainy days. What do you think the reason for this is? I would say – and I guess you also take this line of thinking – that the most obvious reason is that more people in town are looking for transport then. If there are festivals, events or when it's pouring with rain, the demand for taxi rides is far greater. It seems logical, right? But is this true? Or is there different behaviour that can explain this phenomenon? A research team set out to find the answer.[71] NYC taxi drivers all have a trip sheet, precisely documenting the number of rides, the pick-up and drop-off locations, and the ride fees. What the researchers could see by the trip sheet data is that on busy days the tax fares are much higher; and for taxi drivers, these are high-wage days. You would expect that they would use this to do as many rides as possible during that day, bringing in a fair amount of money. You quickly make this assumption about the taxi drivers' behaviour when knowing these two variables: the high demand and the high wages.

However, the researchers found different taxi driver behaviour. It is so hard to get a taxi on busy or rainy days because then there are fewer taxis around. The research showed that most taxi drivers have a daily income quota in mind. Once they have reached that target, most of them stop driving and go home. They make 'one-day-at-time' decisions. That's why it is harder to get a taxi. High wages correlate with fewer working hours. So, now if you are desperately looking for a taxi in the rain, you know why it is so hard to get one; the taxi drivers are cosily at home already. The point I want to make is that this is precisely the fun part of the behavioural analysis: it will help you discover new perspectives and truths. It will unlock insights for you that you couldn't have thought of before. It is shedding a fascinating light on human behaviour that remains intriguing. And it keeps proving to us that we often are more wrong than right.

Behavioural analysis challenges, or looks for evidence as to all the assumptions we make about people's behaviour, and often proves to us that we're more wrong than right

There are several ways to unlock behavioural insights. You could observe people in their daily life. People tend to tell different things about what they intend doing than they will do. Sometimes simply because people do something they are unaware of, and are unable to tell you this. Observing can also help you fight your assumptions. There's a very well-known example of Tom Kelley,[72] one of the co-founders of IDEO. He describes how they were hired by a large toothbrush company which wanted them to develop a new kids' toothbrush. The general and even logical assumption was that kids are small, so they need small toothbrushes. But when they started observing kids in the field, they noticed that those little humans have tiny hands and don't have the grip to hold a small toothbrush. Kids grab hold of their toothbrushes. So instead of making smaller toothbrushes for kids, they need big toothbrushes they can hold onto much better. Kelley tells when their client started selling those toothbrushes; they became the worldwide number one toothbrush brand for kids for months. So, big business.

Another way to 'unlock' behavioural insights is to use data. You could set up A/B-tests and make the first prototypes of digital ads, landing pages or emails. You can then actually measure behaviour: which one is clicked on more. Our preferred way of unlocking behavioural insights is to do interviews. Doing interviews is not just standard qualitative research. We aren't looking for significance or representative samples; we are looking for interesting problems and accurate human insights. Therefore, we only do six interviews at the start of a project. More is not necessary as we're not looking for correlation, were looking for interesting problems.

Where traditional research considers non-coherent answers or stupid decisions, as 'deviants' of the research sample, we as human-focused thinkers start to wake up when this happens. That's where the human comes popping up. Sometimes, a sentence or a word person uses can spark off a whole new idea. You don't find this if you just read research reports. And that's why those reports will never help you to understand why someone doesn't buy your solution, even if they said they would during the research. Behavioural Designers look for the human behind the client, and therefore understand why someone has a specific behaviour or shows certain barriers.

As to both observing and interviewing, YOU NEED to get in the exposure hours. I use capitals. I am that serious about it. The minimum effective dose is two hours every six weeks, talking to an actual person or observing a person that's your influence target. That isn't too bad, is it now? So, go ahead and be a human anthropologist. Apart from it being crucial to the success of your ideas, it is so much fun to do. People will tell you the craziest, funniest, most unexpected, touching and eye-opening things. Let me ask you something. Are you someone who loves to eavesdrop on a conversation? Or loves to observe people on the beach or at an outdoor pub? Well, I assure you – you've always had it in you. This is the perfect empathy-DNA. Humans are a fascinating species, and you now have a valid reason to unleash your unbounded curiosity (and get paid for it while being on top of your empathy game). But the exposure hours are more than just a way to satisfy your curiosity. They are the best self-protection. And we're all full of assumptions about people and their behaviour.

We project our own beliefs on other people all the time

By talking to people, you see and hear what they do, think, feel and say. Why do I keep harassing you about doing insight-work yourself? I have some excellent reasons, but the most important is that we know from practice that this step is crucial in getting you the success you want, or in making the impact you're after. But let me give you the reasons for it:

1. The most important reason is that I want *to protect you from yourself*. A Behavioural Designer knows that they are full of assumptions about people and their behaviour, but these assumptions are primarily projections of their own ideas, beliefs and worldview.
2. The second reason is *bandwidth*. The time you spent doing interviews is not just research time but also 'ideation time'. Every sentence, word and jump of the mind that a respondent uses or makes, can potentially trigger an idea or hypothesis, contain a piece of the puzzle you're trying to solve, or erase a prejudice. Every interview or observation is a potential goldmine for those prepared to listen and observe carefully and non-judgementally.
3. The third reason is *infatuation*. We know from experience that behavioural research helps you to fall in love with a problem. Every conversation teaches you to emerse yourself in the world of your target group. You learn

to appreciate their struggles, fears, pains, hardships to reach goals, their brave yet failing attempts to make something of their life, struggle to break their ineffective habits, etcetera. The more you learn to understand this, the easier it gets to look at your strategy or creative concept as a solution to a real human problem. That's what makes Behavioural Design thinking such fun and so rewarding.

 TO DO: INVITE 5/6 PEOPLE FROM YOUR REAL TARGET GROUP FOR THE INSIGHT INTERVIEWS

 TO DO: MAKE SURE YOU HAVE YOUR PRIVACY STATEMENTS READY FOR READING AND SIGNING

 TO DO: DO BEHAVIOURAL INTERVIEWS AND CREATE YOUR SUE | INFLUENCE FRAMEWORK

 TOOL: DOWNLOAD THE INTERVIEW BIBLE

 VIDEO: WATCH THE VIDEO ABOUT CREATING A SUE | INFLUENCE FRAMEWORK

Recap Behavioural Insights

	What is the SUE | Influence Framework©?	It is a hands-on model that helps you gain a deep human understanding of why behaviour does or doesn't occur.
	What are the elements within the SUE | Influence Framework©?	The **human** you are trying to influence. The current and desired **behaviour**. The underlying motivation for behaviour: **the job-to-be-done** The behavioural bottlenecks: **Comforts** and **Anxieties** The behavioural boosters: **Pains** and **Gains**
	How do we work with the forces within the framework?	We resolve or highlight pains; we enhance gains, we take away anxieties and replace or piggyback on comforts.
	Why is it so important to use the SUE | Influence Framework©?	It helps you eliminate your assumptions. We project our own beliefs on other people all the time. It helps you put psychological intelligence into your decision-making, innovation, solutions, and actions. You will unlock genuine opportunities to influence decisions or change behaviour.

OPPORTUNITIES

– Unlocking opportunities for behaviour change & adding psychological value

Introduction

We are well on our way now. You now know how the people (humans) you're trying to influence arrive at decisions. You are ready to embrace their and your irrationality. And you have unlocked all the forces that stand between current and desired behaviour. In other words, you are at the point of having gained a deep human understanding. Now is the time to turn this deep human understanding into strategies and ideas that will change minds and shape behaviour. We're ready to put things in motion. Quite literally. So, let us look at the building blocks we have right now. You have got your filled-in SUE | Influence Framework.

The next thing to do is to spot opportunities. So, what is an opportunity then? Let me give you a very hands-on definition:

An opportunity is when you can add value for people in a way that they are willing to move from their current to their desired behaviour

In this definition, an interesting word crops up: value. We often use the word quite easily and indisputably. It also seems logical: of course, you need to add value. Without value, no benefit. Without benefit, no desire. Without desire, no demand. But it's essential to have a brief standstill at the concept of value. It is a fundamental building block if you want to influence someone. As a Behavioural Designer, value has always intrigued me, for what does value mean in the context of us all being irrational? To me, and maybe also to you, the first associations that popped into my mind when I heard the word *value* had something to do with economic value – money, income and cash. But there's more to value than that. Before I elaborate further on this, I want to ask you some questions first. Have you ever had the feeling that you are in a competitive rat race? Always trying to make your product or service ten times better, innovating, being a technological frontrunner, catching up with digitally-savvy consumers, creating apps, building platforms, being busy with new product developments? Have you ever had the feeling your competition has beaten you to it? Timewise, budget-wise, or advance-wise? Or do you simply don't have the resources to do what your competition is doing? Fatiguing, isn't it? It is more than plausible that you have answered 'yes' to one of those questions. We all are sometimes pushing against our boundaries of innovation. Sometimes, there is no way to make our product, policy or service any better. Or your organisation simply is not capable of speeding up as much as you would like. There's a way out of this rat race, without losing your shot at success. It's all about that concept of redefining value. And I'd like to introduce you to the ace that Behavioural Designers, have up their sleeve: *psychological value.*

Adding psychological value

Even though you might not be able to make your product, policy, plan or service ten times better, you can make sure that people experience it as being ten times more valuable. That's what psychological value is all about.

Psychological value is the art of making people experience something objectively the same, as subjectively more valuable

Psychological value is a new but immensely important, impactful and potentially profitable concept. I sure hope I've gotten your attention now. But I am not exaggerating. It may sound soppy, but psychological value can lead to substantial cash. It's just another kind of value that we are used to dealing with. It is undiscovered territory. It's where you can outsmart the competition. It's where you can monetize or create success in a radically new way. It's a way of earning money, not by extracting value, but by creating it – for you are taking a deeply human understanding as your point of departure. There are mainly two things of interest now. First of all, what is psychological value exactly? And secondly, how can you make it work for you in practice? Furthermore, there's no time like the present to tell you some more about both. We have learnt so far from behavioural economics that people are irrational, and as to this their perception of value is also completely subjective. Remember, 96% of our decisions are subconscious, are made by short-cuts, are unreasonable, and are not objective. Your system 1 picks up cues in our environment and feeds them into your system 2, turning them into beliefs. This is an essential notion if you want to convince people of the value of your product (and a product can be all kinds of things: a physical product, a service, an app, a policy, etc.). It implies that:

The context in which people use your product is, in their value perception, as important as the product itself

Let me explain this by an example. Just imagine that you're having dinner at a Michelin star restaurant. The chef may be cooking exquisitely, the wine might be in perfect harmony with the food, but if the waiter gives you the feeling you are just one of the many, many guests he has had to wait on, then the food suddenly doesn't taste that good anymore. Objectively you might be eating the best dinner you will ever have in your life, but subjectively the experience will be disappointing because of the context. This may seem like an obvious example, but it goes for everything. I'll give you another example of how context defines our perception of value. The Australian comic duo Hamish & Andy set up an experiment with the famous singer Ed Sheeran. They created the Ed Sheeran Peep Show. In short, they put Ed Sheeran in an actual peep show, and tried to get people in for 2 dollars to come and see him play. It took them well over 2 hours and a lot of extra convincing to get the first visitor in to see Ed Sheeran, whose concert tickets typically go at well over 80 euros apiece. But it was the context that devaluated the whole perception of value, while the product (Ed Sheeran) was the same. The video is hilarious; if you have a spare 6 minutes, you ought to view it.[73]

You can offer someone psychological value by working with the forces and job-to-be-done of the Influence Framework. Think about the Uber taxi rides. They are not objectively better than traditional taxi rides. You still must wait for your taxi to arrive, you still have to pay a considerable amount of fare (sometimes even a lot more than for traditional taxi rides), and you don't know your driver. But Uber does an excellent job of offering psychological value. We, as humans, all hate uncertainty. What Uber did was to design an interface in order to reduce any uncertainty. You can follow the trip of your taxi in real-time; you can see the fixed fee of the taxi ride. You can do the financial transaction from home, so you don't have to hassle with money. You are shown the satisfaction rating of the driver, and you can share your trip with trusted contacts. The taxi ride is not objectively better, but subjectively it is a world of difference. By taking away anxieties, Uber has created a massive business model without even innovating that much, except for radically making their UX human-centred. Reducing uncertainty, is what you also see applied at traffic lights. By indicating the waiting time before the light turns green, it gives people a sense of control, and they are less inclined to drive through a red light. Is this a breakthrough, highly technological innovation that needed years of expensive R&D? No, it is a psychological innovation with a substantial impact on behaviour. That's changing the experience.

I do realise that this concept of psychological value might trigger the feeling that we just have to tamper with reality or change perceptions in order to get people to do or not to do things. However, I would like to stress that we are still in the value-creation business. I think nobody has said it better than Rory Sutherland: 'If you can change people's focus, attention, and their status currencies, so they derive more pleasure from what already exists, rather than from what must be created to satisfy their demands, you can essentially increase wealth without increasing consumption. I'd argue that intangible value, once you learn to respect it, shows that you can make people very content with less.'[74]

Psychological value: It's all about progress

When you come to think of it – thinking about adding psychological value doesn't only solve your innovation, competition, budget, timing rat-race; it also provides a solution to how one delivers more purposeful or meaningful offerings. Behavioural Design is all about helping people to make better choices for themselves. To create psychological value, you have to start thinking in terms of improvement. Again, the SUE | Influence Framework turns out to be the heart of solving this puzzle. Truth is: The SUE | Influence Framework is all about progress.

It helps you to unlock genuine human insights and reveals human needs, struggles and goals. Such human insights are not meant to be treated as static. These insights are there to help someone to progress. You do this by taking away anxieties, allowing someone to realise their jobs-to-be-done, having someone experience gains, or helping them to build better comforts. Through that you bring improvement. You automatically take human needs as your point of departure by using the insights from the SUE| Influence Framework as a starting point for your developing plans, products, policies, services and ideas you are automatically engaged in progress instead of exploitation. It's not about *your* needs, but *their* needs. Giving you ample opportunity to innovate, create or optimise your products without having to produce, pollute or push more.

Let me give you an example to illustrate this. This time it's not a product or service example, but an organisation design. You know that people aren't *econs*, but *humans.* When thinking about attracting or making sure that talent stays within an organisation, psychological value may also do the trick. For years, it was considered that the best way to keep talent happy is to reward them with financial incentives, hence the outrageous salaries and exuberant bonuses. But what did global research within the Google organisation show? Employees feel substantially more appreciated and are much more dedicated to the company if they receive so-called 'experiential rewards' instead of financial rewards. Monetary rewards are individual, rational, and often judged as 'I deserved this'. Experiential rewards tap into the psychology of people. Someone might be experiencing tension at home because they had to work overtime during the last few weeks (anxiety). Google wouldn't give someone some extra financial compensation for this, but it would acknowledge the anxieties: 'Hey, we've seen you've been working late; you must have missed out on some family time. Please take your wife and children to Disneyland. It's on us.'[75] This increased loyalty, feelings of recognition, contribution to the company culture and retention.

Research by the well-known behavioural psychologist Dan Ariely has confirmed this. He and his team conducted research at Intel in order to test different ways of motivating employees, and see what would make them more productive: a cash bonus, a meal voucher, or a verbal reward. Workers were given a production goal at the start of their day, and would receive a bonus if the goals had been met by the end of the day. The result was that the cash bonus had the shortest effect on happiness. But even more so, the day after the bonus was handed out, the workers with the cash bonus were 13% less productive than the workers who received no bonus at all. The voucher and verbal bonuses turned out to be the most appreciated. Ariely believes that cash has less impact because it doesn't show employers are interested in their workers' long-term health and growth. He would suggest looking at different bonuses, like contributing to their children's college funds.[76] This again would make perfect sense from an Influence Framework–point of view. People are not working for the work itself; they do it to reach a goal. In this case, it could be earning enough money to put one's children through college. If you connect with this job-to-be-done, people are more inclined to show the desired behaviour. And psychological value is the name of the game.

By the way, it is not that you cannot make good money by delivering this kind of value, or that you have used behavioural economics to persuade or force people to do things they don't want to do. It's about making the things that people have or need genuinely better. For instance, people already want a taxi ride; they work in jobs; they take aeroplane flights. Only, with the Influence Framework lens, you make sure that it becomes more valuable from a human point of view. And even if you are in the position that you must start from scratch – because you don't have your business, product, service, or policies just yet – if you take the Influence Framework as your point of departure, you will be creating ideas that people genuinely want, need and you will help them to progress. The fact is, you can make money while at the same time helping people to improve their lives, living environments or their experiences. It is still about realising your success and growth. But something essential has shifted in our redefinition of value.

It is not the rate of growth that matters, but the direction of growth

Finding patterns in the SUE | Influence Framework: Spotting the most valuable insights

Look at your Influence Framework right now. This is a treasure box, filled with opportunities to add psychological value. By the way, I would recommend you to stick your SUE | Influence Framework up on your wall, nice and large. So that you can easily read what's in it, and you have a bird's eye overview of your work so far. I recommend keeping it up on your wall for a while, giving you a visual reminder of whom to influence, and when and how. What may, at this point, seem like a piece of paper is your gateway to success.

TOOL: DOWNLOAD THE PRINTABLE OF THE SUE | INFLUENCE
FRAMEWORK

So, finding opportunities starts with finding patterns in your SUE | Influence Framework. The ultimate final goal of your behavioural interventions will be to answer this question: How might we help people to realise their goals in a better way (job-to-be-done) by the desired behaviour or offer? So, look at your Influence Framework. Did you find exciting jobs-to-be-done? Have you spotted insights that provide room for improvement in order to help someone to realise this specific job-to-be-done? You can pinpoint those insights by asking yourself the following four questions concerning the job-to-be-done you've found:

1. How might we find solutions to the difficulties people are currently experiencing (*pains*)?
2. How might we find better alternatives for the advantages of their current behaviour (*comforts*)?
3. How might we take away obstacles that stand in the way of people's progress (*anxieties*)?
4. How might we showcase the advantages of the desired behaviour (*gains*)?

If you doubted at the beginning of this process whether six interviews would give you enough information, the chances are that, at this point, you would instead feel overwhelmed by the number of insights. And you are right – there is a lot of valuable information there, and you will see that more than one opportunity will surface from your hard labour. How do you select the opportunity you want to move forward with? It takes us back to identify where we can add genuine psychological value. Adding psychological value can come from roughly three angles:

1. Functional Improvement
2. Emotional Improvement
3. Social Improvement

When thinking about functional improvement, you ask yourself questions like the following. Can we help save time? Make money? Simplify things? Reduce risk? Avoid hassle? Reduce costs? Integrate something? Organise? Minimise effort? Etcetera. Let's think back to the milkshake example we partly discussed, explaining the job-to-be-done. A functional improvement could make the straw thinner or longer, so someone can enjoy his milkshake for even a more extended time. When thinking about emotional improvement, you ask yourself questions like: Can we reduce anxiety? Can we increase hope? Minimise stress? Help at self-actualization? Add fun or entertainment? Or nostalgia? Add more design aesthetics? Better wellness? Etcetera. In our milkshake example, it could be to design a nice-looking milkshake car cup-holder that people can refill every day, so they don't look like fast food junkies. Or to introduce a flavour that reminds them of being a kid, so that they are in a relaxed modus before work instead of already busy thinking about to-dos. On the other hand, social improvement is all about gaining respect, belonging, attractiveness, affiliation, rewards, etcetera.In our milkshake example, it could spark off ideas such as: Can we reframe milkshake consumption from fast food into a smart solution for commuters? For instance, reframe milkshakes from Drinkable Ice Cream to Breakfast in a Cup?

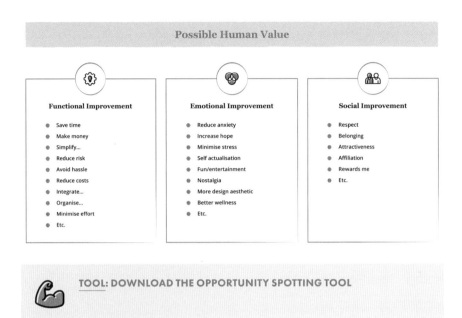

If you have many insights, you can also first use a technique called *dotmocracy* to get some initial visual feedback on what insights matter the most by using the wisdom of the crowd. I've made a video on this technique that you can find on the book website.

Recap Spotting Opportunities

What is a Behavioural Opportunity?	A Behavioural Opportunity is where you can add value for people in a way that they are willing to move from current to desired behaviour.
What is psychological value?	It is the art of making perceive something objectively the same as subjectively more valuable.
How does psychological value relate to the SUE | Influence Framework©?	The SUE | Influence Framework© is all about progress. It shows you where you can add value and turn your ideas into success. It unlocks opportunities to add psychological value.
What is important to remember about psychological value?	It propels you into the value creation instead of the value extraction business. It opens up an entirely new way to innovate that often is quicker and cheaper than traditional innovation but can be just as valuable.

The power of the 'How Might We'-question:
The secret phrase that top-innovators use

I want to introduce you to the secret phrase that top-innovators use to spark off creativity: 'How Might We'-questions.[77] These are questions that help you open your mind to ideation. It is so effective to use this HMW-technique because it ensures you that you'll be asking the right questions to start your ideation. Apart from that, the wording of the phrase itself simply sparks off creative thinking. 'How might we' suggests that a solution is possible. The 'might' part lifts off any restrictions for now. The question doesn't say 'How can we', which immediately makes your mind jump to practical limitations, like budget or time restraints.

The 'might' part is an open invitation to let your mind wander anywhere right now, and to come up with solutions in various ways.

So, how do you come up with great 'How Might We'-questions? A good 'How Might We'-question is a balancing game. It shouldn't be too narrow; it should be able to spark off a wide range of solutions. But it also shouldn't be too broad – you need some helpful boundaries. I'll give you an example of a project we did for one of the national airports in The Netherlands (Rotterdam The Hague Airport). The challenge was that they were undergoing some significant renovation works, which would affect passenger journeys throughout the airport. There was a fear that passengers would experience negative emotions like stress, annoyance, or the feeling of being lost. A too broad 'How Might We'-question would have been: 'How might we make the renovation experience enjoyable for passengers?' A too narrow 'How Might We'-question would have been: 'How can we change the sign on the entrance door when the passengers come in?' To check if your 'How Might We'-question is an excellent stepping-stone for ideation, look at it and ask yourself if it allows for an array of solutions. And if it doesn't, broaden it. If you look at it and have no idea where to start your ideation, you probably should narrow it down. A better 'How Might We'-question could be: How might we direct people's attention to the main task of checking in, from the moment they leave their car?

To come up with the best 'How Might We'-questions, you also must know who you are designing for. From your Insight step, you have most probably found some insights about the human(s) you are trying to influence, insights that most likely allow you to get a bit more focus. Let me give you an example again. Imagine you and I work for the government, and you are asked to come up with ideas that would help adults live more healthily. The desired behaviour we were designing for, is to make people exercise more often. The humans whose behaviour we were asked to design were all adults who are physically and mentally able to exercise. This is a case we teach at our Behavioural Design Academy. When students conducted their behavioural research, they found a rather large part of this population had particular trouble engaging in exercising behaviour. They knew they had to exercise more, but simply didn't do it. I am referring to working parents. They had very emotional jobs-to-be-done, they wanted to set a good example for their children and wanted to live more healthily, so they would still be around to watch their children grow up. However, such working parents have hectic schedules. They have their family to look after; they must manage a multiple-head household, must work, have their commuting time, go for grocery shopping, often look after their ageing parents, etcetera. Going to the gym is just one more task on their to-do list that doesn't fit their schedule (anxiety). They indicated that exercising had given them more energy (gain) in the past, which almost all of them noted to find lacking right now (pain). But instead of exercising, they made the decision to sit on the couch every day after work in order to watch TV with their children, as it gives them the feeling they are at least spending some daily quality time with their offspring (comfort). You can see that taking the Influence Framework as a starting point, you are able to narrow it down to the 'who' as well as spot opportunities that fulfil their JTBD, while you're at it:

1. The humans you are designing for are working parents
2. There is an opportunity to transform exercising from being just another item on the to-do list, to something that creates quality time with the family
3. Helping them to set a good example for their children, and living more healthily and longer

A little 'warning': the opportunities must come from your insights into your SUE | Influence Framework. Often, we see that people already have some creative ideas in mind as we start the intervention phase. And they tend to formulate HMW-questions based on these ideas, but not on the human insights they have found. So, protect yourself from this very human inclination, and always keep your SUE | Influence Framework visible. If you already have any creative ideas, that's fine. Maybe they'll come in handy later on, but put them on your 'Parking Lot' for now. As to now, you must clear your head and be open to the new ideas that come from the insights and opportunities you have indeed encountered, and which didn't come from your assumptions instead. Sometimes it is tempting to write down a solution you came up with much earlier into an HMW-question. Don't fall into that trap. For example: how might we paint colour-coded direction lines from the parking area to the check-in counters? One last thing before we move on: We already talked about opportunities being a breeding ground for adding psychological value. That's why it can be handy (although not obligatory) to:

Write down 'How Might We'-questions in terms of improvement

How might we improve the 'giving experience' of mothers presenting donations to refugees? How might we improve the health of children in their first 1,000 days? How might we improve people's confidence in going to the gym for the first time? How could we improve the well-being of our employees when doing office work? How might we improve the spending budget of families, so that they can give their children the life they want them to have? You don't need to use the word *improve* literally. Often the word *help* also has the same effect.

TO DO: CREATE HMW-QUESTIONS USING THE HUMAN INSIGHTS FROM YOUR INFLUENCE FRAMEWORK

The best starting point for coming up with working interventions: The Behavioural Statement

You can start your ideation with a 'How Might We'-question. That's perfectly fine, and no one will blame you if you do so, and you might be just as able to come up with extraordinary interventions. But it is even better to define a Behavioural Statement. It starts with HMW (so your recent hard work hasn't been in vain), but it does bring behaviour and anxiety into the equation. Do you recall that I explained that no behaviour will ever happen if you don't tackle behavioural bottlenecks (comforts and anxieties)? Change of behaviour often starts with removing obstacles. That is why it is so valuable to include behavioural bottlenecks at the beginning of your creative process. So you won't forget their role in influencing the desired behaviour. And adding behaviour will help you to make your interventions measurable. Did the behaviour occur after the intervention? Giving you more grip on ROI or to impact KPIs. What is a Behavioural Statement? It is your 'How Might We-question on steroids', and it looks like this:

HOW WE MIGHT	SPECIFIC TARGET GROUP IN SPECIFIC CONTEXT	HELP TO ACHIEVE THEIR
JOB-TO-BE-DONE	BY HAVING THEM ENGAGE IN THIS	SPECIFIC BEHAVIOUR
BY REPLACING OR TAKING AWAY THESE	COMFORTS OR ANXIETIES.	

Let me break down the parts for you:

- Specific target group in specific context: the people whose behaviour you are trying to change
- JTBD: the core motivation why people engage in behaviour
- Behaviour: the specific measurable behaviour you want people to engage in
- Comforts or anxieties: the limitations people feel in performing the desired behaviour

A Behavioural Statement makes things measurable. Each one can only be answered by a binary answer:

- You either are the target group, or not: yes/no
- You either want something, or not: yes/no
- You either show the behaviour, or not: yes/no
- You either experience the limitations, or not: yes/no

So afterwards, you can state that of the x people of whom x had this goal, and of whom x experienced these limitations, x engaged in the desired behaviour – the behaviour part is one thing I'd like to give some extra attention to here. In your Behavioural Statement, you already try to make your behaviour as specific as possible. Often people struggle with this. I have some pointers that can help you. Now and then, things go off a bit. because we tend to describe the behaviour almost as an ambition, something you aspire to do. I like to call them 'end-goal behaviours'. The only truth is no one can realise their end-goals overnight. In reality, ambitions, dreams or aspirations are met by a sum of specific behaviours. So, let's stick to our exercising example. Helping people to exercise more, in general, is a tad ambitious – as is losing 15 kilos, saving to buy a house, being more focused, eating more healthily, recycling all your waste, applying for financial aid. If these behaviours were that easy, everyone would engage in them and effortlessly accomplish their goals. Our job as Behavioural Designers is to make these end-goal behaviours realistic – and yes, do-able. We do this by translating them into specific behaviours. How can you check for yourself if you have defined a specific behaviour? By simply asking yourself this question: Can someone show this behaviour, now or elsewhere, very soon? Someone cannot overnight lose 15 kilos, be more focused, eat more healthily, and save up for that home (unless they win the lottery). That's your litmus-test. So, these are the end-goal behaviours that you need to boil down to specific behaviours. It often (if not *always*) takes more than one specific behaviour in order to reach an end-goal behaviour. Back to the losing weight example. Specific behaviours that could be necesarry in order to achieve this end-goal behaviour could be the following:

- Taking the bike to work twice a week
- Eating one piece of fruit every day
- Drinking four glasses of water before lunch
- Doing five sit-ups after waking up
- Taking a walk outside every night after dinner
- Filling in your five-minute journal before you go to sleep
- Eating a vegetarian dinner twice a week

I hope this helps you to get more grip on how to define the specific behaviour in your Behavioural Statement. Just one more thing – it is highly recommendable to go into your ideation with specific behaviour. However, it doesn't have to be set in stone. Sometimes during the ideation step, you come up with more or even better specific behaviours; and that's fine.

You need to safeguard that you are designing behaviour, and not awareness, intentions or ambitions

To wrap it up, let me give you some examples of Behavioural Statements. Let me start with our challenge of designing more exercising behaviour for working parents. We could define the following Behavioural Statement:

> How might we help *working parents* (specific target group) to *set a good example for their children* (JTBD) by exercising *three times a week for 20 minutes* (specific behaviour), and by turning exercise time into family time in a way it *isn't an extra to-do in their schedule* (anxiety)?

Okay, let me clarify one thing here, because I guess you might ask yourself – there is already a solution in this statement: turning the exercise-time into a family-time bit. In this case, the Influence Framework already has revealed an idea: turning exercise-time into family-time. The idea isn't in fact completed yet; it is a start of an idea. The first glimpse of it. This may happen to you when looking at your Influence Framework. Remember I mentioned that insight time is also ideation time? Well, here you have it. Sometimes insights are so strong, and you see patterns so clearly that you can start to see the contours of a solution. However, the Behavioural Statement doesn't require having an idea already. The statement might have been perfect also without the idea in it:

> How might we help *working parents* (specific target group) to *set a good example for their children* (JTBD) by exercising *three times a week for 20 minutes* (specific behaviour) in a way that it isn't *an extra to-do in their schedule* (anxiety)?

Your Behavioural Statement often evolves. In the Intervention step, you will see that sometimes you'll discover better ways to solve your challenge. All roads lead to Rome. Let me give you some more examples of Behavioural Statements, so that you may get the feel of it. These were the actual statements of projects we worked on for an international bank and the Dutch Automobile Organisation:

> How might we help *adult car drivers* (specific target group) who want *to stay connected* (JTBD) to *configure their phones before starting to drive* (specific behaviour) in a way that they *won't have to look at their phone screens while driving* (comfort).

The following statement was born out of the insights we gathered for an investment bank, in which we found that most people who open an investment account don't start investing, because they feel overwhelmed by the myriads of choices.

> How might we help *people who have some extra savings* (specific target group) to have enough money in the bank to provide *for a carefree pension* (JTBD) in order to *open an online stock account* (specific behaviour) by removing their *insecurities to picking stocks or funds* (anxiety).

To give you some more Behavioural Statements from projects we or our academy students have done, in order to help you get the hang of writing Behavioural Statements:

> How might we help *employees of company X* (specific target group) *to report inappropriate intimacies on the work floor* (specific behaviour) in a way they *feel they won't be put in the position of being considered a 'snitch'* (anxiety), and so that they will be able to *flourish in a safe and pleasurable work environment* (JTBD).

Before you get utterly frustrated in the process, I have to warn you that writing Behavioural Statements often takes more time than you might anticipate. Sometimes it is a true struggle to get it right. One piece of advice I can give you is that it is okay to change the order of the elements in the Behavioural Statement. Sometimes your sentence flows more naturally if you switch the parts around a bit. That's okay as long as you include all the building blocks. And as long as these building blocks derive from your Influence Framework. A tip is to put the elements in italics as I did, or to underline them. This way you can check if you indeed have included all four elements. And don't get aggravated too much. It isn't easy to craft a good Behavioural Statement. Just give it a try – practice makes perfect. And it is indeed worth the effort, as it can genuinely spark off the best interventions. So, there you go. You have crafted the ideal starting point for coming up with interventions as to behavioural change. And in the next chapter, we'll move from insight to intervention.

 TO DO: CREATE BEHAVIOURAL STATEMENTS BASED ON YOUR HMW-QUEATIONS AND IF

Recap Behavioural Insights

 What is the SUE | Influence Framework©?

It is a hands-on model that helps you gain a deep human understanding of why behaviour does or doesn't occur.

 What are the elements within the SUE | Influence Framework©?

The **human** you are trying to influence.

The current and desired **behaviour**.

The underlying motivation for behaviour: **the job-to-be-done**

The behavioural bottlenecks: **Comforts** and **Anxieties**

The behavioural boosters: **Pains** and **Gains**

 How do we work with the forces within the framework?

We resolve or highlight pains; we enhance gains, we take away anxieties and replace or piggyback on comforts.

 Why is it so important to use the SUE | Influence Framework©?

It helps you eliminate your assumptions. We project our own beliefs on other people all the time. It helps you put psychological intelligence into your decision-making, innovation, solutions, and actions. You will unlock genuine opportunities to influence decisions or change behaviour.

STEP II
INTERVENTION

How to turn ideas into a success
SUE | Behavioural Design Method©

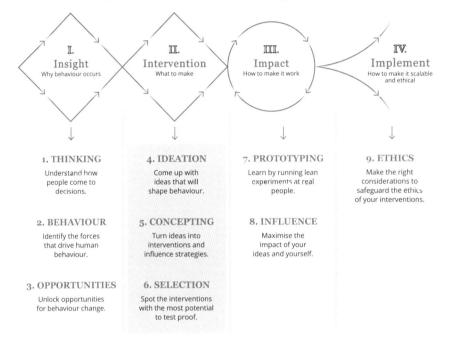

I.
Insight
Why behaviour occurs

II.
Intervention
What to make

III.
Impact
How to make it work

IV.
Implement
How to make it scalable
and ethical

1. THINKING

Understand how
people come to
decisions.

4. IDEATION

Come up with
ideas that will
shape behaviour.

7. PROTOTYPING

Learn by running lean
experiments at real
people.

9. ETHICS

Make the right
considerations to
safeguard the ethics
of your interventions.

2. BEHAVIOUR

Identify the forces
that drive human
behaviour.

5. CONCEPTING

Turn ideas into
interventions and
influence strategies.

8. INFLUENCE

Maximise the
impact of your
ideas and yourself.

3. OPPORTUNITIES

Unlock opportunities
for behaviour change.

6. SELECTION

Spot the interventions
with the most potential
to test proof.

IDEATION

– Coming up with ideas that will shape behaviour

Introduction

We now are moving to the second step of the Behavioural Design Method: Intervention. You have picked the opportunities you think are most promising. You have translated them even into HMW-questions or Behavioural Statements. In a traditional process, this is where the insights get handed over to the creative people. But not this time. I know a lot has been said about creativity being a talent. And of course some people are very talented, but that doesn't mean you have to be an educated, creative professional in order to develop ideas that work. Especially when we're talking about the kind of ideas that we are looking for. These are not just the witty, creative ideas, but ideas that will potentially influence minds and change behaviour – and are built up out of behavioural science. Those ideas can still be very creative, but effectiveness is their foundation. I know it's a common belief that creativity itself is a very intangible, abstract, almost magical process. Still, our experience is that anyone can come up with ideas if one approaches creativity in a truly structured way. For this, one needs a model. This chapter will introduce you to the second mental model in your Behavioural Design toolbox: the *SUE | SWAC Tool*. It explains which buttons to push in order to develop ideas that will influence behaviour. It is partnered with a list of proven concepts from behavioural science, that will spark off your creative thinking, and will help you to find multiple solutions to your behavioural challenge. We will go through a step-by-step process; I believe (and have repeatedly experienced myself) that taking the methodological approach will consistently deliver great ideas.

Designing for behaviour change

Now that you have translated your opportunities into HMW questions, it's time to turn them into ideas that influence minds and change behaviour. And to make it even more ambitious – here we are at ideas that change behaviour over time. Or in other words: our real challenge here is to design new behaviours that will stick. Still, we do have to be realistic at this point. Behavioural change is hard. We as humans would rather stick to less effective behaviours than break through our inertia. Some old behaviours simply feel as comfortable as an old, ragged bathrobe. Instead of getting a new one, you prefer wearing the old rag as it feels so snug and good to you. Even you know it is worn and torn, giving you the sex appeal of a grey pebble stone. We all have very sticky comforts that are very hard to change. Add this to anxieties, and you know you are in for a tough battle in order to change behaviour. Unfortunately, there is no magic formula which is a one-way street towards the ultimate idea that will change all this. We're dealing with humans, which makes it utterly interesting and challenging. Not every idea works for everyone, and even ideas that have worked don't work every time. Change is hard – no doubt about that.

Does this imply that change is impossible? Is it something human beings are simply not willing to do or capable of? For instance, did you know that McKinsey reported that 70% of all organisation transformations fail, or don't even meet their original target's impact? Of which an astounding 72% is accounted to the 'people factor'. Either employees are unwilling to embrace change, or managers are not supporting change.[78] Perhaps you yourself recognise this? Have you ever worked in an organisation or on a team that had to move into a different direction? And have you experienced the resistance that comes with that? Or let's make it more personal. Think back at the (new year's) resolutions you yourself made. Were many of them successful? Doubtful – for you are merely human and changing is hard.

But that doesn't mean we as humans can't change. In our lives, we tend to change many times. And we even do so willingly, and most of the time we even enjoy it. Think of going to university. We can't wait to change our living environment, and move out from our mums and dads. Or think about deciding to go to live together with the love of your life – getting married or having children. These are all changes we voluntarily make (I hope) and that bring us joy (this I genuinely hope, especially as to the kids, as they are irreversible). But even some minor changes we happily undertake and even look forward to. Have you ever have wanted to travel or go on a holiday? Every year, we save up to have ourselves transported to a change in surroundings, and we eat new, exotic food (and take 2,000 pictures in order to never to forget it again, and we share these with the rest of the world). Think about fashion, which changes every season. And even if you are not a fashion addict, I bet that when you look back at some of our old pictures, it is a good thing you did change your looks from time to time. Some hair and fashion choices are better left far behind – well, at least mine are. I do admit I had that entire 'eighties look' going, including fluorescent T-shirts and Wham-like outfits. And don't even get me started on Madonna's influence on me. My catholic grandmother, may God have her soul, is still shocked. Anyway, let's get back to the topic of change. The following is what we can conclude:

Change is hard, but it's happening all the time

How to design behaviour: The SUE | SWAC Tool explained

Much fascinating research has been done into the behaviour-change field of expertise. And it can get quite complicated. That's why I've simplified it again. Without further ado, let's look at the SUE | SWAC Tool. It is foremost a very easy-to-use tool. It explains which four puzzle pieces you need to solve in order to create a context that will persuade someone to do something – and have them keep doing it. What makes this tool so easy to use in practice is that anytime you want to design for behaviour change, all you have to do is ask yourself four simple questions:

Adding SWAC to Moments that Matter

1. How can we make sure someone WANTS to perform the desired behaviour?

2. How can we make sure someone CAN perform the desired behaviour?

3. How can we SPARK the desired behaviour at the Moments that Matter?

4. How can we activate the desired behaviour AGAIN and again?

When the new behaviour doesn't happen, at least one of those four elements is missing. The most important implication of this is that, by using the SUE | SWAC Tool as a guide, you can quickly identify what stops people from performing the behaviours you are looking for.

If a sufficient degree of capability (CAN) to perform a behaviour is matched with the willingness (WANT) to engage in that behaviour, then all that is then needed for the behaviour to occur is to get someone going (SPARK) a number of times (AGAIN) at the Moments that Matter

Maybe you notice that in the tool, it says 'moments that matter'. Not just *one* moment, but *moments*. Behaviour change doesn't happen overnight. Most of the time, someone needs to be reminded of the desired behaviour more than once, for it to happen in the first place. Furthermore, behaviour gets easier when it's repeated. Therefore, we have to make sure that we SPARK someone AGAIN and AGAIN in order to activate the desired behaviour. So, it would be best if you designed several interventions at multiple moments that matter.

Moments that Matter are the relevant decision points to engage in the desired behaviour, or not

Let's take a closer look at all the elements of the SWAC Tool. The one cannot live without the other. If you WANT to perform a certain behaviour, but you CAN't, then nothing will happen for sure. If you CAN perform the behaviour, but you don't WANT to, then that too is a tough battle to fight. So, the best chance for any successful outcomes is when CAN and WANT are both SPARKed, more than once (AGAIN). There should always be both willingness (WANT) and capability (CAN) in order to perform the desired behaviour, but you do not need to always maximise the two. There are two simple guidelines:

1. When someone's really WANTs to change, then someone CAN even show 'hard behaviour'
2. When someone CAN easily perform the behaviour, someone doesn't have to WANT it so badly

You always need a SPARK and a repetition (AGAIN) for the desired behaviour to occur in the first place. Let's address the elephant in the room: SWAC's order seems weird, right? Indeed you're right. I have called it SWAC because that way, it is a system 1-cue to remember the four elements needed as to behaviour change. It sounds like swag (which is a bonus), but it's supposed to stand for this easy to remember formula:

$$\textbf{BEHAVIOURAL CHANGE} = \textbf{S}PARK \times \textbf{W}ANT \times \textbf{A}GAIN \times \textbf{C}AN$$

If you want to make an impression on someone, you can always tell them that SWAC stands for **S**parking off **W**illingness **A**gain and **C**apability. Whatever works for you, as long as it helps you to remember what four elements you need to include a lasting behaviour change. However, I have a preferred the order of coming up with ideas. As to this order, I will now explain the four elements of the SWAC Tool to you.

It all starts with the moments that matter and failure

It all starts with the moments that matter. First, when coming up with ideas for behaviour change, you must understand when you need people to start with the desired behaviour or stop with their current behaviour. Do you remember that Behavioural Design is all about creating a context, in order to trigger people to make a decision or take action towards their goals? The key to creating an influential context is timing. What are the moments then that matter precisely? Well, I guess the easiest way to put it is that

Moments that Matter are decision points, at which people are receptive to changing behaviour or should be reminded to change their behaviour

So, ask yourself: When is someone most susceptible to change? Or what are the moments we must make sure that someone gets triggered into action? These can be existing moments or moments that we must create. But there is another way that you must look at the moments related to the timeframe, as they are needed for behaviour to occur. This has to do with the type of behaviour you are designing for. It is essential to realise that not all behaviour is created equal. Sometimes you need someone to engage in entirely new behaviour (could be when going on a sugar-free diet after being diagnosed as people with diabetes, which may be like doing your banking online for the first time). Sometimes you need somebody to pick up again the abandoned behaviour they were already familiar with, but somehow stopped doing (exercising or going to dentist appointments). Sometimes you need someone to do something once during a one-off behaviour (sign-up for organ donation, apply for university, register online on your website). Still, often we want someone to engage in repeat behaviour (showing up at doctor's appointments on time, not using their phone in traffic, buying multiple products or services from you, making donations). To again make things somewhat simpler, the best starting point is to separate two types of behaviours:

- One-off behaviour (like registering for organ donation)
- Repeat behaviour (such as a healthy eating habit)

You can imagine that if you want someone to only do something once, you will have less convincing to do, and it can probably be done within a shorter timeframe. On the other hand, routine behaviour takes more effort, and you have to be at someone's side longer. So, you need to know which one of the two behaviours you are dealing with in the first place.

What about the new and the abandoned behaviour, then? Well, the fact is, if you want someone to show different behaviour (the whole point of coming up with interventions is causing a behaviour shift), it means they must stop with what they are doing now. Therefore, *you should consider all desired behaviour to be new behaviour.* Even if the behaviour is apparent to someone (like going to school), or if someone knows they need to do it (such as paying taxes). But what about the abandoned behaviour then? This is a fundamental notion to consider.

A key to successful Behavioural Design is the acceptance that people will have moments of weakness or forgetfulness, and slip into old behaviours again

So, to get back to routine behaviours for a bit: I know a lot about building habits and routines that have been written and said. Some tell you to stick to behaviour for 21 days; others claim that 30 or 90 days are needed in order to create routine behaviour. I am not sure what the magic number is. The only thing I am sure of (or have experienced myself) is that there is a dark side to goals, plans and habits – they are very fragile, and therefore you need to be prepared for failure. Failure seems to hit us time and again. That's why I love Buster Benson's 'Chaos Monkey'-approach to life: don't ignore the fact that we are vulnerable to having our goals, plans and habits being disrupted by 'the first rainy day, sick day, vacation day, holiday, grumpy day, low-energy day, or otherwise non-standard day'.[79] The Chaos Monkey comes and disrupts us time and again. If you are designing choice and behaviour, you also must do this with the Chaos Monkey in mind. People will trip despite their good intentions, and will slip back into old behaviours. You need to be there at the tripping points, aka (yes, you know what's coming:) Moments that Matter. As Buster Benson puts it: 'The Chaos Monkey is there to help you. You learn how to switch gears, which helps you become anti-fragile.' So, don't see the people not showing the desired behaviour at first or after a while as a failure from your side. Just make sure you have an intervention strategy ready for it. Accepting that people will fail is a way to create a solid intervention strategy. I've talked about habits or routines, but don't be fooled: Even for one-off behaviour, you should be aware that your intervention strategy cannot be a one-off.

Change doesn't happen overnight for any behaviour. That's why you should integrate multiple moments that matter with your intervention strategy. Make sure you stick by someone multiple times, especially in the beginning, and design for those moments that someone will find it hard to show the desired behaviour. So, when you start coming up with ideas, you first make a list of the Moments that Matter. You will have gained valuable insight into these moments from your Influence Framework. In your Behavioural Research, you have talked to people about successful and failed journeys; this has most probably revealed to you what their make-or-break moments are.

CAN: The hidden gem within the SUE | SWAC Tool

When developing ideas to change behaviour, you always start with finding the Moments that Matter. After this, you can decide if you want to start with thinking about WANT, CAN or SPARKs. But I strongly recommend starting with CAN. Remember that I mentioned that, as a Behavioural Designer, your outset is to design for someone's system 1?

Our job is to help people make better decisions without them having to think

When you look at WANT (willingness) and CAN (capability), something very interesting and important is going on. We are all so used (and trained) to having the best arguments, deals, offers, rewards or promises to convince someone (or ourselves). Historically, we are all shaped around motivation (WANT). If we need to sell something, we are hardwired to try to create the willingness to buy. If a personal resolution fails, our first (conditioned) conclusion is that we must not have wanted it badly enough in order to keep up the self-discipline. What if I tell you that making sure that someone wants something often isn't the most powerful starting point to change a behaviour? Here's why. There is something fascinating about people's willingness to change; It goes up and down.

Wanting to change behaviour requires cognitive action

It is a system 2-activity, like self-control and focus. You cognitively decide you want something. You decide this consciously. I want to lose weight; I want to save money; I want to recycle; I want to spend more time with my kids. We have learnt that our system 2 has only a limited bandwidth. Therefore, your willingness to change will falter; it goes up and down in waves. This is perfectly human but something we must consider when designing for behaviour change. Chaos Monkey Galore! Luckily, as a Behavioural Designer, you have an ace up your sleeve by making behaviour very simple. Our brain L-O-V-E-S simple. The bonus is that we can do things without needing that much willingness when things are simple. That's why we always start with thinking about possible CAN-interventions. This is designing for system 1. The best behaviour change ideas are in their core capability-ideas. Making something very easy to do, re-quires little or no cognitive action from someone.

Working at capability (CAN) is designing for system 1

Let me illustrate how this can work with a real-life example. Most people WANT to save money, but many find it hard to do (CAN). You could design saving be-haviour without stressing the willingness to save too much, but by focusing on making saving behaviour easier instead. This is precisely what the Bank of America did. Their human insight was that people wanted to save money but never did, especially since making regular contributions was very hard. They have introduced the 'Keep the Change' programme.[80] What it boils down to is that every time a client pays with their debit card for daily purchases like buying coffee, going to the dry cleaners and so on, they round up their purchase to the nearest dollar amount and transfer the change from someone's checking account to their savings account – or their child's savings account. From a JTBD point of view, I find the last thing brilliant: a lot of parents want to save money for their children to have a little money in the bank once they go to college or need some extra funds otherwise. So, you must pay something like $4.60, and then $0.40 is automatically transferred. You don't have to think about it; it has been made very simple for you. The result of this Behavioural Design intervention has been very impactful. Ever since the programme launched in September of 2005, more than 12.3 million customers have enrolled, saving more than 2 billion dollars. Of all new customers, 60% enrol in the programme,[81] and the Bank of America reported that 99% of the people who signed up with the programme have stayed with it.

CAN: Taking a closer look at the capability to change

When talking about CAN, we are talking about the fact that a person must have the capability to engage in the desired behaviour. That seems obvious, of course. But designers of compelling experiences often assume people have more capability than they do. You need to be aware of this. CAN-interventions are usually very much needed. So, what are the ways you can go about boosting CAN? There are two paths to make sure someone CAN perform the desired behaviour.

1. You can train people, giving them more skills to do the desired behaviour. That's the hard path.
2. The better path is to make the desired behaviour easier to do. To make it very simple.

Let's go back to a real-life example again. Have you ever had the intention to eat healthily all day? You' really WANT to do so. And then it is 4 pm. You start getting hungry. Someone puts a bowl of potato chips just within your arm's reach, and your willingness to withstand processed foods starts to drop. Before you know it, you catch yourself eating the chips. It was made so easy; you have performed the behaviour without you even discussing it with your 'willing-ness' anymore. But the same goes if someone had put a bowl of cucumber slices nearby. You would have eaten the cucumber. Nothing to do with your strong will, but everything to do with how easy doing things becomes. To make things simple, it is always good to look at the opposite of simplicity. What are the com-plicating factors people face, so we know how people evaluate if they can or cannot perform the desired behaviour? Roughly, we can distinguish six factors that may make things hard for people:[82]

1. Time: If the desired behaviour requires time and someone doesn't have time available, then the behaviour is not simple.
2. Money: A desired behaviour that costs money is not simple for people with limited financial resources. By the way, often wealthy people will simplify their lives by using their money to save time.
3. Physical effort: Behaviours that require physical effort may not be simple.
4. Brain cycles: If performing a desired behaviour causes us to have to think hard, it may not be simple. This is especially true if our minds are taken up by other issues. We all are busy trying to lower our cognitive overload, as Kahneman explained. We generally overestimate how much people want to think everyday.
5. Social deviance: What is meant by 'social deviance' is that it goes against the norm, breaking the rules of society. If a desired behaviour requires you to be socially deviant, that behaviour is no longer simple.
6. Non-routine: People tend to find certain behaviours simple if they are rou-tine, and activities they repeatedly do. They are also referred to as habits or as 'the autopilot'. When people face a behaviour that is not routine, then they may not find it simple. In seeking simplicity, people will often stick to their routines or habits, like in buying groceries at the same supermarket, even if this costs more money or time than other options.

When talking about CAN, there are two ways to go. First, making the desired behaviour easier to do, and secondly, making the undesired behaviour harder to do. The first you perhaps have heard referred to as *a nudge*, but the second is sometimes called *a sludge*. It is all about making it harder to attain to a behav-iour that is not in someone's best interest.[83] For us humans, it can be daunting to change our minds. Especially when we find ourselves in uncertain situations and are confronted with new things (so also new behaviours) that are uncertain. And we are often okay with the status quo, even if it is not optimal. Fact is:

Pushing harder isn't the remedy for behaviour change. We need to start with taking away behavioural bottlenecks, the barriers

And that's precisely what we will be doing when we are working on capability (CAN). We work on taking away friction and lowering hurdles. Or as Jonah Berger states: 'The easier it is to try something, the more people will use it, and the faster it catches on.'[84] We can easily replace 'try' by 'do'. The same goes for behaviour: the easier it is to do something, the faster it will catch on. Just a quick sidestep, in research, in order to see which innovations are the most widely spread, Rogers concluded that one of the essential success factors is triability.[85] Again, referring to how easy it is to try or do something. This is why in The Behavioural Statement, we have only included anxieties. And that's why we will start working on capability interventions.

The best approach is not pushing someone into a desired behaviour, but easing someone into it

It will help you focus on taking away the bottlenecks and roadblocks to a behaviour or specific decisions, and not falling into the trap of overloading people with information. Yes, it is essential to also work on WANT-interventions, but I always feel these are great 'add-ons' completing the influence picture. Not to be denied add-ons, but still: the true name of the game we are in is the removing of obstacles to a behaviour or to decision-making.

CAN: When to boost capability to change

When should you boost the capability to change? Well, always! We like to say that 'simplicity eats willpower for breakfast', or as Dr Kahneman has put it more prosaically: 'Humans are to thinking, what cats are to swimming, we can do it if we have to, but we much prefer not to.'[86] Our brain prefers simplicity. It lowers our cognitive overload. And you know now that our willingness to change can falter, so making things easier for people is the solid foundation of your intervention. The most successful behavioural interventions have capability elements in them. Yes, it would help if you also made sure that people WANT to change, but making certain that people CAN change is your stable foundation. Instead of making the desired behaviour easier, you can also make the undesired behaviour harder. Same thing, different approach.

CAN: How to boost the capability to change

To give you some more context as to how powerful working can be upon making sure someone CAN perform the desired behaviour, I would like to round off this paragraph with some examples. First of all, the 300 million button story.[87] It's about Amazon.com. In the early days of the launch of their online shopping platform, they used to have a 'checkout form' that consisted of two fields (an email address and password), two buttons (login and register) and one link (forgot password). You would say this was quite simple. But it turned out that this form was preventing customers from buying products. They discovered that new customers didn't want to register right away, and returning customers often forgot their login and password, and then gave up after several failed login attempts. What did they do? They greatly 'uncomplicated' the desired behaviour (completing a sale). They removed the register button and replaced it with a button that said 'continue', accompanied by a simple message: 'You do not need to create an account to make purchases on our site. Simply click continue to proceed to checkout. To make your future purchases even faster, you can create an account during checkout.' The story goes that, making the desired behaviour easier by simply changing the button, boosted the sales by 45% ($300,000,000) in the first year.

The second example is somewhat more meaningful, than simply making a lot of money for Jeff Bezos. This is about making sure that talented youngsters in the US from low-income families will start applying for the financial aid needed to make their higher education accessible.[88] However, applying for this financial aid (called FAFSA) is a highly complex task, requiring information such as income tax details. It does frustrate many students and families, yet it is an important application that must be completed in order to qualify for many state and institutional grants. A team of researchers partnered with H&R Block – a tax-filing service company – in order to design an intervention to reduce the application process' complexity. They developed software that extracts information from an individual's income tax form, and uses that information to fill in the FAFSA form automatically. This way, two-thirds of the form would be already have been completed, and the rest could be filled in within less than ten minutes with the aid of a tax professional and the software. The research showed that families with high school seniors or recent graduates were 40% more likely to submit a FAFSA-application, and 33% more likely to receive a Pell grant.[89] One last example is rooted in making the desired behaviour easier to save this precious planet we all live on: The Waterpebble. The Waterpebble is an inexpensive device (less than £10), designed to help conserve water when showering. The first time you use the Waterpebble, it records the time you took for your first shower, and then it uses that as a benchmark for future showers. Rather than displaying the amount of water used, the Waterpebble automatically reduces the showering time's length. It glows green when the water starts running and goes to orange when you should be thinking about de-soaping your heavenly body, and to red when you exaggerate your splash time. It takes away your effort to monitor your water usage and to adjust it yourself. It makes the whole process effortless. The stoplight feature is a very efficient system 1-cue, and it is possible that, over time, individuals will get into the habit of taking shorter showers.[90]

These were all examples of making the desired behaviour easier, but it also works to make the undesired behaviour harder to do. A friend of mine used this on his wife and children. We were in a conversation, and he suddenly said that he has a landline again. A landline? In this day and age of mobile phones? But that was precisely the reason why he got a landline again. His wife and children were constantly on their mobile phones – properly hooked. It wasn't enjoyable to him, but neither was it to themselves. So, they decided to get themselves a phone lockbox. The moment they get home, every family member puts his or her mobile phone into the locker, and closes it. Thus, the undesired behaviour is made impossible. So, why the landline then? Well, by not having their mobile phone, they also lost their reachability. As the grandparents are getting a bit older, they wanted them to still be able to get in touch with them. Hence the landline. So, the landline wasn't an old-fashioned weird idea; it solved an anxiety that stood in the way of getting rid of the mobile phones. I think this is genius.

I wish restaurants would equip themselves with a client's landline and mobile phone lockboxes. Although I suspect some relationships will pretty soon see the end of the day. When dining out, it is shocking to see that some couples are both on their mobile phones, instead of enjoying their time together. Come to think of it, restaurant mobile-phone lockers may solve the 'comfort' of remaining in a bad relationship far too long. It will force people to take the step towards desired behaviour, and release themselves from that boring, grumpy face they wake up to every morning.

A second example of making undesired behaviour harder – well, less pleasant – is an app called 'Little Longer'.[91] Many people have a serious 'snoozing' problem, hitting that snooze button on your phone too many times, instead of getting up when your alarm sounds (the desired behaviour). This app is your alarm clock, but with a special touch: Every time you hit the 'snooze', you are donating to a good cause. You can select the non-profit of your choice and the donation amount in advance, but still, it makes lying in less desirable. Although, come to think of it, for some people it may, in a weird philanthropic kind of way, be extra motivating to sleep in extra-long.

WANT: Taking a closer look at willingness to change

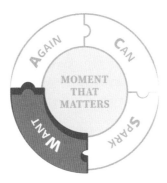

But as said, CAN- and WANT-interventions should be an intelligent interplay. When we are talking about WANTing to change, we cannot ignore the fact that we are beginning to enter the vast territory of research on human motivation.

Willingness to do something is almost always tied to being motivated. There are a lot of theories on motivation out there; most of them explain how motivation is the key concept needed for changing attitude, which then leads to a behaviour change. What is so fascinating about behavioural science is that it has brought to light the fact that it often works the other way around. People tend to change their attitudes in order to be consistent with their behaviour. And it actually works like this: as your brain is in a constant mode of lowering your cognitive load, it again jumps to the easy conclusions. If you do something a couple of times, your system 1 simply concludes: 'I am a person that does this, I must be someone who likes that.' Again, the interplay of your system 1, sending suggestions to your system 2, turns it into a belief – 'I am a person that does this.' In other words:

Attitudes follow behaviour

WANT in the SUE | SWAC Tool, therefore, is not directly focused on changing attitudes; it is all about switching to the desired behaviour. Should we be living in a perfect world, your target group would already want to show the desired behaviour. If that's the case, your only job is to make sure that the new behaviour becomes easier (working on CAN), and to make sure someone is sparked to act again and again. But often, someone isn't that eager to change behaviour. If you want to understand the willingness to change from a human-centred point of view, you must understand that motivation has one role in life, that is to help us to do the hard things. If it isn't hard, you don't need motivation.[92]

We tend to be biased when looking at someone's willingness to change. We all have made *fundamental attribution errors.*[93] When you see people acting in a certain way, or especially not acting in the way you would see fit, you might attribute it to their personality or lack of motivation. That may very well not be the case. The situation is much more likely making them do what they are doing. It's like that colleague at work you don't dig. Then one weekend, you may run into that same person in a bar. And they turn out to be very nice and quite funny. Completely the opposite of that person during your meetings. That's because context prompts behaviour. You've probably also experienced it yourself at one time. Have you ever been in a bad relationship? Ever experienced that it turned you into the worst version of yourself: Cranky, unreasonable, and super impatient? It's not that you aren't a nice person (I am sure you are), but it was your situation that prompted your behaviour. As Kahneman said: Motivation is complex, and people do good things for a mixture of good and bad reasons, and they do bad things for a mixture of good and bad reasons.[94]

Life becomes far more manageable when you live by the belief: 'good person, bad circumstances' – which forces you to have more empathy. A key trait a Behavioural Designer should have anyway. And we all know being judgmental has never brought any progress. So, when we boost willingness to change, we take this positive outtake on human nature as a starting point. We try to develop interventions that help people make the desired behaviour more desirable. We are not in the 'blaming game' but in the 'changing game'.

WANT: When to boost willingness to change

What is interesting about the willingness to change behaviour is that it can be 'way up', but it always comes down again. The best moment to influence someone is at the peak of wanting something. Let's illustrate this with an example. Let's say that you just have taken a wonderful two-week summer holiday. And as you do on a holiday, you enjoy life. You eat out, taste that local beer and wine, and you let your hair down. This is how holidays are supposed to be – carefree. Once back home again, you want to relive that holiday feeling, and you decide to look at your holiday photos. Shock. Is that you? Pictures don't lie, but honestly, there are quite some more kilos on your swimsuit body than you imagined. This photo browsing moment is a moment that matters, in which your WANTing to get rid of that extra body baggage is sky-high. You are truly ready to take action. This is a peak in your willingness to change. Important to know is that, when your willingness is up, you can do more complex things. When your willingness comes back down again, as it always does, you are less able to do hard things. In short: there are temporary opportunities to make people (or yourself) do hard things.

When willingness is high, you can get people to do hard things. But once willingness drops, people will only do easy things

From a business perspective, when your customer, your member, your patient, your user is way up surfing the WANT-wave, that's the perfect time to ask them to do hard things. And you need to do it quickly before the wave goes down, as it will. Make someone sign up for a programme, book an appointment, buy equipment on a willingness high. So, when their willingness is down again, they are enrolled or equipped already. To go back to our summer photo example. It could be it made you very highly willing (WANT) to start eating healthy. So, this is the moment to perform the effortful behaviour to go out and buy healthy foods or prep meals. When your willingness to eat healthily is low again, you have made it very easy (CAN) on yourself. You don't need to want it so badly anymore; you can easily do it because your prepped meals are just in front of you. We always go shopping at the food market on Saturday morning. This allows me to have all kinds of fresh foods in my fridge for the entire week. As I have time on Saturday, I also prep some dressings, soups, and staple foods like rice. I now don't need that much willingness to eat healthy during the week when my schedule is tight again. I just grab and go.

WANT: How to boost willingness to change

Whether you need to work on the willingness to change the behaviour of consumers, employees, citizens or your own, the basis you always must start from is to be very specific about the desired behaviour. Don't say 'exercise more', but say 'do 20 minutes of exercise two times a week'. Don't say 'eat healthy food' but say something like 'eat one piece of fruit every day to finish off your lunch'. Then look at people's jobs-to-be-done. Can you connect the desired behaviour with the job-to-be-done? You can boost the WANT to change behaviour if you can show that the desired behaviour can help someone to achieve the desired outcome. For example, People may not want to exercise (desired behaviour). Still, the result they are looking for by exercising is, for example, 'fitting into their wedding dress' or 'gaining the confidence to find a life-partner' (job-to-be-done). Addressing these jobs-to-be-done have a far greater chance of boosting someone's willingness to change. In other words, you will be most successful if you layer the willingness to change over something people already want. You must be motivation matching.[95] It needs to match what people already want to achieve. It is deep-diving into the why-questions: 'Why would someone want to change the desired behaviour? What would the desired behaviour help them achieve? How would the desired behaviour help them to progress?'

SPARK: Taking a closer look at sparking behaviour change

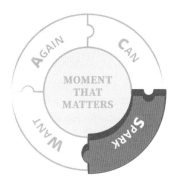

As the SUE | SWAC Tool shows, behaviour is not something that just happens, or is a very spontaneous thing. We as humans don't live in a vacuum, but operate within a situational or social context filled with distractions. You need to be fully aware that just boosting CAN, or working on WANT isn't enough. You need to get people's attention.

No behaviour happens spontaneously. Every behaviour needs to be sparked

Our system 1 continuously picks up cues in our surroundings, and makes behavioural decisions based upon them. One of the cues we want someone's system 1 to pick up is a SPARK. A spark is a cue or call to action that drives desired behaviour. Without a spark, someone may WANT and CAN perform the behaviour, but there's simply no call to action. A perfect example of this is that little optic on your car dashboard showing how much fuel you have left. I think none of us WANTs to run out of fuel, and we all CAN fill up our gas tank quite easily (on European motorways, we have gas stations everywhere). But if we didn't have the SPARK – that little red light flashing up when it is time to pull over and fill up your tank –, I guess a lot more people would need to call road assistance.

Whether sparks will work or not depends on a couple of factors. In the attention department, there are generally four reasons why someone's behaviour isn't sparked:

- *Forgetting*: It may very well be that someone wanted to engage in the desired behaviour but simply forgot to do so, and we need to remind them. In other words: we must spark again.
- *Overlooking*: Perhaps someone didn't notice our spark, and we must make sure we make our sparks more *salient*.
- *Multitasking*: If someone is multitasking – well, then our spark to trigger behaviour is just one extra task. In this case, we should help people to focus (more), so that they will see our spark.
- *Distractions*: Maybe someone is suffering from so many distractions that we must take away whatever keeps them from paying attention to our spark.

There are roughly three categories of SPARKs: *reminders* (to remind someone of the desired behaviour), *obstructions* (to have a pause in the undesired behaviour) and *interruptions* (to interfere with automatic behaviour). But reminders, obstructions and interruptions can come in many shapes and forms, and they have some characteristics to be effective: A spark should be noticeable, actionable, sensory. For a spark to work, someone should be able to spot the spark (could be with one of all of your senses), and they should know what to do when noticing the spark.

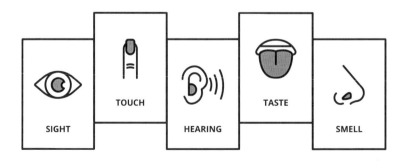

A very well-known spark is a traffic light. You see it. We all know we must stop when the light turns to red. And we know we can drive when the light is green. Another spark that has probably brought yourself into action multiple times a day is that little red notification on your mobile. You see it, and you know what to do: check your email. If someone comes up to you and extends his hand, that's a spark. You see it, and you know it means you can shake his hand. The arrows on the shop floor in Ikea's are sparks: your system 1 notices them almost subconsciously, and you're very inclined to follow them. At Schiphol Airport, they experimented with reducing the spillage rate in the men's toilets. They decided to put a little black fly into the toilets deriving from the idea that men like to 'aim and conquer'. The experiment was a raving success; reportedly, the spillage rates dropped, and the cleaning company responsible for doing the toilets said the cleaner's costs decreased by 20%.[96] The tiny rubber flies did cause some splattering, so toilet manufacturer Sphinx was ordered to make toilets with the flies engraved. These are now installed across the airport. Who would have guessed a fake fly could be a successful behavioural spark? Sparks can also be internal. Think about a rumbling stomach; it sparks you to eat something. Only for us, it's hard to design those kinds of inner sparks. So, you'll have to focus on the external sparks. Sparks can come to us through all our senses: Sight, hearing, smell, touch, taste. An example of a tactile spark is one of those watches that vibrates when you've got to take some more steps to keep fit. A well-known example of an odorous spark to promote buying behaviour is making sure you have just baked a fresh apple pie when selling your house.

SPARK: It's all about timing

You can spark someone at exactly the right moment or exactly the wrong moment. These are closely linked to timing. Again, for a spark to work, you need to return to the Moments that Matter you have identified.

Sparking is triggering behaviour at relevant decision points

Let me first give you an example of sparking at a wrong decision point: A friend of ours once booked a flight to the US with United. He was supposed to take the flight: but the truth is his flight got cancelled. Yet on the same day, he got an email with the following question: 'On a scale from 1 to 10, how likely are you to recommend United Airlines?' Automated ice-cold spark moment. On the other hand, if you own a road assistance service that spans Europe and helps clients in their mother tongue, when would it then be the best time to get someone to become a client? On the first of January to secure a year of road assistance? No, that is the time when most people have spent too much money already. A better sparking moment would be just before the summer holidays. A lot of people go on vacation by car in Europe. A lot of them go to France, though not many of them speak French. And only a few French people speak English (excusez-moi if I just offended all the French). So, joining a European road assistance that speaks your language makes a lot of sense before the holidays – just think about the nightmare of your car breaking down on the Route du Soleil with two crying kids in the back seat, while you must explain the problem in French to an only French-speaking mechanic. This is more than enough to convince someone to join your service.

Choosing the right sparking moment can make all the difference between an intervention being successful or not. Let me showcase this with a real-life example again.[97] An example that also shows why a psychological understanding of the Moments that Matter is crucial concerning people who have kept paying their rent too late, which has complicated their lives as they ran seriously behind in their rental payments. This all changed when they examined the spark moments. Traditionally, the next month's rent was due by the end of the month. When this was changed to the beginning of the month, they noticed rent payments had gone up. Why? At the beginning of the month, people receive their salaries. And even people in debt at that moment have the psychological feeling (entirely subjectively) that they've got money. When they were sparked to pay the rent at that time, more people did pay their rent. And their 'putting off'-behaviour very much declined (the red line in the graphic).

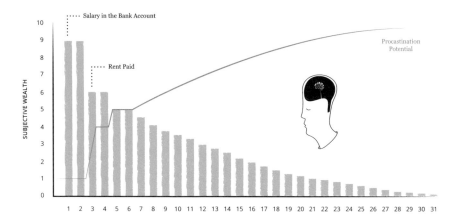

Data source: Hogeschool van Amsterdam

More recently, a behavioural experiment conducted by the Common Cents Lab of Duke University in collaboration with the Beneficial State Bank (BSB) showed the same importance of matching income flows as to payments.[98] Banks cannot influence the situations people have to face, like loss of income or a job, but they can affect the timing of the 'sparks' by closing the gap between salary payments and loan payments. If you buy a car, the default spark moment to pay for your car insurance is often the day you purchased the vehicle. Offering the bank's clients the opportunity to change this default spark moment has helped them to perform far better in terms of 'on-time payments, and total payments'.[99] If you think about it, this is significant, or as the research team put it: 'Even a single late payment on your car loan can result in late fees, and damage their credit score. Not to mention the worst-case scenario of repossession, which can jeopardise a person's ability to work and earn an income.' So, here you see that a small intervention in the timing of sparks can positively impact people's financial independence. As a bonus, at the same time, adding some smart Behavioural Design can help banks to turn around their reputation of being the 'big bad money machines'. Win-win. I've come across another example of a beautiful collision of a job-to-be-done and a perfect spark moment. This is the true story of a nine-year-old girl scout who sold out 300 boxes of cookies within 6 hours ... outside a medical marijuana dispensary.[100] Her simple but very effective message was: 'Satisfy your munchies.' It was a record-breaking sales campaign. There was some debate whether it violated girl-scout rules – but from a Behavioural Design point of view, it was (literally) right on the money.

A spark type that can be very successful is a *planning spark*. These are gentle reminders helping to set someone into action at the moments that matter. These planning sparks can have a very positive impact on a person's life. Take this example from Uruguay. In Uruguay, children of four and five can attend pre-school. Doing so is crucial in their development: Pre-school children develop cognitive, socio-economic as well as motor skills. Children who do not participate in pre-school regularly, often insufficiently develop these skills, which impairs them reaching their full potential in later life. Literature shows that children with frequent pre-school absences are likely to have lower academic results later, and perform worse in the labour market.[101] In addition, absences decrease as the grade level increases.[102] It was time for a behavioural intervention at Uruguay's public pre-schools (*Consejo de Educación Inicial y Primaria* [CEIP] centres).[103] In this case, the intervention covered the whole SWAC-approach. The researchers decided to work with personalised text messages, delivered to the parents. Four behavioural interventions were applied, but the planning spark looked like this: '[Parent name]: Think on the reasons that may have prevented your child from attending school last year. Create a plan to avoid them this school year!' Messages were sent 3 to 4 times a week.[104] The intervention had no average treatment effect on attendance; results ranged widely across groups, from increased attendance from 0.38 to 1.48 days throughout nine weeks. Children in remote areas increased attendance on average by 1.5 days. Among all children in the study, the intervention increased language development by 0.10 standard deviations, an impact similar to that of very labour-intensive programmes, such as home visits. Willingness and planning sparks could be introduced at minimal expense using the government's mobile app.

Let us now look at another behavioural intervention strategy making use of planning prompts, this time in Kenya. What was the case? Unfortunately, in Kenya there are many people infected with HIV. Luckily, there is treatment now. However, medicine needs to be administered regularly for this treatment to be effective. Patients' obedience in taking their medication has declined, especially in rural areas. This can be a challenge as medical assistance isn't around the corner. Researchers decided to see if planning sparks, reminding people to take their medication might help.[105] This was achieved by sending people SMS notifications either daily or weekly. They experimented with short and long messages. The short message was designed solely as a reminder; the longer message included social support. As only 45% of the patients owned a mobile phone, these were provided to those in need.

	English	Swahili	Dholuo
Short reminder	This is your reminder.	Hili ni kumbukumbu lako.	Ma en ote ma iparonigo.
Long reminder	This is your reminder. Be strong and courageous, we care about you.	Hili ni kumbukumbu lako. Uwe na ujasiri, tunakujali.	Ma en ote ma iparonigo. Bed motegno kendo bed gi chir, wageni.

Data source: Pop-Eleches, Thirumurthy, Habyarimana et al. (2000)

The researchers didn't find any difference between the long and the short messages, but the results were promising. The weekly SMS-reminders increased the taking of the medicine (at least 90% throughout the study) by 13 percentage points on average. This is 13% fewer people facing the chance of dying of AIDS! I love how, in this study, SWAC comes together. The repeated text messages (SPARK AGAIN), the personalisation and social support (WANT) and the handing out of mobile phones (CAN). The willingness may be further boosted by trying out different social or identity messages in the long reminder, but that's just a game of testing, learning and optimisation. But also look at the JTBD; framing a message from a JTBD point-of-view can be so powerful. For example: 'protect or care for your loved ones'. It is a matter of tweaking until you find the ultimate formula.

Are you ready for another example from the health-care realm? It is another example of Behavioural Design to increase medication intake. In this case, statins are a group of medicines that are very effective in managing chronic diseases such as high blood pressure and diabetes. The drug itself is pretty cost-effective, much more than the treatment needed if people do not take it. The researchers working on this intervention decided to approach behaviour change by sending diabetics patients letters in order to nudge them to make an appointment with their doctor to check if statin could be the right medicine for them. They experimented with two letters sent by the Oklahoma Health Authority: one containing no behavioural interventions and the other with a more persuasive design. I wanted to show you how they used a very original spark. A magnetic post-it was included in the behavioural designed letter that reminded people to make an appointment. It is a brilliant 'little big idea': a capability and a spark in one. People will themselves put this post-it (spark) at a spark moment that makes them see the post-it regularly. Probably at the fridge, where they will 'encounter' the spark several times a day. Having someone subconsciously pick their spark moments is something we can 'steal like an artist'. Oh, by the way, it also had a positive effect.' After 60 days, nudge recipients were 7% more likely to have obtained prescriptions than 4% of those who received a simple recommendation to see a doctor about their cholesterol levels. While the absolute numbers were not large, the data revealed how effective an inexpensive nudge could be – in this case yielding a 75% increase in impact.[106] By the way, a $5 gift card didn't affect the patient's behaviour.

AGAIN: Taking a closer look at repetition in order to shape a desired behaviour

Remember, you need to always consider the desired behaviour as something new for people. Even the one-off behaviour. Therefore, it is so vital to spark behaviour AGAIN and AGAIN. You need to get people over the *Behaviour Change Threshold*. If you are designing for behaviour change, it looks like this:

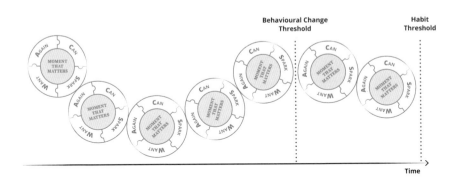

Let me illustrate this with an example from my private life. I live in the city centre of Amsterdam, and every month we get this door-to-door paper about things happening in our neighbourhood. I always read it (my willingness to do so is relatively strong as it concerns my immediate living environment). One day I read a tiny ad from two retired technicians located in the community centre. It stated that they had started a free consultation hour, in which you could get broken electrical devices checked and repaired by them. I had this beautiful lamp of which the switch hadn't worked for over a year. I am an absolute no-no as to all electric things, so the ad was a lifesaver. I was very willing to go over and see them, and this was something I could do (it was across the street and the service was free). Then it was dinner time; I folded up the paper; and three days later, it landed in the paper bin, and a week later outside in the recycling container. I forgot (one of the attention blockers – remember?). No behaviour happened. The lamp was still sadly dark. If I had come across a flyer in the neighbourhood, a sign near the community centre, or could have sent a direct message to the technicians, I would have been reminded of it. In the end, I repaired the lamp myself (yes, unexpected capabilities!). But I hope it sheds some light on why you need more than one intervention (oh yes, I love a good old word joke).

For behaviour to happen, it should be made available to us. It should be sparked AGAIN and AGAIN

Byron Sharp has 'coined' this helpful *mental and physical availability* concept to be the keystone as to a brand's success. And which I think might also be relevant at behavioural success. He states that mental availability isn't awareness or salience. 'It refers to the probability that a buyer will notice, recognise and think of a brand in buying situations. It depends on the quality and quantity of memory structures related to the brand.'[107] In this case, 'buying situations' is just a specific form of behaviour (to buy); we can replace it with any desired behaviour. It concerns the point someone makes at a decision. In Sharp's case about a brand, we can replace this with your specific offering. The fact is, you need to build memory structures. We can do this by creating more SWAC- interventions. They are our gateway to the mental and physical availability.

Mental and physical availability make us remember to perform behaviour

To recap, adding AGAIN to your behavioural interventions is helping someone to continue with a desired behaviour. There are several ways of doing this. Making the behaviour easier (CAN) is essential, and making sure people WANT to continue is essential. And, of course, SPARKs like those reminders do help.

AGAIN: How to design for sticky behaviour change

It almost goes without saying that if your objective is to design a repeat behaviour, adding AGAIN is of even more importance. Most behavioural intervention strategies aim not only to change behaviour, but to change this new behaviour into a routine behaviour (a habit), so that the new behaviour will stick. For something to become a habit, the desired behaviour must become system 1. It must become automatic. Someone shouldn't need to think about the new behaviour anymore; a person simply does it. This can be achieved if you are able to make someone perform a new behaviour over and over AGAIN, and can help them to pass the *Habit Threshold* – as illustrated in the visual on the previous page. As Aristotle already stated:

We are what we repeatedly do

To this he added: 'Excellence, then, is not an act, but a habit.' The habit-building subject is utterly fascinating, but also very comprehensive. Out there you will find dozens of books dedicated entirely to the subject of habits. This isn't one of them. However, you and I do have to deal with the habits of people. They are firmly located in the comfort zone of our SUE | Influence Framework, and you will come across them more than once. Next to this, designing automatic behaviours (which habits are) is a Behavioural Designers' ultimate desire. If we can make positive behaviours automatic, we will be able to save the world and the people that live on it in 'one fell swoop'. As Behavioural Designers, we do owe it to ourselves to know a little more about habits. The most essential insight from all the habit books I've read is that:

A small-changes approach helps to create sticky behaviours

In one study,[108] volunteers who wanted to lose weight were randomised at a habit-forming intervention, using a small-changes approach and a non-intervention control group. The small-changes approach consisted of a leaflet with ten simple diet and activity behaviours. The control group only had the end-goal of wanting to lose weight. After eight weeks, the small changes group had lost 2 kg, compared to the 0.4 kg in the control group. At 32 weeks, the habit-forming group had still lost only an average of 3.2 kg. What was most interesting is that interviews with the small-changes group revealed that they considered their new behaviours' second nature. They even felt odd not doing them.[109] The behaviours had become habits. So, why do small steps help? Not engaging in the desired behaviour – so-called *procrastination* – often is about starting that behaviour. Once you have started a behaviour, it becomes easier.[110] This again refers to the importance of capability: if habits are small or easy to start, someone is less likely to procrastinate. One way to do this is to break up behaviour into smaller units. There's this example of the writer Trollope, who wrote over 50 novels, giving proof of an unbelievable productivity. He didn't judge his progress as to the number of chapters or books he wrote, but he measured it in 15-minute units. And every day, he set a goal of 250 words every 15 minutes, and made it a habit (custom) to do this for three hours a day.[111] In his own words: 'It had at this time become my custom and is still my custom though of late I have become a little lenient of myself, to write with my watch before me, and to require of myself 250 words every quarter of an hour. This division of time allowed me to produce over ten pages of an ordinary novel volume a day, and if kept up through ten months, would have given as its results three novels of three volumes each the year.'[112] Another way to make habits easier, is to use the two-minute rule: 'When you start a new habit, it should take less than two minutes.' Here are some examples based on the book *Atomic Habits:*[113]

- 'Reading a book every week' would become 'Read one page every night'
- 'Do 30 minutes of stretching', would become 'Do one stretching exercise'
- 'Fold the laundry' would become 'Fold one pair of socks'
- 'Run three miles' would become 'Jog for 2 minutes'

People must master the habit of starting by making new behaviours easier to perform

An automatic behaviour first needs to be established, before it can be improved: 'You have to standardize before you can optimize. The more you ritualize the beginning of a process, the more likely you can slip into the state of deep focus required to do great things.'[114] As you master the art of starting, the first two minutes simply become a ritual at the beginning of a more extensive routine. Apart from making the desired behaviour smaller, there is another effective behavioural intervention. For, in psychological research, habits are seen as 'actions that are triggered automatically in response to the contextual cues associated with their performance'.[115] To phrase it easier: Cues in our context can trigger our action. For example, you put on your seatbelt (action) when getting into your car (contextual cue) or wash your hands (action) after going to the toilet (contextual cue). Therefore, making behaviour smaller and attaching it to a relevant context, helps us to form habits. How might this work? Looking back at previous examples, you can start by coming up with a stable context, and then add an 'every time' rule:

- I will read one page every time I get into bed
- I will do one stretching exercise every time I get up
- I will fold one pair of socks every time I start up my computer
- I will put on my running shoes every time I get dressed

If you are looking for a relevant, stable context, you may see if you can piggyback to an existing habit (or behaviour). This makes the new behaviour easier to perform. Referring to our examples: You already have to get out of bed, go to sleep, get dressed, or start up your computer. These are stable contexts. In order to make the behaviour easier in these chosen contexts, you can add the cue:

- Already put a book next to your bed
- Already lay out your exercise mat in your living room
- Already put one pair of socks next to your computer
- Already put your running shoes in front of your closet

This approach context, the cue, the small-changes approach may seem trivial, but can lead to significant results, such as contributing to children's health, happiness and learning capabilities. Let me give an example from practice. More and more children are not sufficiently active physically, which is critical in helping their bodies and minds to stay healthy. The *Daily Mile* programme uses the concept of a stable context, combined with a small changes- approach in order to get children moving. The programme gets pupils to run, jog or walk a mile in the school grounds (stable context) every day. This takes only 15 minutes (a small change), and they can do the daily mile in their regular clothing. Often, schools have pre-marked tracks in the school grounds (cue). These have had excellent results. Teachers report that children have improved levels of alertness, mood and verbal memory (7% increase),[116] it does help children to focus better in class and makes them happier,[117] it promotes positive peer-to-peer and teacher-child relationships,[118] it enhances learning outcomes,[119] it has a positive effect on the school environment,[120] while children report feeling calmer after the daily mile,[121] it improves their attitude towards psychical activity,[122] it improves their fitness (9% increase)[123] and their leg strength (5% increase),[124] and it reduces their body fat (4%).[125] It helps children to reach one-third of the WHO's daily psychical activity target[126] cost-effectively.[127] The Daily Mile programme is now a habit in almost 14,000 schools in 85 countries. Which means that over 3 million children are now getting more physical activity on a daily basis.[128] Easy does it.

I can imagine that at this point, a question crops up like: how many times or what length of a period does it take before something becomes a habit? I wish I had a clear-cut answer for you, but I don't. Literature seems to have different opinions on how often you must repeat something before it becomes a habit – varying from 21 days to 66 days. However, I've looked into some scientific research. A research team in London[129] decided to figure out how long it takes to form a habit. They examined 96 people over 12 weeks, and checked up on them every day to see if a new behaviour had become automatic. They both tested easy behaviour 'drinking water at lunch', and more complex behaviour like 'going for a 15-minute run before having dinner'. After these 12 weeks, the researchers asked people at what point the behaviour had felt automatic to them. The answer – I warned you there was no clear-cut answer in the study, varied between 18 to 254 days. When they took the average, it boiled down to 66 days. So, on average, it takes more than two months in order to build a habit, but (there's the 'but') it varies as to the behaviour, person and circumstances. If you are good at arithmetic, you will have noticed that 254 days are more than 12 weeks – the length of the study. And you're right – the researchers used the data to do an estimation over longer timelines. So, to conclude, anyone who claims to have found the golden rule of the number of repetitions or days as to forming a habit, you should not take seriously. It all depends on the behaviour, the person, and the circumstances. But if you are doing a pop-quiz and have to give an informed answer, your safest bet is:

It takes between 2 to 8 months to build a habit. Not 21 days

However, there is one way you can make an informed estimation of how long it takes before your user will pass the habit threshold. You do need data. When we worked for the fitness chain, they could see by their member's data how many times someone visited one of their gyms, and when most people cancelled their subscription or renewed it. By these data, they could see that they would become long-term members if someone regularly came to the gym for three months. Knowing this, we created Behavioural Design interventions in order to help someone make it through those first three months, so that we could help them to build a lasting healthy exercise habit. Thus, crossing the habit threshold. This is the only way I can tell you to gain more certainty over the needed period. When you don't have data, you can start collecting them. Now for some good news. The same research found that missing one opportunity to perform this behaviour did not affect the habit-building process. 'Repeating a behaviour in a consistent context, automaticity increases it.'[130] You should stick to new behaviour for a more extended period, but you can give yourself some 'slack' when you miss a few days. Building habits is not an all-or-nothing game.

Another good reason to spark AGAIN and AGAIN: Usage and retention

You will probably run into some resistance when trying to convince your manager that you need to confront clients more than once with the desired be-haviour when this desired behaviour is about sales. Many executives strongly favour masking costs in order to boost sales, and they certainly don't want to have them mentioned more than once. Therefore, we see so many all-inclu-sive packages that neatly bundle a stack of small prices together, promoting pre-paid yearly subscriptions, season tickets or reductions for auto-enrolment payments. This sounds logical: clients get payment out of the way, and suppli-ers have their money in the bank. Therefore, it may sound counterintuitive, but from a behavioural science perspective, this is not always the most effective road to take. It can be very beneficial to cut up prices and confront clients more than once with it in order to boost product usage and repeat sales. Researchers found that timing follows consumption.[131] That sounds abstract. Let me explain what the researchers discovered when they examined the actual behaviour of gym members. Researchers wanted to know which gym members a) visited the gym most frequently, and b) who of them renewed their gym subscriptions. As you know, most gyms try to promote yearly subscriptions. The longer your gym contract, the higher the price reduction you get. However, the people on an an-nual payment plan attended the gym far less than those on a monthly payment plan. This matters as a client who doesn't use a product is not inclined to buy that product again. In other words, by using the psychology of pricing, you can see to it that consumers keep returning.[132]

The frequency with which you pay has a dramatic impact on how much you consume[133]

This is what the analysis of the gym's records showed: 'consumption closely follows the timing of payments'. Whether members made annual, semi-annual or quarterly payments, gym use was the highest in the months immediately af-ter following payment, and declined steadily until the next payment. Members who paid monthly used the gym most consistently, making the price scheme most likely to generate membership renewals.[134] Generally, acquisition costs exceed retention costs, so there is another good reason to SPARK AGAIN and

AGAIN. Especially when you realise that quitters are also not likely to become your ambassadors.

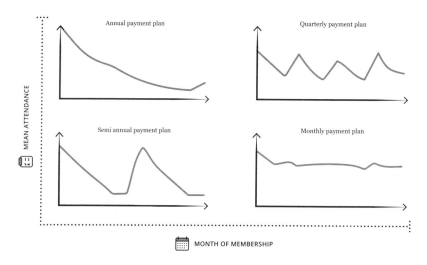

Data source: John T. Gourville and Dilip Soman (2002)

Interestingly though, this same insight is not just relevant to marketing and sales. The same researchers suggest the same concept could be applied to healthcare. Most of us pay an insurance fee that covers our medical costs. However, do you exactly know how much your visit to your GP costs? Or a mammogram? There is little to no cost transparency in health care insurance. One could argue that more cost transparency might help people reconsider the number of health care visits they make, helping to reduce overall health care budgets. That's true, but in this case, cost transparency could also help tackle another health care challenge: Making sure that people get their so much needed health care. According to the researchers '15% of insured children do not get all the immunizations they need, 30% of insured at-risk women fail to get mammograms within any two-year window, and 50% of insured men over 50 fail to have physical exams within any three-year period'.[135] If you could remind people every month that they are paying amount X for their health care anyway, this might spark them to get the care they need: 'I am paying for it, I am not going to let it go to waste.' Therefore, this interesting side-effect of sparking behaviour, AGAIN and AGAIN, can be explained from the *sunken cost effect*. People tend to engage in the behaviour if an investment in money (or effort, or time) is made. We don't want to waste what we have already spent.

Recap Developing Interventions

What is important to know about the SWAC Tool©?	You need to remember that you should treat every desired behaviour as new. Therefore, you need to ensure someone can and wants to show the behaviour. And you must spark the desired behaviour more than once.
How does SWAC help us come up with ideas?	It is a system 1 cue to remember the four elements needed for behavioural change. It sounds like swag (which is a bonus), but it stands for this easy-to-remember formula: **Behavioural Change = Spark x Want x Again x Can**
What are we looking for?	People need both capability (CAN) and willingness (WANT) to shift to the desired behaviour, we are looking for ideas to boost both. However, no behaviour happens spontaneously or overnight. Therefore, you need to SPARK the desired behaviour AGAIN and again.
How can you develop SWAC interventions?	By asking these four questions: **CAN:** can someone perform the desired behaviour? **WANT:** does someone want to perform the desired behaviour? **SPARK:** is someone set into action at the right moment? **AGAIN:** more than once?

Using the SUE | SWAC Tool in practice: Asking the right questions

Adding SWAC to Moments that Matter

1. How can we make sure someone WANTS to perform the desired behaviour?
2. How can we make sure someone CAN perform the desired behaviour?
3. How can we SPARK the desired behaviour at the Moments that Matter?
4. How can we activate the desired behaviour AGAIN and again?

However, understanding the SWAC elements is one thing, making them work is another. We had to design behaviour in practice; we had clients who came to us with real behavioural challenges that needed real answers. So, I wanted (and needed) more. I wanted to know how you can boost WANT to change or how to grow CAN. That's why I turned to behavioural psychology again. And I found answers, or better put: I found behavioural principles rooted in behavioural science. I not only read about the principles that were only test-proofed in lab settings, but I also read all about the successful application of these principles in real-life situations. Some turned out to be a clear showcase of applying behavioural science to boost capability; some were helping to increase willingness. Others were intelligent ways to spark someone into action or to add repetition. I loved discovering all these scientific principles and working interventions. But again, it was pretty overwhelming. There were days the research reports were stacked up on my desk. In almost every one of them, I found interesting, working Behavioural Design interventions that I wanted to remember. And I couldn't. Also system 2, I guess. I needed to bring back simplicity again to prevent myself from drowning in this whirling pool of information. So, I did. Instead of trying to remember all possible behavioural principles or the working combinations, I found out that life becomes much easier if you realise that:

1. *Finding the right intervention is a matter of asking the right questions*
    Some people know all behavioural principles by heart. Still, you can now
    breathe a sigh of relief. That is unnecessary for you to do, and not even the
    most productive. Even if you can recite all behavioural principles, which
    still doesn't make it easy for you to apply them. You need to know what they
    help to solve. So, I did they work for you. I have read dozens of Behavioural
    Design success cases, and our SUE team has solved dozens of behavioural
    challenges themselves. This gave me a treasure box of input from which
    I could back-engineer. I carefully analysed the underlying questions that
    needed to be answered. And then, I researched which principles were
    put in place to help to do this. Let me give you an example to make this all
    less abstract. I already mentioned Robert Cialdini. In his bestselling book
    Influence,[136] he has identified six principles of persuasion that explain the
    psychology of why people say 'yes'. You could learn these principles by
    heart (reciprocity, scarcity, authority, commitment/consistency, liking, so-
    cial proof/consensus), but they become much more workable if you know
    how and when to apply them. So, for instance, I back engineered 'social
    proof' to 'Can we make sure we show that similar others are already show-
    ing the desired behaviour?' This way, I created a workable set of SWAC In-
    tervention Questions© both to boost CAN and WANT.

2. *By starting with a question, you begin looking at the behavioural
    principles as possible lenses*
    Behavioural Design is not a one-trick pony. You often need a combination
    of interventions to make someone change behaviour. Our SUE teams often
    refer to the ideation process as 'gathering pieces of the puzzle'. The shape of
    the SUE | SWAC Tool isn't just based on semantics; solving a Behavioural
    Design challenge is solving a complex puzzle. It is seldom the same. Inter-
    ventions are context-dependent, and not one size fits all. Therefore, as a Be-
    havioural Designer, you need more aces up your sleeve. By starting with a
    question, you begin to look at the behavioural principles as lenses in order
    to look through at your challenge. It helps you come up with as many pieces
    of the puzzle as possible in a structured way.

To make it even more straightforward, I want to introduce you to *The Magnificent Ten* of CAN- and WANT-intervention questions. In the appendix, you can check out the whole set of SWAC Intervention Questions, and you can find more information about the book website. For now, if you have these two sets of ten questions, you'll go a long way. They have been selected as the intervention questions we use most at SUE and have consistently yielded results. There's no specific order in the questions; it is simply your toolbox with different lenses to solve your behavioural challenge.

 TOOL: DOWNLOAD THE SUE | SWAC TOOL CHEAT CARD

Using the SUE | SWAC Tool in practice: Coming up with ideas

Okay, time to get practical again. You have the insights from your SUE | Influence Framework that you have translated into a HWM question or a Behavioural Statement. This is the starting point for your ideation. Now, follow this four-step process:

1. Take your Behavioural Statement (or an HMW question) and start by identifying the Moments that Matter in solving this Behavioural Statement. There are always more moments. Think back about the successful and unsuccessful journeys people have described to you in the Insight step. This should help you to pinpoint the key moments in their decision-making process. What were the moments at which the desired behaviour could have a lift-off? What are potentially drop-out moments? Which moments had very strong emotions tied to them: both negative and positive? Emotions are always a good indicator to pinpoint moments that matter, as emotions are signals that inform you whether someone is getting closer (or not) to achieving their job-to-be-done.

2. Now, ask yourself these four questions as to the specific Moment that Matters:

    a. Must I make the desired behaviour easier (CAN)?
    b. Must I boost someone's willingness to engage in the desired behaviour (WANT)?
    c. How can I set the desired behaviour into action (SPARK)?
    d. How can I make sure someone will engage in the desired behaviour AGAIN?

The rest of this chapter (up to concepting) can be seen as your 'Behavioural Design Playbook' in which you will find the 'Magnificent 10' lists of SWAC Intervention Questions. Each intervention question is explained with examples in which the specific behavioural intervention has been applied, so that you understand what that intervention can bring you and give you inspiration for solving your own behavioural challenge. Just browse through the following pages. You may want to read them all first, so that you know what behavioural interventions are possible. But I expect that later on you will use this chapter much more as a reference (hence the name Playbook). I also hope that on these pages of the book, you will write down most of your own notes: what worked and what did not.

Your task now is to develop as many ideas as possible that will help you design behaviour for the specific Moment that Matters using the intervention questions. So look at a Moment that Matters. Decide whether you need to do a CAN, WANT or combination of both intervention there. Suppose you need to do a CAN intervention, then browse to the 'Magnificent 10' CAN questions and select 3 or up to 5 intervention questions that you think might influence the behaviour at that Moment that Matters. You will see that you instinctively already know which of the ten questions will be the most relevant to answer, because you have spoken to people. Now take one intervention question at a time and try to think of answers for it. So, take one intervention question, think of ideas, take the next intervention question, think of ideas, and so on. Do this for each intervention question you have chosen and for each Moment that Matters. If necessary, read first the explanation of the chosen CAN and WANT intervention question and the example cases on the following pages. This will help to inspire you. I have made a video for you that takes you through the process of ideation (and how to use this book) in a little more detail.

 VIDEO: WATCH THE VIDEO USING THE SWAC INTERVENTION QUESTIONS AND THIS BOOK IN IDEATION?

We use a creative technique called brainwriting in ideation. This is working individually and trying to come up with as many ideas as possible within 5 to 10 minutes per question, writing each idea down on a separate post-it. I made a video to explain this technique. Do a brainwriting round for all your chosen CAN and WANT intervention questions.

 VIDEO: WATCH THE VIDEO HOW DOES BRAINWRITING WORK?

3. After this, think about SPARK and AGAIN ideas. Which order you want. For SPARKS, ask yourself: can you think of ideas for reminders, obstacles, or interruptions for the Moment that Matters? For AGAIN ideas, choose 5 intervention questions from the AGAIN 'Magnificent 10' list. In either case, do brainwriting rounds to develop a range of ideas.

To summarise, for each Moment that Matters:

a. CAN intervention needed? Choose 5 CAN Intervention Questions, do brainwriting for each individual question.
b. WANT intervention needed? Choose 5 WANT Intervention Questions, do brainwriting for each individual question.
c. Choose 5 SWAC Intervention Questions for AGAIN, do brainwriting for each individual question.
d. Do a 5-10 minute brainwriting round to come up with SPARK ideas.

You'll end up with a stack of ideas on loose post-its; in the next chapter, "Concepting," I'll show you what to do with them. OK, now that you know what to do, it's time to do it. Time to introduce you to the SWAC Intervention Questions. I start with the CAN and WANT Intervention Questions, illustrated with examples. Followed by the AGAIN Intervention Questions and an overview of possible SPARKS.

TO DO: IDEATE TO COME UP WITH CAN, WANT, SPARK AND AGAIN-IDEAS

Designing behaviour in practice: CAN and WANT Intervention Questions

On the next page you find the two Magnificent 10-lists in order to come up with ideas to boost CAN and WANT. They are followed by explaining the behavioural principle attached to the Intervention Question, and then illustrated with real-life examples. I have made a download of these two lists, so you can keep them at hand when you're developing ideas to shape decisions and behaviour.

TOOL: DOWNLOAD THE 'MAGNIFICENT 10' CHEAT CARDS

THE MAGNIFICENT 10

CAN we make the desired behaviour(s) easier (Or undesired behaviours harder) to do?

C1.	Can we give less options to choose from?	Option Reduction
C2.	Can we ask an easier question?	Question Substitution
C3.	Can we make it more distinctive?	Salience
C4.	Can we add or take away hurdles?	Friction
C5.	Can we use easier words?	Clarity
C6.	Can we break-down the behaviour into smaller steps?	Chunking
C7.	Can we show what people have to do next?	Specificity
C8.	Can we provide personal guidance?	Assisting
C9.	Can we add a deadline?	Forcing Function
C10.	Can we pause people in their behaviour?	Decision Points

THE MAGNIFICENT 10

WANT how might we make someone willing to show the desired behaviour(s) or unwilling to show the undesired behaviours?

W1.	Can we show the behaviour of others?	Social proof/bandwagon effect
W2.	Can we remind someone of their social image/identity?	Social identity/signalling
W3.	Can we make it personal?	Personalisation
W4.	Can we present information in a different way?	Framing
W5.	Can we make people feel they are losing out on something?	Loss aversion
W6.	Can we make someone aware of their future self?	Hyperbolic discounting
W7.	Can we show progress in percentage or in abstract measurements?	Feedback
W8.	Can we make the end-goal of the behaviour visual?	Feedback
W9.	Can we add meaning to a number or statistics?	Anchoring
W10.	Can we design a positive state-of-mind?	Priming

C1. Can we give less options to choose from? OPTION REDUCTION

We live in a liberal society, and tend to feel that our freedom of choice is one of our greatest accomplishments. However, from a behavioural psychology point of view, offering someone too many options to choose from will negatively influence people's behaviour. This is also called *the paradox of choice*, a concept coined by Barry Schwartz: 'Learning to choose is hard. Learning to choose well is harder. And learning to choose well in a world of unlimited possibilities is harder still, perhaps too hard.'[137] He claims that less is indeed more, when it comes to directing someone in making a decision. So, what negative effects might there appear when we have too many choices?

1. First of all, having too many options causes may result in *apathy*, simply because it requires too much cognitive activity. This might lead to decision fatigue, or even to not making any decision at all.[138] This phenomenon is called *choice paralysis* (also called *choice deferral*). There is a cognitive bias related to this phenomenon called *regret aversion*. When people anticipate regret due to a choice, they tend not to act at all. This might have severe consequences. A meta-analysis has shown that people's behaviour in accepting medical treatments are more influenced to avoid regretting the making a wrong choice, than they are influenced by other kinds of anticipated negative emotions.[139] Therefore, in designing a choice, you need to be aware that the number of options you present to someone also will increase the probability of choice regret, which might enhance inertia. In the mentioned example, this was shown to seriously impact behaviour as regards health.

2. Secondly, if we have more options to choose from, we tend to make worse decisions as we rely even more on our system 1-cues, which might be biased.[140] Examples of this are our tendency to stick to defaults, recommendations, or reliance on peer choices.[141] Have you ever said in a restaurant: 'I'll have what they are having'? Well, probably this was caused by the option overload on the menu. Research has shown what happens when there are six or thirty food options on a menu. In the first case, people tend to choose for themselves. In the second case, they choose what their partner chooses.[142]

3. Thirdly, we tend to make more *conservative* choices and avoid making more innovative and maybe even better decisions. Again this has to do with our tendency to minimise the potential for regret.[143]

4. And finally, the more options we have to choose from, the *less satisfied* we are with the choice we made. The more options, the more we feel we 'missed out on them.' In his book, Schwartz described two experiments. One in which people had to choose between 20 varieties of jams, and another where the choice was between six models of jeans. The experiment showed that the more choices people had, the less satisfied they were about their final choice. This matches Sheena Iyengar's research – a professor at the Columbia Business School and author of *The Art of Choosing* – which taught us that 'the existence of multiple alternatives makes it easy for us to imagine alternatives that don't exist – alternatives that combine the attractive features of the ones that do exist. And to the extent that we engage our imaginations in this way, we will be even less satisfied with the alternative we end up choosing. So, once again, a greater variety of choices makes us feel worse.'[144] Therefore, having too many choices has been associated with feelings of unhappiness.[145] Or, to put it more positively: Limiting the number of options may lead to more satisfying choices. Now, let me tell you a bit more about the jams' study: On a regular day at a local food market, people came across a display table with 24 different jams.[146] Then, on another day at the same food market, people were offered only 6 different types of jam to choose from. The result as to the buying behaviour? The six choices showed a sales uplift of 1,000%.

Paradox of Choice

LESS IS MORE – TOO MUCH CHOICE IS STRESSFUL

When is option reduction the most effective? A meta-analysis[147] comparing 99 scientific studies on *choice overload* showed that option reduction will work the best:

1. When people want to make a quick and easy choice
2. When the product is complex (so that fewer choices help to decide)
3. When it's difficult to compare alternatives
4. When consumers don't have clear preferences

From an ethical point of view, it is good to distinguish between options and choices. We feel it could be very effective Behavioural Design:

It is possible to help someone make better decisions by limiting an option, but you shouldn't forbid a choice

Let me illustrate the difference with an example. Limiting the number of options or omitting some has proved very effective in helping people who are struggling with obesity. One way to combat obesity is to change eating habits. Many interventions have been developed and tested to help people change their eating patterns. In a meta-analysis that pooled data from nearly 96 behavioural experiments on successfully promoting healthy eating, the most effective intervention was found to be changing the number of plate and cup size options. In many restaurants you can choose between different cup sizes. In the study, simply removing the largest option (in this case, large 16-ounce cups) helped people eat less and still feel satisfied. Although you are taking away options with this intervention, you are not taking away people's freedom of choice. They still have the choice to refill their cup or buy a second serving. Only, not many people seem to do that. By simply limiting the options, it became easier for people to adjust their behaviour. Changing the size of tableware can also be very effective. A variant of option restriction is the so-called *default option*. An option that is chosen for you by default. You can still choose another option (freedom of choice), but since people would rather make less effort than more, many will stick with the option they have already chosen (the default). When researchers served food in smaller dishes as the default option, the daily sugar intake was reduced by an average of 21 sugar cubes.[148] You could build a nice sugar pyramid of this every day. I don't know why you would want to, but you can. In short, what can you do to reduce options?

1. Limit or remove options: Terminate products or services that are not doing well
2. Organise options: Create categories, or ease people into choosing from more options
3. Frame options: Present information to someone in a way that choosing becomes easy
4. Help people to understand their personal preferences: Help them limit their options to the ones that fit them
5. Offer expert advice: This way people can ask a specialist to help them choose to outsource the decision

Limit or remove options

How far you should limit options depends on the behaviour you are designing. If you want someone to click on a button on your website, it is better to have a single clear option. If you want someone to pick a health regime, it works if you have three options, with your preferred option positioned in the centre, for people tend to gravitate to the middle. If you want someone to buy a specific product, it works to show two options of which the left product (in Western countries) is a decoy that is priced much higher than your target product. This higher-priced product will act as a mental anchor that makes people feel your product is a perfect deal. These are best practices from behavioural science, but it is always a matter of experimenting with what works best in your situation. One thing remains the same for every situation: Less is always more when shaping decisions and behaviour.

Organise options

However, you can make people more capable in choosing from more options. You just must do it gradually. A research team at a German car manufacturer's ran an experiment[149] with the manufacturer's online car configurator. Potential clients using the configurator had to choose from 60 different options in order to configure their entire car. Every option again consisted of sub-options. For instance, in order to pick your car colour, you had 56 colours to choose from, choosing your engine also four options and so on. It seemed logical to have people select an 'easy' option first. For example, colour is something that most people have a set preference for. And then they move to the 'harder' options like the engine. The experiment made half of the customers go through the configurator as to many options (e.g., colour) to fewer options (e.g., engine type). The other half went from fewer options to many options. The researchers found that they 'lost' the second group: They kept hitting the default button or aborted the process. The first group hung in there. They had the same information and the same number of options, only the order in which the information was presented varied.

If you start someone off easy by limiting options first, you can teach them how to effectively choose out of more options

Therefore, if someone must make several choices, present the choices with little options first and build it up from there. Even if you think that a choice that has many options is simple to make, do not feel tempted to put this first in the decision chain.

Frame options

Sometimes option reduction is a matter of framing. In other words, you are thinking about how to present information to someone. Maybe you have kids, and well, most kids aren't big on eating veggies. Mine isn't, anyway. We, as parents, often tell our kids: 'Eat your peas.' You'll probably have more success if you give your kids a sense of control, designing the options differently. 'Do you want to eat your peas or your carrots first?' It can also work in our professional life. Let's say you are in negotiation with a talent you like to attract for your team or organisation. Make sure you frame your negations so that the options are limited yet allow for autonomy. Often, negotiations boil down to challenging the salary offer. Suppose you give someone the option to get awarded a higher salary, but you wish to tie a condition to it. For example: sure, you can have a higher salary X, but it implies X fewer days off. Your candidate still has the freedom of choice, but at the same time you've framed your offer as to *bounded options*. Thus, it was prevented from setting the stage for a limitless salary/bonus battle, nitpicking over secondary employment conditions. So, 'it's an either *this or that* kind of framing'.

Identify personal preferences

We have seen that when we experience option overload, we tend to rely on system 1-cues, such as following the choices of others. If you can help someone identify their personal preferences, you will be able to rule out many options. Shopping bots or online filters help us to navigate through options. Once you have set your preference, you only get to see a selection of all options available to you.

Offer expert advice

A different way to reduce options is to outsource the decision process to an expert. In this case, we can learn from the 'healthcare realm'. If you have a condition that can be solved by treatment A, B or C, most people would follow their doctor's advice for a specific treatment. He will rule out some of the options for you. What if we could also provide trusted experts from other realms? If you knew them, wouldn't you rely on an exercise, nutrition, finance or education expert? That would save you many hours of researching, and going down that rabbit hole of endless possibilities. You could also follow the lead of a trusted specialist.

C2. Can we ask an easier question?
QUESTION SUBSTITUTION

Let's say you want someone to do something that requires some thinking. For example, you want someone to vote for you. You could try and convey your points of view on specific subjects, or highlight a section from your political programme. Wait, you might think that doesn't work – that's system 2! And you're absolutely right. Question substitution is a system 1-technique that will make someone vote for you without you having to convince them through arguments. What is question substitution all about? It replaces a complicated question with an easier question, which results in the same behaviour. So, in politics, you see it happening all the time. Politicians (especially populists) don't ask you to support the ins and outs of their foreign policies in order to make you vote for them (the desired behaviour); they replace it with a much simpler question: 'Do you want refugees to come over and take your jobs?' An easier question to answer the same behavioural result is getting you to vote.

But it goes beyond politics; which holds for every problem that is hard to solve for people. Whether to invest in a stock, choose a mortgage, pick the right candidate to fill a position or choose an insurance policy, your system 1 will kick into action in order to lower the cognitive load it needs to solve this problem rationally. In *Thinking Fast and Slow*, Kahneman writes: 'When confronted with a problem – choosing a chess move or deciding whether to invest in stock – the machinery of intuitive thought does the best it can. If the individual has relevant expertise, she will recognize the solution, and the intuitive solution that comes to her mind is likely to be correct.'[150] But what happens when the question is difficult, and a solution is not available? We then will answer a more manageable and related question. If the question is 'Should I invest in Ford Motor Company stock?' the easier question to answer is 'Do I like Ford cars?' This is how our system 1 helps us. I'll give you the last example as to how this system 2/system 1-interplay works. In the book, the so-called 'Linda Problem' is described. Kahneman and Tversky did an experiment where they introduced participants to an imaginary woman named Linda – and this is how she was introduced to them. Please read the following statement about Linda and then intuitively answer the question about her:

Linda is 31 years old, single, outspoken, and very bright. She majored in philosophy. As a student, she was deeply concerned as to issues of discrimination and social justice, and also participated in anti-nuclear demonstrations. Which is more probable?

1. Linda is a cashier
2. Linda is a cashier, and is active in the feminist movement

What was your answer? If I had to bet, you choose option 2, which is the option that most people pick. But the correct answer is option 1. The astounding response in Kahneman's and Tversky's original research, was that 85% got the answer wrong and thought the correct answer was option 2 (even though the participants were students of *Stanford's Graduate School of Business*, and among them there were both novice and experienced statisticians). Why is option 2 the wrong answer, and what happened just now? What went wrong here is that our brain substituted the more difficult question (*how probable is it?*) for an easier question (*how logical is it?*). You read about her student activities, and as to this story, your system 1 thought it was logical or coherent. Linda was still involved in the feminist movement, so your system 1 jumps to a conclusion, and your system 2 lazily endorsed it. And it happened very quickly without you even noticing it. However, this goes completely against the laws of probability (Linda is a cashier is more probable; adding the detail of her being a feminist only lowers the likelihood) because feminist cashiers are a tiny cashiers' subgroup.

When faced with a difficult question, we often answer an easier one instead, usually without noticing the substitution[151]

So, now that you know how question substitution works, the question remains what you might do with it. If you want to influence someone to perform a certain behaviour, probably the behaviour itself is not something people are inclined to do. This is the 'difficult' question to answer: go to the gym, separate plastics from paper, look at your pension plan, give me an okay as to this budget, and join my service. There is an influence opportunity if you replace that question with an easier one. And that is where the JTBDs you found could be providing you with an answer, as then you can replace the question with a deeper lying motivation. 'Do you want to be able to play with your kids?' (JTBD) Yes (an easy answer to an easy question). Then join the gym (desired behaviour). 'Do you want to travel the world after pensioning?' (JTBD) Yes (an easy answer to an easy question). Then look at your pension plan (desired behaviour). Opportunities for question substitution can be found in JTBDs, but they don't have to. It's just a tip I found useful in order to come up with question substitution.

Unfortunately, question substitution is specially mastered by extreme-right winged politicians. Why did people vote for Trump? Not because he asked the people to support his political programme. He asked them a far simpler question: 'Do you want your country to be led by a Dealmaker?' 'Yes! We all want a good deal, right?' The entire Brexit wasn't about Europe. The question most Brits answered was 'Do you want to take back control?' which was supported on a system 1-level by a visual of a stream of refugees. Fortunately, not all question substitution is used as dark wisdom. I hope these two examples will help you to better recognise how your system 1, or the system 1 of the people near to you, is tricked by populists. But let me also give you some examples of question substitution in daily life, that help people to make better decisions or help them to lead better lives.

Have you ever given any thought to taking a life-term insurance? Most of us don't like thinking about that inevitable end to our life, or of those who are dear to us. However, the costs of giving someone a decent 'send-off' are rising. *The Fair Funerals Campaign* is talking about 'funeral poverty'. That is 'where the price of a funeral is beyond a person's ability to pay. It is a growing national crisis most affecting those with the lowest incomes'.[152] According to this organisation, the average costs of a funeral in the UK were £3,785, a substantial amount that many households don't have in their bank account. And it's not just the lack of money that causes a problem; there are psychological effects too. There is an enormous stigma as to not being able to provide your loved one with a warm and decent farewell. Katie Williams, a former hospice nurse, had witnessed this far too often. She came up with a brilliant question-substitution solution. Instead of asking people to take a life-term insurance, she asked people to join 'The Coffin Club'. It's a membership club that meets regularly at where you can plan your final send-off. It gives people control as to their end-of-life celebration. Members of the coffin club decorate their own coffins with memorabilia that represent them, making the final stage of their life a lot less impersonal. But the club also provides them with a safe place to gather information about the costs and planning involved in a funeral, taking away the shame of not knowing how to deal with death. You might think this is a small-scale initiative, but the truth is Coffin Clubs are now a worldwide phenomenon. I love the Coffin' Club's credo, which you can find on their website: 'Don't leave it till you're dead – plan ahead! Empower yourself to sort out the end of your life and then you can forget about it and get on with living!'

Another more positive example of question substitution is: Have you ever had a parking ticket? I did. Although we know what we did wrong, the desired behaviour – 'paying a fine' is not something we happily do. We don't like to spend money on this, unless one asks a different question. In Las Vegas, the city council decided to agree upon a month-long plan to take another currency than money to pay your fine with.[153] Instead of asking for money, they asked for school supplies. Items like pens, post-it notes, pencils, rulers, etcetera. These were donated to Teachers' Exchange, a non-profit associated with the Public Education Foundation. Well, that's a different matter, right? One that I am far happier to answer to. Do you want to pay a fine or donate? In the end, the Las Vegas City Council also uses the money that comes in from parking tickets so as to build a better community; only, it feels a lot more satisfying and enjoyable to contribute to it directly yourself.

Las Vegas City Council Approves Program Allowing Parking Tickets To Be Paid With A School Supply Donation For A Limited Time

City of Las Vegas sent the bulletin at 06/10/2019 10:54 AM PDT

News Release

David Riggleman | Director of Communications | 702.229.2207
June 19, 2019 | FOR IMMEDIATE RELEASE

MEDIA CONTACT: JACE RADKE | 702.229.2205 | 702.249.3514

Las Vegas City Council Approves Program Allowing Parking Tickets To Be Paid With School Supply Donation for a Limited Time

Program to Run From June 19 Through July 19, 2019

Las Vegas City Council unanimously voted in favor of the allowing parking tickets issued between today and July 19, 2019, to be paid with donations of school supplies. Any supplies taken in by the city through the program will be donated to the Teachers Exchange, a 501(c) 3 non-profit that is associated with the Public Education Foundation.

Those who have a parking infraction in the city of Las Vegas between now and July 19 may satisfy their tickets by bringing new, unwrapped school supplies of equal or greater value to their fine to the Parking Services Offices at 500 S. Main St. This must be done within 30 days of the citation date and a purchase receipt for the donation is required. In addition, only non-public safety citations are eligible for this program.

In July of 2016, the City Coucil adopted an ordinance authorizing the establishment of this occassional program allowing for charitable donations in lieu of payment for parking fines.

Some of the items accepted include:
- Pencils
- Pens
- Erasers
- Dry erase markers
- Index cards
- Paper towels / Disinfecting wipes
- Card stock
- Copy paper
- Storage bins
- Rulers
- Scissors
- Pencil sharpeners
- Post-it notes

Las Vegas City Council
Mayor Carolyn G. Goodman | Mayor Pro Tem Lois Tarkanian
Stavros S. Anthony | Bob Coffin | Michele Flore | Cedric Crear
City Manager Scott D. Adams

C3. Can we make it more distinctive? SALIENCE

Our system 1 subconsciously picks up distinctive features, such as colours, logos, taglines, etcetera. It activates associations without requiring any cognitive effort. You can use them as system 1-shortcuts that help people to remember and value you and your ideas. A specific way to activate *salience* is to use the so-called *rhyme as reason* effect: 'The rhyme as reason effect is a cognitive bias that causes a rhyming statement to be judged more accurate than an equally valid non-rhyming one. The rhyme as reason effect occurs because people evaluate a statement's truth according to its aesthetic qualities or the ease with which it is processed by the brain.'[154] That's why it is used in so many expressions:[155] 'An apple a day keeps the doctor away', 'A friend in need is a friend indeed', 'Shop until you drop', 'Walk the talk', 'Make-or-break', 'Nearest and dearest', 'Meet and greet'. And whoever needed to 'explain' the purchase of this Jaguar e-type at home, was given a persuasive argument in the Jaguar advertising. For under the car's image it says: *Grace, Space, Pace*. Who could resist that?

In a scientific study, researchers have found that the statement 'What sobriety conceals, alcohol reveals' is judged as far more accurate than 'What sobriety conceals, alcohol unmasks'. 'The results in the study suggest that rhyme, like repetition, enhances processing fluency [my interpretation: system 1-capability] that can be misattributed to heightened conviction about their truthfulness.'[156] It also works with alliteration by the way (a form of repetition). So, now you know why you always thought that the saying 'the bigger, the better' just felt so damn good. It makes no sense if you think about it a little longer: if you wake up tomorrow morning weighing 40 kilos more than you do now, I'm not sure that then you'll think: 'bigger is better'. So, to bring it back to you one more time: do use the power of rhyming one-liners. You can use them, as they are more distinctive and repetitive, 1 + 1 = 3. For it is always nice to be super effective on the influence scale, right?

A lot has been written about the subconscious effects of colour usage. You might have seen articles yourself of certain colours that are supposed to activate specific emotions – like yellow evoking joy and purple evoking spirituality.

I haven't found any conclusive research on the one-on-one relation of specific colours linking to particular emotions, but I have noticed the powerful impact of green, orange, and red. These colours have a robust universal meaning, and are able to provoke automatic behaviour. In Santa Fe (Argentina), they've sent letters to taxpayers who failed to comply with paying their property tax. The original letter was redesigned by adding colours to make parts of the information stand out to help reduce cognitive effort, and increase an understanding of the benefits of participating in tax amnesties; the redesign encouraged a 30% higher participation rate than the original notice.

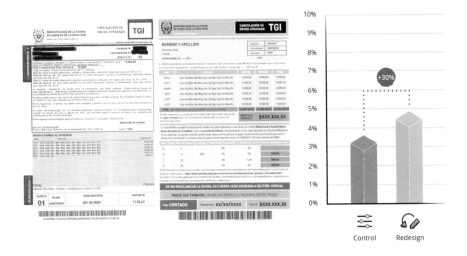

The food industry currently uses these colours to make it easier for people to arrive at better dietary decisions for themselves. Many people struggle with bad eating habits; and reading food labels and understanding nutritional facts is part of the solution. But those labels are very system 2. A lot of information is hard to read and hard to understand. By adding colour to the labels, you add a system 1-cue which makes it far easier to choose healthy foods. In Britain, for instance, the stoplight labels below were introduced.

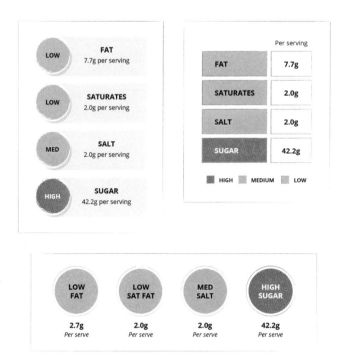

Data source: UK Department of Health

The power of the use of colours is fascinating. You would think that people on a diet are more intrinsically motivated to read labels, and remember the nutritional information on these labels. And that non-dieters would be less intrinsically motivated and therefore more suspectable to the 'traffic light cues' that require little to no cognitive effort. However, a study comparing dieters with non-dieters found that the non-dieters were less affected by the colour coding than the dieters. The non-dieters don't look at the labels at all. The dieters used the colour-coded labels and perceived the green-coded ingredients to be the healthier option. Even when very unhealthy ingredients were colour coded green.[157] Overall, results suggest that green labels increase perceived healthiness, especially among consumers who attach great importance to healthy eating.[158]

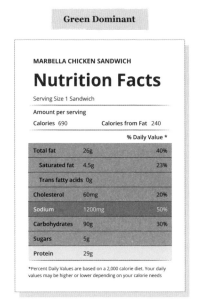

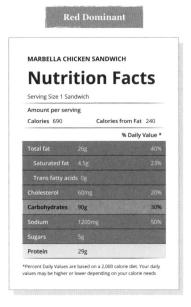

Note that there is an essential word I used here: 'perceive', which brings me to a fundamental notion in Behavioural Design. You can come up with all kinds of interventions, but:

You must prototype in the real world to test-proof whether your intervention will have the desired impact on the behaviour of the desired target group

This is the difference between scattering some 'persuasion principles' over your ideas or designing behaviour. As it turned out, yes, the colour coding did influence perceptions of a product's being healthy. Research has undoubtedly shown that a candy bar was perceived as healthier when it had a green rather than a red calorie-label, even though the labels conveyed the same calorie-content. Nevertheless, studies have also shown that changes in perceived healthiness are unlikely to influence actual behaviour as regards food choice and consumption. 'Attempts to establish the informed consumer with the hope that informed choices will be healthier choices are unlikely to change consumer behaviour and will not result in the desired contribution to the prevention of obesity and diet related diseases.'[159] This is why you should always test your interventions and why this is included in the third step of the SUE | Behavioural Design Method.

But let's end with a very effective way to use the colour red which did influence behaviour and helped people to stop mindless eating. A lot of people overeat because of unaware snacking. Behaviourist Brian Wansink[160] has conducted a study in order to find out if colour could be used to alert the brain as to the amount that someone had been snacking. He did a test with 98 students and gave them a tube of crisps. Half of these tubes, he filled with a red coloured crisp at intervals suggesting a serving size (seven crisps being one serving size). Half of the group of students were made to consume these out of 'normal' crisp tubes (the control group) and the other half out of the tubes with red crisps every other seven crisps. Students who were served the tubes containing the red marker crisps, consumed an astounding 50% less than the control group. The study shows that adding visual markers to snack food packages can help people monitor how much they are eating by interrupting their automatic eating habits. This study, and also other studies, demonstrate that people use visual warnings to indicate to them when to stop eating. I believe that making these visual indicators distinctive, might contribute to helping people to make it even easier to arrive at better decisions themselves.

Another way to be distinctive is to use sound. You may probably recall that the jingles of brands can subconsciously work on your preference – that's one way of using sound. But I'd like to mention a different usage of sound that can help you to be more distinctive as to steering behaviour. That is the absence of sound – researchers at Stanford Medical School[161] have shown that music works upon the areas of the brain involved in paying attention. What was particularly inter-esting is that a peak brain-activity occurred during the short period of silence between musical movements (when seemingly nothing was happening). We can use this effectively: distinctiveness is all about attracting attention in order to activate behaviour. This perfectly explains why the beeping sound in your car works so effectively when you are not wearing your seatbelt. The fact that it bleeps at minor intervals of silence causes it to attract attention, and most of us tend to react by putting our seatbelts on.

C4. Can we add or take away hurdles? FRICTION

This intervention makes undesired behaviour harder to engage in, decreasing someone's capability by introducing friction.[162] Or to put it more simply: to raise barriers. Let me illustrate this with an example in which adding friction helped to prevent some severe behaviour: like accidental poisoning and even suicide. Maybe you knew it already but overusing paracetamol (a widespread household drug), is a frequent method of suicide and of 'non-fatal self-harm' worldwide.[163] 'Suicidal behaviour is often impulsive, and people tend to use drugs already available in their homes. People are also more likely to consume more than 25 tablets, the amount associated with acute liver dysfunction when they are in a loose pack instead of a blister pack'.[164] In 1998, the British government decided to change the legislation on paracetamol packaging. The drug could no longer be sold 'loose' in big containers and was restricted to blister packs that are far harder to open. Also, the number of tablets in this blister packaging was limited to 32 tablets in pharmacies and 16 tablets elsewhere. But they even put up more friction: you couldn't buy multiple packs at one shop. These seem only relatively small, and that it is easy to get around the frictions that were introduced. Someone could still go to several shops and purchase more than one package, and then spend a night taking out the pills from their packagings, but the numbers showed that these small interventions indeed had a significant impact. Putting up these barriers resulted in 'an estimated 43 per cent reduction in suicides in the 11 years following the legislation – that's 765 fewer deaths: 990 including accidental poisonings. There was also a 61 per cent reduction in registrations for liver transplants caused by paracetamol poisoning.'[165]

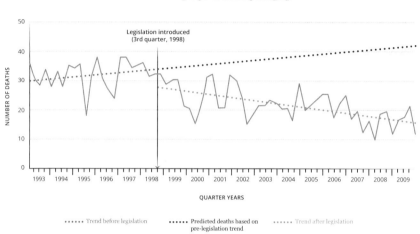

Figure 3:
Reduction in UK deaths by overdose after change
in law relating to paracetamol packaging

Data source: WISH Behavioural Insights Forum[166]

But there is an even more significant upside to all of this. Evidence suggests that people do not find a different route to suicide when faced with these kinds of costs, but rather discontinue the attempt altogether.[167] Therefore, limiting the ease of access to painkillers may be a very effective means to combat suicide rates. Another example of introducing a hurdle is by a 'waste container-garden' intervention. In many cities, people dump their garbage next to the waste containers, causing litter and making neighbourhoods far less pleasant places to live in. Turning the space around a waste container into a small garden does make this behaviour a lot harder to carry out. People are less inclined to dump their waste in a garden, and as a bonus it can also turn the street into a nicer place. Experiments in The Netherlands have shown that littering decreases, and that the municipality needs to spend less money on cleaning up the mess. Next to the fact that these gardens brighten up the streets, there's another side-effect: They act as a drainage for any excess rainwater.[168]

So, there you are: Putting up hurdles can be positive. A hurdle can also be a hurdle in perception only. You don't always have to install a physical hurdle in order to influence behaviour. Let me tell you about this example from Iceland.[169] By painting a 3D pedestrian crossing on the road, it feels like a physical hurdle has been raised, but it is merely a painted one. However, it does tend to influence car drivers' behaviour: For they to slow down. When car drivers came up close, they realised that they were braking for a visual illusion. So, after they showed the desired behaviour, this is also a reason that cyclists are not 'tricked' by this intervention. They often cycling quite close and slow enough to recognise the crossing as a painting.

Now that we are on the subject of hurdles, let's also look at friction from the other way around: What about removing friction? Sometimes people are more than willing to display certain behaviours, but are up against very practical barriers. The *hassle factor* is one of the UK's homeowners' main barriers towards making energy-efficient changes to their homes, such as 'loft insulation'. Research has shown that one significant practical and psychological barrier to a loft insulation is a requirement to clearing out a cluttered loft.[170] This has led to an intervention to remove friction. A trial is being launched in London in order to test the effectiveness of offering subsidized loft insulation, paired with a loft-clearing service. Added to this offer will be the opportunity for residents to donate their unwanted loft contents to a local good cause.[171]

Another example of taking away frictions that positively impact sustainable behaviour is a case at University College Cork. In 2007, UCC-students initiated a pilot Green Campus-programme that would lead the university to become the first one to be awarded a Green Flag by the Foundation for Environmental Education.[172] They noticed that students were more than willing to use re-usable cups, but a barrier to doing so was that your cups become very dirty after using them. Nobody wants those little bits of left-over coffee dripping in their bags. So, they decided to remove friction by installing 're-usable cup-washing stations' all over the campus. This increased the re-usable cup-use by 20%.[173] Let's look at another example on a different Campus where one had realised that hassle factors were preventing students from engaging in another more environmentally friendly behaviour, to wit cycling. On the Aalto University campus in Finland, they do not only provide campus bikes, but they also designed a capability intervention to make sure that the desired behaviour would stick.[174] Because riding a bike is one thing, but repairing one is another. They took away the hassle of going to a bicycle-repair shop by installing the campus bike repair units, making it incredibly easy to fix any (easy) bike problems yourself. These examples of thinking about removing friction link back to the SUE | Influence Framework again; it's an intervention to remove anxieties in order to get people to come up with the desired behaviour.

C5. Can we use easier words? CLARITY

This intervention question has everything to do with the fact of being crispy clear as to what you want people to do. We often use too difficult wording or ambiguous sentences, which people don't know what to make from. We tend to overestimate the reading level of people, and use a lot of complicated, inside-out terminology. There's this example from Disney's.[175] They had a website on which the average password length was 35 characters. Which is quite long for a website, right? What happened however was a lack of clarity. The website's headline stated that: 'Passwords must contain at least six characters.' The thing is, most users of the website were kids. And to them the word *characters* had a completely different meaning. They found this out by looking at the passwords at the back-end of the website: MICKEYMINNIEGOOFYPLUTOSNOWWHITEMOW-GLIDUMBO. Children had gone out of their way to name six Disney characters. This may sound like a peculiar example, but the truth is that we as adults also like easy language. And even if you're educated above average, you do. Your system 1 thrives on clear language: it is perfect for reducing the cognitive overload. Furthermore, easy words aren't just easier to understand – they also make the communicator far more likeable and trustworthy. Looking at words from a human psychology point of view can help you to become a lot more persuasive. I won't bother you with a full-on training in persuasive copywriting, but here are some easy words to use that were scientifically proven to be influential:

The word free
There's has been research by Dan Ariely[176] that studied the persuasive effect of the word *free*. We all like to get things for free, but he showed how we change our behaviour at the word *free*. He started his study by asking people to choose

between two kinds of chocolate: a 15-cents Lindt truffle (of superior quality, and half the price that is usually paid for this sort of thing) or a 1-cent Hershey Kiss. 73% of the participants choose the Lindt truffle. When they reduced the price of both chocolates by 1 cent, the Lindt truffle ended up at 14 cents, and the Hershey Kiss was now for free. The Lindt truffle now was even a better deal for such a good chocolate, and the price difference between the two chocolates remained the same. However, people did change their choice drastically. Now 69% had the Hershey Kiss instead. Ariely explains it by 'loss aversion': people cannot resist a good deal (or steal). Of course, be careful with the word *free*: you don't want to attract freeloaders. But linking it back to clarity: if you want people to subscribe to your newsletter, tell them that joining your newsletter is free. Not all people understand the word *subscribe*, but the word *free* does add extra per-suasion.

The word because

The word *because* can also help you to be more persuasive. The following exam-ple is described in the book *Influence* by Robert Cialdini.[177] They wanted to know how someone was allowed to cut the line at a Xerox machine. Would another phrasing help? At the first test round, the person stated: 'Excuse me, I have five pages. May I use the Xerox machine?' Indeed, 60% of the people agreed to let him skip the line. At the second test, the wording was 'tweaked' just a little bit: 'I only have five pages. May I use the Xerox machine for I'm in a hurry?' 94% of the people agreed. According to Cialdini: 'A well-known principle of human behavior says that when we ask someone to do us a favor, we will be more suc-cessful if we provide a reason. People like to have reasons for what they do.' Connecting it to clarity:

If people understand why you want something, it becomes clearer

The words now, fast and instant

People love easy words that spark that something is going to happen right away. Words like *now, fast* or *instant*. We, as humans, are driven by instant gratification. Again, this has to do with an aversion to loss. Our emotions are much stronger when we're thinking about the fear of losing something, than our emotions are at the prospect of winning something. So, we love things we can get our hands on quickly.

God terms

In general, we as humans are drawn to words that inspire positive feelings in us. These words were labelled *God terms* by Kenneth Burke.[178] Although they aren't religious by definition, they are words that spark moral value within us. Think about words such as *blissful, love, save, wonderful, passion, power, winner* and *strength*. You can use these words in your texts. When choosing which words to use, I would like to end with a quote from Frank Luntz, author of the book *Words that Work:*[179] 'People want to be inspired. They want to aspire to something. You can have the best product, the best service, and the best argument in a debate. But without effective words, you still will lose. In the end, you need good principles and good language if you are to succeed.' You should be especially careful if you are involved in corporate and brand strategy. These are realms that are often characterised by 'abstract wording' galore. If you just want to enjoy yourself for a moment, take a look at the mission statement generator.[180] The mission statements it generates may sound hilarious, but I am afraid you will recognise parts. And if anything, it will give you a glimpse of what not to do.

C6. Can we break-down the behaviour into smaller steps?
CHUNKING

Chunking is all about doing the steps someone must take to show that the desired behaviour is far more manageable. You can do this by breaking the desired behaviour down into some smaller bits, also referred to as 'chunks'. For instance, if you want someone to quit smoking, that's hard behaviour which CAN be very difficult. Still, you can make it simpler by breaking up the behaviour. The NHS has introduced a perfect example of this thinking. They help people to stop smoking not by focussing on quitting smoking right away, but by helping someone step-by-step. First, you can apply for a free 'stop smoking kit'.[181] It contains nicotine patches and a squeezy toy to give you something in your hand as a substitute for your cigarette. But they guide you towards the end goal of quitting smoking easily by, for example, first sticking on the patches and sending you motivational emails. Chunking behaviour into smaller steps helps people to focus on one thing at a time, so that psychologically the overall behaviour seems more manageable.

By the way, the same goes for goals. If you break down a goal into smaller steps, people feel more confident that they will be able to reach the final goal. Let's check out some more examples of companies which do a good job of adding simplicity to their offerings. The first example is the blogging platform *Ghost*. Maybe you have heard of the *aha moment* describing the point at which people start to get value from a product and keep on using it. *Ghost* introduced a simple five-step process for guiding users to the essential steps to get value out of the platform. These steps are laid out for the users, and they see a satisfying green checkmark and a strikethrough for the tasks they've completed. The only challenge with having someone take a step on your website is to be online to see the website. Ghost solved this by sending users, who had left the online set-up process, conditional emails depending on where they left off in the process. These were emails giving clear guidance for how to finish the step. Eventually, they were able to boost the efficiency of their conversion rates by 370%.[182] Simply by breaking up the behaviour into smaller steps and guiding people through them.

Another company that helps people develop good financial behaviour by chunking tasks is HelloWallet.[183] They do this via a weekly Sunday email, containing just one small manageable financial task for users to focus on – perhaps simply setting up a holidays' savings fund, and no more. HelloWallet points out that it takes just three minutes to set up. By chunking savings behaviour into smaller steps every week, people begin to develop better financial habits and are more likely to meet their goals. HelloWallet's research shows that success at these small tasks does build up people's confidence, and makes them feel more able to manage their finances.

Chunking is all about presenting information in a way that makes it easier for people to process

The upside of chunking is that our capacity to receive and remember information improves. You probably have experienced it yourself: have you ever better remembered a phone number by chucking it? For instance, the SUE | Behavioural Design phone number is: (+31)202234626. But I remember it by chunking it: 20 223 46 26. This works psychologically because the chunks are seen as one 'unit' of information,[184] so instead of remembering all the separate digits, I just must remember four chunks. You are making the cognitive steps smaller.

Talking about cognitive steps. I came across another example that helps people to make two essential daily steps very easy by offering chunks – I am talking about oral healthcare. Most dental experts agree that a pillar in oral healthcare is brushing your teeth twice a day. Most people know this, but not all of us do. This is where Lenny Kravitz may help. Lenny? Yes, Lenny! Not by rocking your hips from side to side on one of his hit singles so as to make your brushing duties more enjoyable (could be, by the way – *let love rule* also for your ivory chewers). But in this case, it is by buying his toothpaste. After seeing oral mishaps in the Bahamas, he decided to co-found a toothpaste brand to help people fight tooth decay on the island. And I think they did some brilliant chunking: not only did they name the toothpaste brand Twice. They are literally translating the chunking in the brand name. But they also developed two tubes of toothpaste: The Early Bird and Twilight. One to use in the morning, and one before you go to bed. On top of this, they provided the packaging with a system 1-colour code: a white tube representing the light in the morning, and a black tube representing the dark evening. They chunked the product into two, and gave the chunks a name and colour to match. How easy can you make it to help people brush twice a day? I think it is a brilliant capability booster. We all know that saying with the apple twice a day and the doctor, right? I think we can now safely add: 'If you brush twice a day, you keep the dentist away'. Perhaps now a question may have come to your mind. Is there anything known about the optimal number of chunks? Well, this has been researched. Early behavioural research revealed that humans best recall seven pieces of information plus or minus two.[185] However, more recent studies show that chunking is most effective when four to six chunks (or steps) are created.[186]

C7. Can we show what people have to do next?
SPECIFICITY

We often overestimate that people know what they have to do next. We assume that they know which follow-up steps they need to take in order to achieve the desired behaviour. But often, this isn't true. This is why providing follow-up information is vital in boosting someone's capability to take further action. A fascinating study[187] demonstrated that providing follow-up information makes it easier for someone to take the next step. It also affects the engagement with the message you are trying to convey as a whole. In this study, the researchers ran an experiment with two groups. One group received a public health pamphlet with information on tetanus. The second group received that first pamphlet, but it also stated they would receive follow-up information with an action plan. What happened was again fascinating human reasoning. The second group could recall more specific information from the pamphlet than the first group, even though the follow-up information wasn't comprehensive. The first group blocked out all info that evoked a sense of urgency, thinking that if there weren't any instructions on what to do next, they needed not to worry about it. 'It won't happen to me.' The second group didn't feel this way as they had a plan to take action. In short, adding follow-up information or providing an action plan with the next steps, makes it easier for someone to engage in the behaviour, but they will also be more attentive to your messaging.

Another way we can shape behaviour by using specificity is by aiding people with *action planning*. Action planning is an approach that helps people decide which steps they need to take to achieve a goal. Researchers wanted to see if they could help participants aged 18–56 to build up an exercise routine.[188] The research revealed that while the intention was an important predictor of behavioural change, cultivating habits by action planning was the most effective intervention to bridge the intention-behaviour gap in order to increase overall physical exercise behaviours. Improving an individual's mental and physical well-being, and potentially alleviating the costly burden on public health services. Action planning worked far better than *coping planning*, the making of specific plans to overcome possible barriers that may stop individuals from acting upon their intentions.

C8. Can we provide personal guidance? ASSISTING

Some behaviour is simply hard to perform, and you can help people increase their capability by providing a coach or giving them personal assistance. A great example is the Pedal Project[189] in London and Birmingham, which offers free cycle training to refugee women. Upon arrival in the UK, refugees are prohibited from working and must wait as to their asylum claim for years on an average of 38 pounds support per week. This leads to emotional, psychological and financial problems for a large, disadvantaged group. By refurbishing abandoned bikes (about 28,000 are left alone in London each year) and by training the refugees in biking, journey planning and bike maintenance, the programme doesn't just give women access to bikes, but foremost the power of moving freely, meeting other people, getting active, gaining confidence, and getting out of social isolation.[190] The programme there was born out of the need to 'break stereotypes and social barriers for women to ride bikes, while promoting a healthy and eco-friendly mode of transportation'. Fortunately, the Pedal Project is not unique; for instance, the Bike Project teaches all refugees to bike (not just women). Giving someone the capability to do something can have a major impact; as the Bike Project states: 'A bike helps refugees and asylum-seekers access food banks, legal advice, healthcare, education and much more.'[191] Another example of personal assistance is the 'Reading Partners' organisation. They believe that 'the ability to read transforms lives and changes outcomes for children and communities'.[192] Children have some critical school years that build the foundation for the rest of their life. Reading Partners assists children falling six months or more behind on the reading grade level. A volunteer teams up with this child twice a week to help them read. This assistance has been impressive: 90% of all students master the expected skill levels, and an astonishing 85% of these children even exceed their end-of-year literacy goal. But just as important, it helps them gain confidence, pride, and feeds their hunger and capability to learn even more.

Finally, providing personal assistance could also come as a coach or partner to someone in order to increase their capacity to achieve success. An example of this is the 'Nurse-Family Partnership'. About 400,000 children born in the US each year are born in poverty. Many of their mothers are still young, single, lack higher education and a solid social network. If lucky, those children and their mothers get some help during labour, but they are left on their own after this. Therefore, children born under these circumstances face significant difficulties in escaping poverty or growing up healthily. The Nurse Family Partnership helps these first-time mothers succeed in raising their children. From the beginning of the pregnancy, until the child is two years old, they provide for a nurse, to partner up with the new mom, that visits them at their own home twice a week – educating them, sharing resources, performing health checks, and lifting the weight of having a child – all voluntarily for free. Over 300,000

mothers have already been helped this way. Thus, they gave them far more capability to create a better life for themselves and their family.[193]

317,000+
FAMILIES SERVED
Since replication began in 1996

40
STATES
The U.S Vigin Islands and
some Tribal Communities

5x
$ RETURN
Every $1 invested in NFP saves
$5.70 in future costs for the
highest risk families served

Data source: nursefamilypartnership.org

C9. Can we add a deadline? FORCING FUNCTION

Many people find it hard to get into action, and putting things off is a relatively
widespread human tendency. We all start dieting tomorrow. Or set aside money
for our holiday next week. Or edit that work report later. Often, this is blamed
on a lack of motivation or willingness to act. This might certainly be the case,
but it can also be that people lack self-confidence, that the action steps can be too
overwhelming, or that people believe they simply cannot do it. Telling themselves, they are simply the kind of person without self-discipline. The truth is
you can help someone transform into a getting-things-done powerhouse by
a small intervention – i.e. adding a deadline. Dan Ariely ran an experiment[194]
with his students. At the beginning of the 12-week semester, they had to deliver three papers that would make up most of their grades. He didn't give the
students deadlines when these papers were due. They had to set the deadlines

themselves and commit to them. So, once they had chosen the deadlines, they couldn't change it anymore, and they had to meet them in order to score a good grade. They could freely choose to set the deadline at any day during the semester. You would expect that students, who are procrastination champions, would all opt for deadlines by the end of the semester. Rationally you might say that if they had set an earlier deadline, they would run the risk of not being able to meet this deadline. So better give yourself some slack and push the deadline backwards. What happened in practice is that the majority of students picked earlier deadlines. And what was even more interesting is that these students' capability to commit to this earlier deadline resulted in higher grades.

A deadline can make someone feel more capable to perform a task

The effect becomes even more impactful if you make someone commit to that deadline. Preferably publicly, or in writing. Knowing this, you can imagine how you will be able to help people make progress. If you want people to apply for something, or reply as to a thing you've offered them, then helping them to set a deadline can be a boon. Perhaps this could be built into apps. And if you want people to save money or not miss out on subsidies, you might consider adding a deadline for them. Researchers once ran a behavioural experiment[195] at the Toddington Medical Centre and Wheatfield Surgery. If people didn't show up at their outpatient appointments, apart from the fact they don't get the medical attention they need, it will cost money. In Britain alone, approximately 6 million appointments are missed every year, resulting in direct costs estimated at £700 million.[196] The most common practice is that the doctor's assistant writes down our next appointment. Or sends us an email about it. But in the experiment turned things around: they made the patients themselves write down their appointments on an appointment card. This is the same as publicly committing them to a deadline. And this dropped the 'no-show' rate by 18%.[197]

Kiva partnered with the Common Cents Lab.[198] They added a deadline to the email which participants received when they didn't finish the sign-up process:

Hey Astrid,

I saw you started an application with us - the first big step in receiving your Kiva loan! Applying for a business loan can be a daunting task, and it doesn't have to be that way.

To make you application process easier and give you tools for success, I invite you to take advantage of some best practices, which can be found in our **Borrower Hub.**

Keep in mind that you have until **[date]** to submit your application.

All set to go? Just follow the link below to continue.

 **Continue My Application**

The result was there were 24% more completed applications. But they even went a step further: they added an extra deadline with a positive incentive. This resulted in an additional 26% of completed applications.

Hey Astrid,

I saw you started an application with us - the first big step in receiving your Kiva loan! Applying for a business loan can be a daunting task, and it doesn't have to be that way.

To make you application process easier and give you tools for success, I invite you to take advantage of some best practices, which can be found in our **Borrower Hub.**

Keep in mind that **you have until [date]** to submit your application.

However, if you submit your application **by [date],** I'll move it to the front of the line!

All set to go? Just follow the link below to continue.

 *Continue My Application*

Data source: Kristen Breman[199]

But adding a deadline could also be an effective intervention when it comes to your capability to finish things. When looking at your productivity, you could set a deadline. I've set a deadline for the press release of this book. I am now nearing that deadline, and I wish you could see me: I am a dedicated 'lean-mean productivity machine'. Sort of... Well, it does work. Otherwise, you wouldn't be reading this book, right? I did combine it with breaking down my action steps. So, I set up multiple ambitious but achievable deadlines. Which I think, were essential psychologically. I always like to refer to these as avoiding 'design for disappointment'. If you are going to set unachievable deadlines, you wouldn't even start. You would destroy someone's notions of capability. Every time a person misses a deadline, their self-confidence gets a beating. But having a manageable deadline and 'firing up' your pride of the achievement does work like a charm.

The power of deadlines was proven in other cases too. You would think that, as people, we mostly put things off which we don't like. However, behavioural research has demonstrated that this is not solely the case. Even when things are pleasurable and can have immediate benefits, people tend to procrastinate, and deadlines can help to get them into action. The researchers found that, for example, recipients of gift certificates and gift cards with extended deadlines, tend to procrastinate in reacting to them more than those with short deadlines, resulting in an overall lower reaction.[200] So, if you want people to react towards something, it could be a coupon, some free advice or a free download, but do make sure to add a deadline. It might also be that you want people to visit an exhibition or a showcase: a deadline works to stimulate reaction. The study showed that:

People tend to act closer to a deadline, regardless whether the message is aversive or enjoyable[201]

As you can see in the figure taken from the study, procrastination occurs in both cases (as regards signing up for a pension plan, and as to visiting an exhibition).

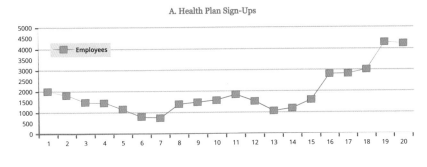

A. Health Plan Sign-Ups

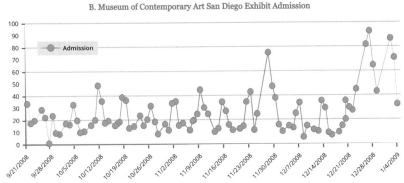

B. Museum of Contemporary Art San Diego Exhibit Admission

Data source: Gneezy, Shu (2009)

And you see the spike in the number of active participants when getting closer to the deadline. So, here's the behavioural science that might have backed you up when your parents went bonkers when you as a kid didn't start studying on time. It is perfectly explainable human behaviour to only start to get active when the deadline draws a bit nearer. It's just human nature, mom! You realise this knowledge also obliges you to give your kids a bit more slack. And deadlines; even better. In order to round things off, I just want to show you a case from everyday practice that illustrates why you shouldn't shy away from using deadlines, even when you need people to do something. This is an example of work done for Kiva. Kiva crowdfunds loans for small businesses but in order to qualify the businesses must provide eight pages of very detailed information. You can imagine that this isn't a very lightweight sign-up process, and it has shown that only 20% of the applicants did finish all the steps. It would feel counter-intuitive to add deadlines, but it did work.

C10. Can we make someone pause their behaviour?
DECISION POINTS

Working on capability is a two-way street. Instinctively we would choose to develop interventions to make the desired behaviour easier. However, sometimes making the undesired behaviour harder can be effective. We have talked about the fact that our system 1 is trying to lower the cognitive overload, and, as we are designing for system 1 that's what we often try to do. We design with a view to minimal decisions. But sometimes it is better to design for more decisions. Adding intentional decision points make someone pause their behaviour and reconsider what they are doing.[202] A lot of people for instance find it challenging to spend less money than intended. You can make this easier for them by giving them a 'pause' in their behaviour. Let me illustrate this by a real-life example that took place in India. There are quite some low-income households in India, with very little cash to spare. Salaries are often paid in cash, making it very easy for family providers to spend it, for instance in the bar after a hard days work. Still, people also needed for instance money for the children's upbringing. Those households typically earned 670 rupees per week (£6.60 or $11.20), and most families only managed to put aside 5 rupees per week (0.75%).[203] Their intervention was to divide the money into envelopes before handing it over to the beneficiary. It made any undesirable behaviour harder to perform, as it added extra decision points. Instead of giving money in one single envelope, people saved more if the same amount of money was divided over several envelopes. People had to pause to physically open the envelope, and created a decision point during which they considered whether they wanted to spend the money.[204] This increased the savings rates from 0.74% to 4% (27 rupees per week).[205]

The same researcher, Dilip Solman, researched whether adding decision moments would also work in other areas, thus helping us control our consumption.[206] They found that this is indeed the case as to eating chocolates, but it also worked in order to limit gambling behaviour. Maybe you recognise their chocolate research findings. If I asked you: 'Would you like to eat a chocolate bar of about 700 calories?', would you be joyfully jumping at to getting such a fast calorie intake? I don't think so. The same goes for bags of potato chips, buckets of popcorn at cinemas, or anything else you can buy in bulk. Once something is in a big bag or box, there's just one decision point. If they had put the same amount of chocolate in separate bags, people would have restricted their choco-late intake. Every time someone had to open a pack (decision point), they recon-sidered their consumption. I know that putting candies in separate wrappers is not the most environmentally friendly solution to fight our sugar-rush craving grazing behaviour. But if you want to limit your calorie intake or reduce spend-ing your money, you may consider putting your money or food into separate units that take some effort to open. This will help you to pause. The researchers saw the same effect in gambling. Participants could get 100 tokens or chips to gamble with. Some got 100 chips right away; others got ten envelopes with ten chips. The only requirement for them was that they could not gamble with their winnings. Every participant gambled, but the participants who had to open an envelope in order to get to the next ten chips were far quicker to stop gambling.

These are research settings, but stop and think for a moment (yes, indeed just pause) about how these findings could help one to design positive outcomes in realms that require our attention in daily life. Attached to the examples of this intervention is that the mentioned objects of behaviour – whether money, choc-olate, or fiches – were very physical indeed. For instance, if we look at the realm of finance, the challenge is that we have often overspent because we lack this visibility. We all rely extremely upon credit and debit cards, which makes our spending invisible, almost as if we are not dealing with real money. Adding de-cisions points, in this case, could still be very effective. What if every time you slide your debit or credit card through the machine in order to make a payment, a notification would pop up saying something like: *'Are you sure you want to spend these 25 euros?'* I would stop and think for a tad. So, how can you get people to pause? Generally, you have three interventions at your disposal:

1. Transaction costs: you can add the effort, time or energy that will stop someone in their tracks
2. Reminders: you can remind someone of what desired behaviour is
3. Interruptions: you can tackle the undesired behaviour

Adding money or food in separate units, which require some form of effort to open up, are examples of the transaction costs; and reminders are quite self-explicatory, right? The notification at a debit machine is an example of an inter-ruption. But let me give you another example of an interruption. If, for instance, you want to design a more sustainable behaviour, you could very well install or develop products that automatically switch off. For instance lights, and the same could go for air conditioning, heating or shower water. Although, I do have to admit I've got some horrible memories of taking a shower in a camping ground and being all 'soaped up' when the water supply was interrupted. There are no good memories of touching and feeling my way to the on-button again, eyes burning due to soap. To conclude, we all have two sides in us. The person who wants to be impulsive and the one that wants to be in control. This intervention of adding 'decision points' is helping to balance the two. Whenever we are too impulsive, a decision-point literally hits the break which we so badly need to regain control.

W1. Can we show the behaviour of others? SOCIAL PROOF & BANDWAGON EFFECT

We, as humans, are social animals. We learn by watching others; we don't like to be excluded from a group and tend to comply with social norms. When an idea increases in popularity, people are more likely to adopt it. This is a shortcut our brain takes for satisfying two human needs. First of all, we need to belong; we want to fit in. We genuinely dislike being excluded from a group, a community and social events, or being the odd one out. Therefore, adopting a group's norms, attitudes and behaviours, is our way of making sure that we are socially accepted and included. So, if we see other people supporting, buying, liking, favouring, or doing a particular something, we are motivated to do the same, and tend to go along by copying the group behaviour. Secondly, we need to be right; we want to win (or at least be on the winning side). Our brain subconsciously scans for information and behaviour, in order to judge what is accepted and considered right within a group, and turns this all into a belief that if everyone else is doing something, it must be the right thing to do.

Social proof is a psychological and social phenomenon, whereby in a given situation people take on the doings of others in an attempt to reflect correct behaviour

Social proof is especially prominent in ambiguous social situations, where people cannot determine the appropriate mode of behaviour. It is driven by the assumption that the surrounding individuals know more about the current situation.[207] To humans, it is far easier to comply with the decisions and beliefs of the majority, than to go against the popular belief of a majority or group. Several decades of psychological research have proved the power of social influence, the tendency that people adopt the opinions, judgements and behaviour of others.[208]

The upside is that this social influence or the relying on social proof helps us to reduce our cognitive load; we simply 'hop on the bandwagon'. But the downside is that 'it can override the individual critical thinking that often goes into making good decisions. Decisions that benefit many other people do not always benefit us.'[209] Perhaps everyone is intermittently fasting right now, but your body needs more fuel to function. Social proof or the *bandwagon-effect* is basically a form of *groupthink*, also referred to as *mob-mentality* (something we try to get rid of in our ideation process). When it seems that everyone is doing something, there is immense pressure to conform. This pressure to fit in has an impact on all kinds of human behaviour – what we wear, who we vote for, what decisions we make as to health, wealth, work and education. And so on. You must have experienced it yourself more than once. If people start wearing a specific item of clothing, chances are you will have bought one too. If all of your friends are on WhatsApp – well, the chances are that you have joined up too. If you are in a multi-storey carpark and you don't know where the way out is, the chances are that you tend to follow people walking in a certain direction, instead of looking at the way finder.

This need for us to fit in also creates the dysfunctional decision-making in groups. Individual team members will seek recognition by adapting their views to the group's views. This makes for a tendency to produce groupthink. Our need for conformity shuts out the consideration of different points of view besides ruling out *exploratory thought*[210] – which, in return, can negatively influence the quality of group decisions. Peer pressure is also the downside of social proof. This is also why most parents hope their children will have the right kind of friends – because we know that it is tough for children, especially young adults, to go against the grain. So, if all your friends are smoking, skipping classes or worse, it is tremendously hard to choose not to do so yourself. Social shaming or social exclusion is our worst fear. This also implies that, as parents, we will need to set the right example. If you smoke, chances are you're setting a social norm for your child. We love to see ourselves as individuals and independent thinking creatures, but most of the time we are simply not. We follow the herd. And though you might not notice it, but how you act also influences the people around you more than you think. Moreover, every trend is catapulted by social proof. However, the bandwagon-effects can be more flimsy. If the herd decides to do something else, we'll simply jump off the bandwagon again. That's why trends often are so quickly to come and go.[211]

These are all relatively harmless examples, but the social proof and the band-wagon effect also fuel other, harmful or dangerous behaviours. When a lack of individual critical thinking is widespread, it can have damaging implications. History has shown that they can fuel social and political movements which damage both people and society. Especially populists misuse this lack of critical individual thinking, by sending out political messages that resonate loudly in today's political discourse and that tap into the beliefs of 'ordinary' people. World War II has been one of the most devastating examples of a fascist movement propelled by crowd acceptance. Unfortunately, also in recent history, there are examples of the dangers of the bandwagon effect. Research has shown that when people learn that a particular candidate is leading in the polls, they are more likely to change their vote in order to conform to the winning side.[212] In one study carried out during the 1992 U.S.-presidential election, students who learnt that Bill Clinton was leading the race in some polls switched their intended vote from Bush to Clinton.[213] Another research showed that individuals influenced by the anti-vaccination movement, became less likely to get routine childhood immunizations for their children. This large-scale avoidance of vaccinations was considered linked to a recent measles outbreak.[214] And the bandwagon-effect can also negatively influence professions.[215] The 2008 housing crisis is a painful example of this. Prices went up due to widespread speculation, in which one investor followed the other. This resulted in a buying frenzy known as a 'price bubble' – which ultimately crashed with devastating consequences for investors and for especially average homeowners who got trapped in the highly speculative financial products.

But we wouldn't be Behavioural Designers if we hadn't also seen the upside of things, and started thinking about how to use this phenomenon for an intervention that might positively affect human behaviour. Sometimes there are advantages to being part of a herd. There's power in numbers, and crowds may bring about a real change.[216] Just look at the #metoo- and #blacklivesmatter-movements. They may be different from the social justice movements in the roaring sixties. But still, the interconnected era has enabled movements to gain traction by a mass of people fighting behind their computer screens. Who says activism has died? It has shifted into a different place! Chances are, at this point you are not looking to start a movement. So, how can you add social proof to your idea?

Remember that we had learnt that social proof especially kick-starts our system 1 into action in ambiguous situations? As Cialdini puts it: 'Especially when people are uncertain, people will look to the actions and behaviours of others to determine their own.'[217] So, see if you can add numbers to the users or people already showing the desired behaviours. It could boost the willingness to switch to the desired behaviour. Especially if the people you are referring to are similar others. While the bandwagon effect can have harmful consequences, the good news is that it can also lead to an adoption of healthy or desired behaviours. If most people seem to reject unhealthy behaviours and then embrace healthy choices, people might become more likely to avoid any risky decisions and engage in beneficial actions. The BIT-team discovered another way of leveraging the power of social proof in the UK. They wanted to see if they could increase payroll presentation among government employees. They reached an astounding 220% increase in employees signing up for the programme, by simply adding a picture of a co-worker who had already registered.[218] What else could you do? One of the most general forms of social proof is the publishing of user reviews. A study[219] showed that 'the average consumer spends 13 minutes and 45 seconds reading reviews before making a decision and reads ten reviews before feeling able to trust a business'. A separate study revealed that 'over 88% of online shoppers incorporate reviews into their purchasing decisions'. Therefore, adding reviews to your offers can be a potent mechanism, so be sure that you get them to stand out.

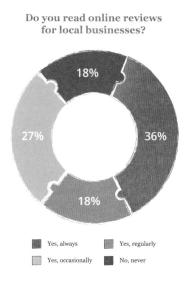

Do you read online reviews
for local businesses?

Yes, always
Yes, regularly
Yes, occasionally
No, never

Data source: BrightLocal.com

If you want this behavioural intervention to work, it is best to present more people who tend to show the desired behaviour. If you only present one person, you might run into a *translation problem*: 'That person is not like me or someone I'd aspire to, so why follow his/her behaviour?' We preferably follow similar others. When you are booking a hotel room online, you value reviews of people who are like you more than those of rather random others. If you're a young couple, reviews of families with several kids will be less relevant to you.

Therefore, tell folks the number of people that have already bought your product. Or the number of those who were happy with the way your service works. This is what hotel-booking sites often use, stating the number of positive reviews or reciting the number of times that the hotel was booked. You can also boost someone's willingness, by referring to other people in a similar situation as the person you're trying to influence. A well-known example is the research on towel re-usage in hotel rooms. Two field experiments examined the effectiveness of signs requesting hotel guests' participation in an environmental conservation programme, by asking them to re-use their towels. First, they compared the more traditional message that focuses solely on environmental protection, with a message that adds social proof to this. These were the two messages:

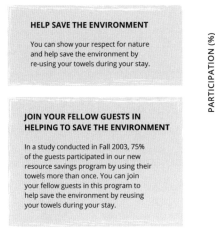

HELP SAVE THE ENVIRONMENT

You can show your respect for nature
and help save the environment by
re-using your towels during your stay.

**JOIN YOUR FELLOW GUESTS IN
HELPING TO SAVE THE ENVIRONMENT**

In a study conducted in Fall 2003, 75%
of the guests participated in our new
resource savings program by using their
towels more than once. You can join
your fellow guests in this program to
help save the environment by reusing
your towels during your stay.

Data source: Goldstein, Cialdini, Griskevicius (2018)

TOWEL HANGER MESSAGE

Data source: Goldstein, Cialdini, Griskevicius (2018)[220]

It caused a 26% uplift in towel re-use. However, the most compelling message described group behaviour in the setting which most closely matched the individuals' immediate situational circumstances. The message that 75% of the guests in this room (including the room number) did re-use their towels, will lead to 33% more re-use. They also tested whether identity could have a positive effect. It did, but it wasn't as effective as comparing someone to similar others.

JOIN YOUR FELLOW GUESTS IN
HELPING TO SAVE THE ENVIRONMENT

In a study conducted in Fall 2003, 75% of
the guests who stayed in this room (#xxx)
participated in our new resource savings
program by using their towels more than
once. You can join your fellow guests in this
program to help save the environment by
reusing your towels during your stay.

JOIN YOUR FELLOW CITIZENS IN
HELPING TO SAVE THE ENVIRONMENT

In a study conducted in Fall 2003, 75% of
the guests participated in our new
resource savings program by using their
towels more than once. You can join your
fellow citizens in this program to help save
the environment by reusing your towels
during your stay.

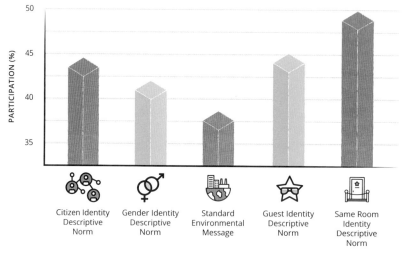

> JOIN THE MEN AND WOMEN WHO ARE
> HELPING TO SAVE THE ENVIRONMENT
>
> In a study conducted in Fall 2003, 76% of the
> women and 74% of the men participated in
> our new resource savings program by using
> their towels more than once. You can join
> the other men and women in this program
> to help save the environment by reusing
> your towels during your stay.

Data source: Goldstein, Cialdini, Griskevicius (2018)

There was this (literally) funny experiment at LaTrobe University aiming to identify the impact of this similarity effect.[221] Perhaps you have heard of 'canned laughter', the pre-recorded laughter used during TV shows. Former repeated research shows that, when others laugh, people start laughing and smiling.[222] According to Cialdini, 'People laugh in response to canned laughter because of automatic, non-thinking conformity, simply hearing others laugh leads us to laugh as well.'[223] However, these researchers wanted to know if it also mattered *who* was laughing. According to *the theory of self-categorisation*,[224] we all categorise ourselves in several ways, on the extremes as human beings or individuals or somewhere in the middle as group members. The theory has shown us that we become psychologically interchangeable with others due to the fact, which makes group processes such as 'social influence' possible. Self-categorisation is therefore closely tied to *similarity*. But the researchers[225] wanted to know if the strength of self-categorisation would have a boosting or limiting effect on social influence. In other words, does similarity count? The researchers tested this by making students listen to canned laughter. One group was told they would hear the laughter of fellow students (in-group), and the other group was told they would hear the laughter of politicians who the students had no interest in (out-group). The results confirmed the researchers' hypothesis: 'Participants laughed and smiled more, laughed longer, and rated humorous material more favorably when they heard in-group laughter rather than out-group laughter or no laughter at all.' Or as the research was titled: 'It is not funny if *they're* laughing.'[226]

However, in the absence of 'another you', quantity counts. Simply because it is harder to argue vis-à-vis more people. Adding on to this, the more that (different) sources say the same thing, the more that it provides social proof. People need to hear from multiple sources to change beliefs. Social proof also may work in our favour another way – It can create network effects. If we can get more people to change their minds, the people surrounding them may change their minds as well. The question remains: how many people does one need to create network effects? The answer is: It depends – if you deal with people with weaker attitudes and beliefs, you don't need social proof from many sources. However, if you are dealing with people who have stronger beliefs, you need more social proof sources in order to corroborate your point. How can you make this work in practice? Jonah Berger differentiates *a sprinkler- and a fire hose-strategy*.[227] Or to put it otherwise, *a scarcity or concentration approach*. If you are trying to convince people who have firm beliefs about their current behaviour (in a 'zone of rejection'), a concentration strategy is more effective. That is to say, focusing on a smaller group of people whom you confront with social proof multiple times within a short period (the more time there is between social proofs, the less impact it will have). However, if you deal with people leaning towards a zone of acceptance, one or two people will be enough proof to others in order to shift their beliefs and mimic behaviour. In this case, you can provide less social proof, and you can focus upon influencing more people at once.

I've just one addition to using social proof as to influencing someone. It is something you can use for personal influence. You might find yourself occasionally in a situation where you have to convince one person. It could be your manager or partner. Let's suppose you must convince someone to grant you a budget for a project. We would tend to go to that person right away, trying to convince them the best we can. Next time we should try adding social proof by showing your plan to a colleague or another manager first. Preferably two or more. Creating a movement of your own that provides you with 'buy-in' as to your plan. If you can tell your manager that person X and X have reviewed your plan and are willing to back it, you could add social proof to your selling pitch. You are enhancing your manager's willingness to grant your wishes. I love this quote of Derek Sivers:[228] 'The first follower is what transforms a lone nut into a leader.' So, go ahead and use social proof to transform yourself from that lone nut into a leader. You know you have that leadership potential. And social proof can help you, simply just like that.

W2. Can we remind someone of their social image/identity? SOCIAL IDENTITY/SIGNALLING

Let's carry on with the importance of social context; another intervention could be pretty successful: reminding someone of their (past) social identity. In the Insight chapter, we have already seen that humans are strongly influenced by their beliefs, and how they see themselves as to their identity. You and I have carried out behaviour that we tend to describe as 'typically me'. The truth is that those beliefs about us can make it feel strange to behave differently ('that's just not me'). It can withhold us from engaging in a new behaviour. Identity can therefore also be a breeding ground for inertia. But it may also work the other way 'round. We know from psychological research that humans seek to be consistent as to our past behaviours in order to avoid what psychologists call *cognitive dissonance*. And we feel discomfort when our attitudes and beliefs do not match our behaviour.

Therefore, we can shape behaviour by reminding someone of their identity, and how it fits this desired behaviour. Let me give you an example I love. Researchers found that people are more likely to vote if they are reminded of their identity as a past voter.[229] Voting is an essential behaviour, as it is crucial to a well-functioning democracy. One of the challenges in voting is that it is a pretty individual kind of behaviour. You have to go and vote in private, and usually not one of your reference networks will check if you showed up at the ballot. The channels used to getting people to vote are often quite individual, like social media or TV ads – and we ourselves take them in. Before the 2010 U.S.-elections, an experiment[230] was conducted in order to get people to vote amongst people with a low to moderate likelihood of voting. They sent get-out-the-vote letters and incorporated some behavioural interventions. The letter started by emphasizing somebody's identity; it read: 'You're a voter. Thank you for voting in 2008. Public records show that you voted in the most recent election. It is people like you who decide the future of our country by getting out to the polls on Election Day, November 2, 2010.'

I already mentioned that Behavioural Design is often a mix of interventions. In this case, some extra socially related interventions were added. Some voters received an additional message which added social observability, stating: 'You may be called after the election to discuss your experience at the polls.' In addition, social proof was added: 'This year, voters like you will join HUNDREDS of THOUSANDS of other [State] and cast a ballot on Election Day.' They then combined social identity and the social norm with signalling behaviour, allowing someone to feel good about their behaviour. By handing out 'I voted'-stickers and -signs. Signalling is a critical mechanism; it helps people to express their social identity, stand out from the crowd, and be respected for their identity. This respect was also emphasised in the letter: 'We hope the public record shows that you were a voter again this election so we can thank you again. Remember, when you see people wearing *"I voted"* stickers and waving signs on Election Day, it is time to *join the millions of Americans who will vote this year.*' They have added to a commitment mechanism, by making people fill in their 'voting plan' (I'll come back to commitment later). This is what the letter looked like:

A

You may be called after the election to discuss your experience at the polls.

[Date]

Dear [Name],

B

You're a voter. Thank you for voting in 2008! Public records show that you voted in the most recent election. Again, thank you. It is people like you who decide the future of our country by getting out to the polls on Election Day, November 2, 2010.

C

This year, voters like you will join HUNDREDS OF THOUSANDS of other [State] and cast a ballot on Election Day.

This election is important, and people like you will choose who represents us in Washington. You were a voter in 2008, you are still a voter.

D

Voting takes a plan.

○ Will you vote on Election Day Tuesday November 2nd? _____

○ What time will you vote? _____

○ How will you get to your polling place? _____

B

We hope the public record shows that you were a voter again this election so we can thank you again.

E

Remember, when you see people wearing "I Voted" stickers and waving signs on Election Day, it is time to join the millions of Americans who will vote this year.

A

We may call you after the election to learn about your voting experience. We are interested in what voting on Tuesday was like for you. PLease pay careful attention, and possibly even take notes. We look forward to talking with you after the election about your vote.

Sincerely,

Joan Fitz-gerald

This was the impact of the letter on voter turn-out:

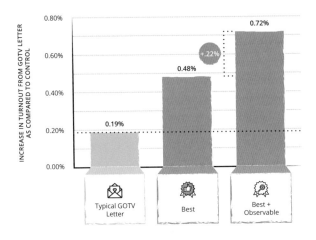

Data source: b-hub.org

Researchers in Switzerland dealt with a similar challenge. They asked themselves what the potential effect upon behaviour would be now that citizens were offered the possibility to vote by mail. When voting can only be done in person, it makes the behaviour visible – as this can act as an identity signal. 'People may therefore vote because they want others to see or know that they voted, and will thus think of them as civic-minded or public good oriented and doing their part to contribute to society.'[231] In contrast, voting by mail reduces this visibility. The study[232] showed that voting by mail had little effect on the overall total voter turnout. However, they did notice a considerable voter turn-out-decrease in smaller communities. The researchers' interpretation was that in smaller communities, people know one another to a greater extent and also are more tightly linked to the community. The smaller the community also implies that your social group is more likely to know if you voted. The conclusion is that more people in small communities were likely to vote, just because they wanted others to see them voting, due to social image concerns – rather than it being a question of them wanting to vote. The vote-by-mail option shut off some of the social-image effects, by reducing the signal contained in (not) voting. We can learn from this that designing for visible identity-signalling may be very effective in steering desired behaviours. Efficiency (in this case, voting by mail, did provide cost reductions) may erode the behaviour you are truly after.

The example from the US was all about stressing someone's positive identity, but stressing a negative social identity can also be effective. In Guatemala[233] individual taxpayers and companies that had failed to pay their taxes in 2013 were randomly assigned to three groups, so as to receive different notifications from the tax administration-entity. One traditional notice urging to pay taxes, one notice adding a negative social identity, framing the failure to file a tax return as a deliberate choice rather than as a mistake: *'Before, we saw your tax filing delay as a mistake. However, if you fail to file your tax return now, we will consider it your choice, and you may be audited and subject to legal procedures under the law.'* The last message added a descriptive norm, mentioning that 64.5% of the taxpayers had already paid that tax: *'According to our records, 64.5% of Guatemalans filed their income tax returns for 2013 on time. You are part of the minority of Guatemalans who have not filed their return on this tax.'* These two interventions increased the rate of payment, and the average amount paid conditional upon paying, overall, more than tripling tax receipts. So, there you go, never underestimate the power of identity in changing behaviour. Still, I hope you also grasp now that stressing past identities can be a powerful way to boost someone's willingness to show a desired behaviour.

W3. Can we make it personal? PERSONALISATION

You can boost someone's willingness to go ahead with you, if you make your offer more personal. In one interesting study, researchers wanted to find out how waiters might get more tips in restaurants. Researchers found that waiters who personalised the check – by writing 'thank you' or by drawing a happy, smiling face on the back – increased the tips they received.[234] But also, a more personal interaction can increase tipping behaviour. Briefly touching customers, squatting during the initial contact, making additional non-task contacts, and showing a maximum smile when introducing yourself – all this has been associated with an increasing amount[235, 236, 237] of tips with a view to increasing the compliance rates for questionnaires. Compliance rates are typically low. The researchers worked with personalisation by adding a post-it to the questionnaire. They also send out questionnaires without this intervention, in order to have a benchmark. The 'no personal message'-batch's compliance rate was 34%; while adding a post-it without any text already raised compliance to 43% (as people feel that someone has made some effort). But the post-it with a message increased the compliance rate to an astounding 69%. I must stop you now, before you go out of your way and send all your clients handwritten notes – getting such cramps in your hand like you had not experienced since you learnt to write. The research also noted that computerised handwritten messages had almost the same effect. So, go ahead and install a lovely handwritten font, and run some experiments yourself. Another experiment like quickly testing yourself is something the Unbounce company learnt us.[238] When they were looking to increase the number of people subscribing to a 30-day trial subscription, they were able to increase the clickthrough ratio by 90% within three weeks. They tweaked one word in the website's 'call to action-button'-text, making a change in the way of personalisation. The new button read 'start *my* free trial' instead of 'start *your* 30-day trial'. So, just a tad more personal. Don't you just love it when small ideas can significantly impact compliance with a desired behaviour? That's truly one of the beauties of Behavioural Design.

You can also kill personalisation, by the way. If you still have a no-reply email in place, replace it. And even if you send out automated emails, use real names. People appreciate the personal touch. A personal touch can also be a phone call, as the following example[239] illustrates. Tax delinquency is a major problem in Colombia. The National Accountant Office has estimated the total outstanding debt to the National Tax Agency of Columbia at $2.5 billion, representing about 20% of the estimated total tax evasion within one year. The agency conducted a field experiment using phone calls to have person-to-person communications with taxpayers, in order to recover unpaid debts. I can imagine that you're thinking that calling is a pretty expensive way of customer contact. And you're right. But in this case, the payment rate among taxpayers who received a personal phone call was about 25 percentage points higher than that of the control group (about a fivefold increase), while their average payment was almost three times higher.

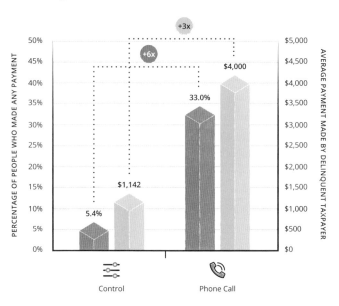

Impact of Phone Calls on Debt Collection

Data source: Mogollón, Ortega, Scartascini (2019)

But personalisation can also help to solve more severe problems. Opioids have caused many deaths in the United States. It is estimated that between 1999 and 2016, over 350,000 Americans died due to an overdose. Opioid addiction and related fatalities are becoming a national epidemic. Over 2 million Americans suffer from opioid addiction. The root of the problem is getting the prescription of an opioid. The problem is that physicians don't always see the effect of the pre-scriptions they fill. Therefore, researchers set up a randomised experiment[240] in the San Diego area. They sent clinicians personal letters, signed by the Chief Deputy Medical Examiner of San Diego County, notifying them of their former patient's death. The letter referred to the patient as to name, address, and age, thus turning the patient into a real person.

County of San Diego

DR. GLENN N. WAGNER	MEDICAL EXAMINER'S DEPARTMENT	DR. JONATHAN R. LUCAS
Chief Medical Examiner	5570 Overland Ave, STE 101, San Diego, CA 92123-1215	Chief Deputy Medical Examiner
(858) 664-2896	https://www.sandlegocounty.gov/me/	(858) 694-2895

San Diego County Medical Examiner Office
{Address}
{Phone}
{Email}

[Date]

Dear _____(name prescriber),

This is a courtesy communication to inform you that your patient (Name, Date of Birth) died on (date). Prescription drug overdose was either the primary cause of death or contributed to the death.

The San Diego Medical Examiner's office sees between 250 and 270 prescription medication-related deaths each year. A significant proportion of deaths are due to the combination of multiple prescription medications. Patients may obtain legitimate prescriptions for opioids, benzodiazepines, muscle relaxants, and sleep aids from more than one prescriber. When taken in any combination, these medications put patients at greater risk of death. We also see many deaths that are a result of long-term therapeutic prescribing.

Data source: Doctor, Nguyen, Roneet, Jonathan et al. (2018)

The researchers found that the letter sent to clinicians reduced the opioid prescriptions which were provided up to four months later by 9.7%, compared to prescriptions by clinicians who did not get a letter. Clinicians who did receive a letter were also 7% less likely to start a new patient on opioids, and also between 3% and 4.5% less likely to prescribe high-dose prescriptions. Let's end with a European example. In 2011, the UK Ministry of Justice faced over £600 million in unpaid fines. Researchers from the UK Cabinet Office's Behavioural Insights Team[241] had targeted debtors who failed to pay their court fine on time. All subjects had already received a written notice warning them that a bailiff could enforce the penalty through carrying out an arrest or the seizure of property. They tested whether personalisation could also help with the fine payments. These were the messages they sent out to the debtors:

Text Condition (Abbreviation)	Text Message
Standard (Standard)	You have not paid your fine. Pay immediately or a warrant will be issued to the bailiffs. Call 03007909901 quote ref [number] div [number]
Personalised Name (Personal)	[Name], you have not paid your fine. Pay immediately or a warrant will be issued to the bailiffs. Call 03007909901 quote ref [number] div [number]
Personalised Amount (Amount)	You have not paid your fine of £[amount]. Pay immediately or a warrant will be issued to the bailiffs. Call 03007909901 quote ref [number] div [number]
Personalised Name & Amount (Personal / Amount)	[Name], you have not paid your fine of £[amount]. Pay immediately or a warrant will be issued to the bailiffs. Call 03007909901 quote ref [number] div [number]

Data source: povertylab.org

The most effective message, personalised in order to include the subject's name, increased the average amount paid by 189%, from £4.46 to £12.87.

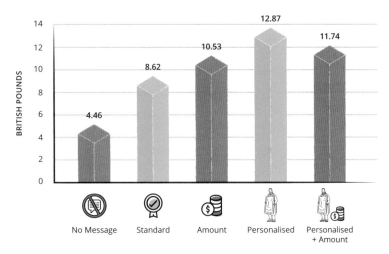

Data source: povertylab.org

Of course – the most personal is to show up in person. They often say 'don't blame the messenger', though in Columbia the messenger shouldn't be blamed but praised. In a field experiment[242] trying to get tax debtors to pay their taxes when these are due, the research team decided to see if the way of collecting the tax would make any difference. Whereas most behavioural research focuses on behavioural interventions within a message, this experiment focused on how a similar message was delivered. They sent out emails, letters and added personal visits.

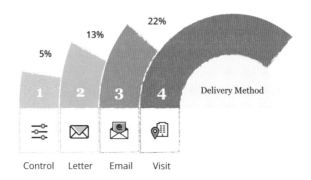

22%

13%

5%

1   2   3   4   Delivery Method

Control   Letter   Email   Visit

Among those who received the messages

Data source: Ortega, Scartascini (2015)

The results were fascinating. Debtors who received a letter made a payment as to their outstanding debts that was about eight percentage points higher than people who hadn't received a message. Sending out an email proved to be 17 percentage points higher than for those receiving an email, and if you had received a personal visit, the payment was about 88 points higher. Almost every person who had a visit from a tax inspector made some payment. I understand that making a personal visit isn't always an option. It's far more time-consuming and expensive than sending a letter. However, we are also creatures of habit: we often send out emails just because we always do. And it is an easy way to do things. But next time, if you need to convince someone of something, decide whether it isn't worth making a personal visit. The tax agency in Columbia estimated that it cost them $0 per email, $0.50 per letter, and $8 per personal visit. The average amount collected was around $590 per email, $ 550 per letter, and over $2,000 for in-person visits. Moreover, they found significant spill-over effects. People who received the in-coming messages started to make payments, also as to other due taxes too. So, it may be worth the money if you need to convince someone of a 'bigger' plan you have, whether it is a budget or an idea: Try the personal approach. Visits are often regarded as costs, but once you start thinking of them as an investment, you might learn they could be highly profitable.

There is another exciting way to use personalisation. Have you ever wondered why the Coca Cola-bottle is shaped like a curving human body? Why does the front of a Volkswagen Beetle looks like a happy face? And why do so many brands use cartoon characters? This is all about a personalisation phenomenon called *anthropomorphism*.[243] It means that one sees human qualities in non-human entities, or to phrase it otherwise it's about the 'personalisation' of objects. Have you ever seen a face in the clouds? Well, you weren't simply dreaming away, but you were certainly 'anthropomorphising'. Research has shown that this specific form of personalisation tends to influence our decision-making, and that we can use it to design positive behaviour. For instance, in order to promote recycling behaviour and donation behaviour. In two experiments, personalisation was used to measure the effects of *object personalisation* upon behaviour. The first setting was a little sign on the counter of a coffee shop requesting the donation of money in order to save trees. One sign was a plain sign with a tree on it that said 'save the trees'. In the second sign the tree had a face saying: 'save me!'. At both expressions, people donated money; only in the plain condition, 40% of the people donated, and in the second condition 65% of the people did so. But not only this, at the personalisation condition the amount of money donated increased by 70%.[244]

The same happened in promoting recycling behaviour. Again, there were two conditions that looked like this:

This second study replicated the findings of the first study.[245] Why does this work? This form of personalisation triggers *anticipatory guilt* – we feel guilty if we don't help other human beings in need. The mere presence of humanlike features often leads us to think that an object may also have humanlike mental states, such as feeling sad, unhappy and stressed.[246] We want to help to avoid someone feeling like that; and therefore, we adjust our behaviour with a view to prevent experiencing future feelings of guilt about not helping someone. Therefore, this is an effective intervention to get people to act more 'socially'. This form of personalisation can be a simple, low-cost intervention for policymakers or non-profit campaign managers in order to change behaviour.

I would like to finish this behavioural intervention with an example of the personalisation that I love because of its potential impact as to solving a wicked problem, i.e. crime. In the UK, the government wanted to help law offenders to avoid becoming recidivists.[247] They did this by adding personalisation to the custody setting. On the cell walls, they added handwritten messages by rehabilitated offenders. The writings explain how the offender was able to change. The form of the messaging (the handwriting) and the messaging's content was important. It combined personalisation with psychological research, which had shown that people are far more likely to succeed and rebound from their failures if someone expresses a belief in their capability to grow and develop throughout their lives.[248] The trial is still in process, so I cannot give you any results yet, but it may turn out to be quite promising. I wanted to show you this example so as to illustrate that something that seems so inconspicuous as adding a personal touch can help to solve big problems. That's it for now as to this intervention.

W4. Can we present information in a different way?
FRAMING

I must give you a head's up: we have arrived at one of the most potent behaviour-al intervention mechanisms that are out there: *framing*. It is the principle used abundantly by populist politicians and other people with doubtful intentions. It has been used to influence and mobilise flocks of people successfully, though unfortunately not always for the sake of good. The flipside of the same coin is that if you are more aware of this intervention, you have the same power tool in hand that you may use to design a positive change. So, what in fact is framing?

Framing is presenting the same information in a different way

The result is that precisely the same information may be perceived differently, as well as the judgements, decisions and behaviours attached to it. Kahneman and Tversky[249] have explored how a different phrasing might affect choices. So, let me do the same experiment with you. Right now, you need a bit of imagina-tion. What if I told you that I am a doctor, and you are visiting me because quite a lot of people are ill. As a matter of fact, at present 600 people in total are not feeling well. Unfortunately, their illness can be quite severe, lethal even. And what if I tell you that I've got two treatments for the 600 people – which one would you then choose?

- Treatment A will save 200 lives
- Treatment B means that 400 people will die

I bet you chose treatment A. You joined the 72% Kahneman and Tversky, and encountered the choice for a positive framing in their research when you did. Objectively, the effect of both treatments is the same. In both scenarios, 200 people survive and 400 die. But our system 1 picks up the word *save*, and our brain prefers positives to negatives. I think this example illustrates very well how framing works. But it also reveals the potent power, as only subtle changes in phrasing can make a big difference. A lot of research has been done as to framing and how it is able to influence decisions by changing the descriptions of choices. For instance, people prefer meat labelled as 75% lean to meat that is labelled as 25% fat.[250] I always love it when I come across real-life examples. I found a study[251] on framing which described framing experiments in two fields needing better decision-making: finance and health. Let me share them with you, as they can inspire one how to use framing yourself. Again, let me do the same experiment together with you. First, let us start with buying a sofa. Imagine you have just recently purchased a couch. It costs you $1,000, but you were able to finance it. You had to make a 20% down-payment; the rest you had to pay off within a year in equal monthly payments against 0% interest. So, which payment plan would you choose?

- Loan: payment framed as the amount required to pay off the loan
- Paying off the sofa: payment framed as the amount required to pay off the sofa
- Owning the sofa: payment framed as the amount required to own the sofa

Remember, in all three options the price of your sofa is the same. Would you like/Do you want a loan, would you like/do you want to pay off your sofa, or would you prefer a payment plan in order to own your sofa. Take your pick. I have another question for you. You will get a $300 tax refund. How much are you willing to put towards paying your sofa? I am curious what you decided. Let me share what happened in the research, and see if it corresponds with your choices. Participants who opted to 'own the sofa' contributed significantly more of their tax refund, than participants who chose the 'loan' or 'pay-off' option. The researchers noted that the 'owning' participants focused on progress; they perceived the tax refund as progress towards owning the couch. The other participants focused on the loan, and on how much of the loan still had to be paid. The tax refund was just a tiny percentage of this loan, so it felt like less progress, and it decreased their willingness to deposit the tax refund. What does this tell you? Well, if you are selling products and services, and offer clients the opportunity to take up a financial plan, you can see how frames can have a genuine impact on the willingness to make payments. The industrial standard is to use financial framing, but it might be helpful to use ownership frames. This has proved to influence payment behaviour, which decreases the chance of people gathering debt.

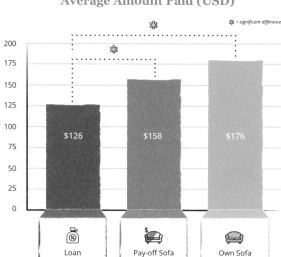

Average Amount Paid (USD)

❋ = significant difference

Data source: Holzwarth, Berman, Schwartz, Schanbacher et al. (2020)

Another example in the finance department. You probably know that there are savings products around that lock your savings for a certain period. As the account holder, you are unable to withdraw your money until a certain date. You might recognise this as a great capability hindrance: making the undesired behaviour harder to carry out. These products have indeed shown great results as to increasing savings.[252] Researchers explored whether framing might have an effect too. They framed these locked savings products, called CDs, either as a 'certificate of deposit' or 'super-locked savings'.

- Product was framed as a Certificate of Deposit
- Product was framed as Super-Locked Savings

What would you choose? The participants preferred the 'Super-Locked Savings', most probably because of the positive associations with the word *super*. However, there was no difference in the amount they would put in. Their willingness depended on the money they had in their savings account. They then also changed the interest rate:

- Product was framed as a Certificate of Deposit with 2% interest
- Product was framed as a Certificate of Deposit with 3% interest
- Product was framed as Super-Locked Savings with 2% interest
- Product was framed as Super-Locked Savings with 3% interest

However, when the interest rate changed from 3% to 2%, people were prepared to put in more money. What was fascinating though, is that having people switch from a 'Certificate of Deposit' to a 'Super-Locked Savings'-product had the same effect as a switch from a 3% to a 2% interest rate. People deposited more money. This shows that you do not necessarily need financial incentives to have people save more. By reframing your product, you can achieve the same results as to saving behaviour.

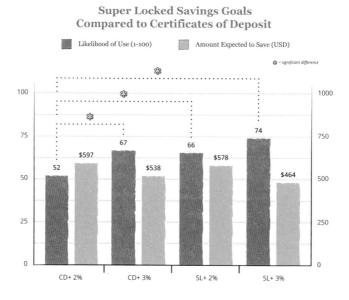

Super Locked Savings Goals Compared to Certificates of Deposit

Data source: Holzwarth, Berman, Schwartz, Schanbacher et al. (2020)

Let's move to another realm that needs a shrewd Behavioural Design: promoting health. One important way of not contracting diseases is getting vaccinated. How could you, for instance, use framing in order to get people a flu vaccine or a COVID-19 vaccine? This research team developed frames on a genuine human insight: people's sceptic attitude towards health insurance companies. 'Many people feel that the cost of their health insurance is too high relative to the benefits they receive, and don't believe that insurers have their best interests at heart.'[253] So, what if you could frame the flu vaccine as a way of getting the most out of your insurance? They tested three frames that measured the intention to get a flu shot:

- Control: flu shot framed as a way to stay healthy
- Maximise: flu shot framed as a way to maximise your insurance benefits
- Grudge: flu shot framed as a way to spite your insurance company

Intention to Vaccinate (%)

Data source: Holzwarth, Berman, Schwartz, Schanbacher et al. (2020)

I want to share one more framing research[254] as regards a subject I can relate to, and probably you also: exercising. Can framing help boost your willingness to exercise? I already have come across research stressing that we as humans can adapt very well to coping with negative situations. Our brain can re-evaluate stressful or negative events as valuable or beneficial, even at 'cognitive reappraisal'.[255] Simply put, you can change how you perceive a feeling before you have experienced it. We can regulate our emotions. When it comes to exercising, many people are put off, due to the aching muscle that exercising gives you. What if you could use reframing in order to prompt a cognitive reappraisal? In other words, could framing be used to see to it that the muscle pain is perceived as positive? And how would that affect future accomplishments? The researchers asked 78 participants (aged 18–55) to do as many bench-presses as possible in order to measure their baseline performance. After this, the group split up in two parts. Each group had to listen to a voice recording presenting a different frame as to muscle pains that are caused by exercising:

• Helpful: pain framed as a sign of muscle-building
• Harmful: pain framed as a sign of teared muscles and possible injury

And then one would have to do as many bench-presses as possible again. The cognitive reappraisal indeed kicked in. Participants felt less pessimistic about pain when it was framed as a sign of muscle building. However, there was no difference as to the bench presses that were completed. Participants lifted weights the same number of times in both conditions, but felt less negatively about their pain when it was reframed positively. So, there was a change in psychology, although there was no change in physiology. This is an important finding. The way you feel about something (the way it affects you) is a driver of your future willingness to do the exercises.[256]

Pleasantness of Pain

100 = Most Pleasant Imaginable, 0 = Neutral,
-100 = Most Unpleasant Imaginable

❋ = significant difference

	Helpful	Harmful
	-12	-24

Data source: Holzwarth, Berman, Schwartz, Schanbacher et al. (2020)

You can imagine using these insights to influence emotions positively as to all sorts of negative experiences. While we are on the subject of the negative, let's talk about debate and criticism. These are often seen as negative behaviours. However, if you must find solutions to complex problems, or for instance in learning situations, then criticism and debate are essential features. These spark creativity and innovation, as they allow different viewpoints to flourish. By reframing debate and criticism as contributions to the group, they therefore become an asset. Researchers think this reframing can help people to feel free. It is almost considered as 'a prompt to do something normally forbidden – at least considered impolite – yet may be liberating in and of itself'.[257] So, think about this when you have a team meeting or need to solve a complex problem with a group of people. You might get more and better ideas by starting your meeting with reframing the debate, feedback and criticism. Now let's go from us to Africa. The government wanted to promote health care in Zambia by training people from local communities to become community health assistants. They used posters to recruit people to take up different frames:[258]

- Community-focused frame: Want to serve your community? Become a *CHA*!
- Career-focused frame: Become a *CHA* to gain skills and boost your career!

What was fascinating is that the CHAs recruited via the career frame made on average 94 more household visits than the CHAs recruited through the community frame did. 'This is a meaningful difference: if each of the 147 CHAs in the community incentives group had done as many visits as their counterparts in the career incentives group, 13,818 more households would have been visited over the 18 months.' Areas where CHAs were recruited via the career frame showed better health outcomes for community members, especially for women and children.

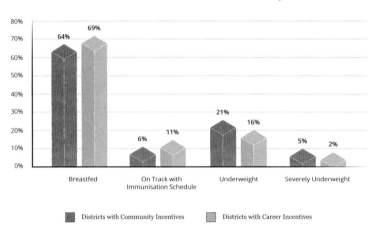

Health Outcomes for Children under 2 years

Data source: www.poverty-action.org

So, as you can see, frames are everywhere. I am happy that my parents weren't consciously aware of this behavioural intervention. When I had to do something as a child, they would tell me things like: 'Astrid, will you brush your teeth now?' If I didn't step into action, they would say: 'Let me *rephrase* this: brush your teeth now!' It was pretty effective, but if they would have said: 'Let me re-frame this: do you want your teeth to fall out? Brush your teeth.' I would have been away to my pink glitter-covered toothbrush at a speed that would even make Usain Bolt proud.

W5. Can we make people feel they are losing out on something? LOSS AVERSION

The following behavioural intervention that can spike someone's WANT to change (or not) is called *loss aversion*. Loss aversion is a cognitive bias, which explains that human beings feel the pain of a loss more intensely than the equivalent pleasure of a gain. More simply put: it feels better not to lose 10 euros, than to win 10 euros. Perhaps you have already heard of the *prospect theory*?[259] This was a theory constructed by Kahneman and Tversky. They demonstrated how people tend to react differently to negative and positive changes. More specifically:

The pain of losing is psychologically twice as powerful as the pleasure of equivalent gains

This is important to us, as it can strongly influence people's behaviour. There are a couple of psychological explanations for loss aversion. First of all, there is a phenomenon known as the *sunk-cost fallacy*. If people have spent their effort, time or money on something, they will commit to the behaviour related to it – for otherwise, they feel they will lose out. For example, if people spend 60 euros on a four-course dinner but are already full at the third course, most of them will eat dessert anyway. 'I paid for it!' Thaler calls this *mental accounting*.[260] He explains that people will make an effort to drive a few hours through a bliz- zard storm in order to attend a concert that they (only) paid $20 for. So, it feels like a loss not to go, or not to finish all your plates. Another famous example by Richard Thaler is about a man who joined a tennis club, and paid a $300 mem- bership fee for the year. After just two weeks of playing, he develops a case of tennis elbow. Despite being in pain, the man continues to play, saying: 'I don't want to waste the $300.'[261] Secondly, there is a psychological tendency called *re- gret avoidance*. The regret people feel for bad outcomes from novel actions is far greater than their regret as to bad consequences from inaction.[262] So, why risk 'new behaviour'? You often see regret avoidance coming back in the comforts of the Influence Framework. I know I should work out, but the thought of the muscle pain feels a lot worse than me having to take a breather when going up the stairs.

Loss aversion is a fascinating phenomenon as it is also activated as to some- thing we don't own yet. Just the potential thought of losing out on something, already triggers the bias. That's because loss aversion is about tension – the tension between what people *have* and what they *want to have*. Let me give you an example of loss aversion kicking in by not actually losing something you possess – it has to do with decision-making. You would think that people are more satisfied with their choices if they have carefully considered their options. But the opposite is true because of loss aversion. Research[263] shows that close consideration of choices may create a mental attachment to options, a so-called sense of ownership. In other words, when someone chooses one option, they feel they have 'lost' all other options. As a matter of fact, it can have the unde- sirable consequence of people feeling less satisfied with their decisions. Maybe you have experienced it yourself. You set out to buy a pair of jeans. You go to a department store, and you have an ample choice. Flared jeans, skinny jeans, high-waist, stonewashed, dark blue, light washing, black, etcetera. You try on a few, and three of them fit you like a glove. After some turns in front of the fitting-room mirror, you decide to go for the dark blue skinny ones. So, you 'lose' the skinny black one and the dark blue flared jeans. You never actually owned them, but it does feel as if you had to part with them. This feeling of mental ownership can be so strong that it increases the abandoned option's attractiveness, compared with its appeal previous to the choice. The researchers didn't investigate how long this discomfort would lasts, or what would happen if all the options were negative (choosing between two painful treatments). However, we can take from this that a loss aversion can be related to both tangible and intangible assets. Loss aversion does have its boundaries in a few ways. First of all – and this seems obvious – people feel more loss averse if the stakes of their choice are larger.[264] In fact, some research[265] even struggles to find effect for small losses. Secondly, the strength of loss aversion differs among cultures. There is a study[266] researched in 53 countries with a view to understanding how cultural values affect someone's perception of losses compared to gains. They discovered that people from Eastern European countries tend to be the most loss averse, contrary to the individuals from African countries who were shown to be the least loss averse. This can be explained[267] by the variety in the level of support from friends, family and communities in the different countries. Some countries are more individualistic, others more collective. You can imagine that in collectivist cultures societal and family ties are closer, as they provide a social safety net. If you have a social safety net it becomes less risky to make decisions. You simply have a support system in place. Therefore, the feelings of loss decrease. And of course, this also works the other way round. If you are on your own, losses will feel more intense.

But there is more to loss aversion. Sometimes we need to make some riskier decisions in life. At one point or another, we as individuals and corporations and societies will be faced with complex problems for which there are no clear-cut answers. The COVID-19 crisis is a recent example. However, difficult situations need innovative thinking and new approaches. Innovation is about discovering unknown territory; and therefore it always feels risky. But riskier solutions sometimes are precisely what we *need* to get to break-throughs. Thus, insight into loss-aversion psychology is crucial, for something as seemingly minor as loss aversion can significantly impact the progress that countries make and the way that they handle complex difficulties such as COVID-19. The level of loss aversion can potentially determine the rate of innovation, welfare and sustainability of a country. Let me give you an example of this. Brazil is a typically collective culture, and this has helped them to tackle a problem that a lot of countries face: infectious diseases. In Brazil, some very innovative research was done by Oxford University in order to fight Dengue fever and the Zika virus with genetically engineered mosquitoes that produced enviable offspring. It was a big success: 'mosquito larvae were reduced by 82%, which led to a massive 91% drop in dengue fever cases'.[268] The second point is that no longer insecticides can be used to fight the mosquito. These modified mosquitoes leave no trace in the ecosystem, making them far more eco-friendly. A similar innovative gene technology could be seen in fighting other crop pests. At this moment, field trials are carried out in the Cayman Islands, Panama, Brazil, the US and India – all of them collective cultures. However, Europe remains lagging behind. 'Loss aversion within their decision-making bodies has potentially prevented European nations from trying new and emerging technologies, due to the fear of risk and loss.'[269] So, you see, loss aversion can influence system interventions that may boost or block the progress of an entire nation or continent.

But what about individuals? Is there also a difference in the perception of losses and gains among individuals? There most certainly is. It has to do with power. People in a powerful position often have more wealth and a wider network. This makes it easier for them to accept a potential loss, as they are better positioned to deal with such losses. Therefore, people in power tend to care less about losses; and simultaneously they value gains more.[270] But you need not necessarily be in a powerful position yourself to have a greater willingness to take on risks. If you have a relatively high income or live in a wealthier village or city, researchers noticed the same effect: people are less loss-averse and are more willing to take on risks.[271] So, suppose you want to grasp the level of someone's willingness to make decisions that are perceived as challenging or innovative. In that case, it is essential to look at someone's socio-economic status and environment, as both have turned out to be very influential at the level of loss aversion. So, it's time to translate this into practice. How can we use loss aversion to help people make better decisions? There are roughly five ways in which you can apply this intervention.

1. Framing
2. Allocating or labelling
3. Imagining your future self
4. Providing perspective
5. Directing attention

Framing

First of all, the way you frame a question – as either a loss or a gain – can change the decision someone makes or the response they give. It may be far more helpful to present something within a loss frame instead of a gain frame. Let me give you an example. Let's say you are in the business of selling home insulation. You could then approach me with either of these sales pitches:

*   You'll *save* 120 euros a year by replacing your insulation
*   You're *losing* 120 euros a year by keeping your current insulation

The second will be more effective. Let me give you an example from practice.[272] In Great Britain, there are about '250,000 unlicensed cars, representing around £40m in lost revenues'.[273] Researchers have sent offenders different kinds of letters in order to urge them to pay their taxes. In one of these, they added loss aversion by using messages such as *'Pay Your Tax or Lose Your [Make of Vehicle]'*. Unfortunately, this didn't have the desired impact. Until they turned the loss aversion up a notch, when they included an image of the offender's car in the letter, this didn't only make the letter more distinctive (the 'salient effect' we mentioned earlier). It also combined a strong element of personalisation, which far more emphatically triggered the feeling of potentially losing their car than words did.

DVLA relicensing rates

40% — Original Letter

42% — New Letter

49% — New Letter + Image

Data source: Behavioural Insights Team

Another example I love is the website www.stickk.com, which helps you stick to personal goals. It could be anything from losing weight to running a marathon. You commit to a goal at the site, but then loss aversion is added. You have to put money at stake. You then log into the site once a week and update your progress. If you haven't achieved your weekly goal, you lose your stake. But there is more to it. You don't just lose your money if you don't accomplish your weekly goal. You can (don't have to) select an organisation you hate that will get your money. You can take your pick from a list of what *stickK* calls 'anti-charities'. You can choose your own anti-charity. You also can give the money to a random charity, friend or foe, or not have any money on the line at all (although that is not recommended). Furthermore, you must appoint two referees in order to check if you are sticking to your desired behaviour. The programme is hugely successful. When I checked the website today, there was an astounding 50 million dollars on the line - as 521,000 commitments had been created, 1 million workouts completed, and over 40 million cigarettes had not been smoked.[274] The success of the programme is the addition of loss aversion. It makes it different from just any other goal-setting or coaching programme. If you put your money and your reputation on the line, you will be far more likely to stick to your training schedule – particularly if the money you might lose would be funding an organisation you can't stand.

Another example from health care. In health care, caregivers often must deal with two different cognitive biases of patients – first, the *optimism bias*. Patients often underestimate the probability that a disease might affect them.[275] And secondly, the *false beliefs* that make patients underestimate the consequences of a disease. To counter these biases, a loss-framing could be used. Researchers did so in order to help prevent breast cancer. Unfortunately, this is one of the most common types of cancer among women. However, early detection can be critical and decisive for a positive outcome. Having timely and frequent mammograms is essential. Still, many women do not make use of them as often as they should. In a study[276] conducted in the United States, women were invited to watch educational videos about breast cancer and mammograms. These used both a loss and a gain frame:

Gain-framing	Loss-framing
Describes how early detection of breast cancer can save your life.	Describes how failing to detect breast cancer early on can risk your life.
Although all women are at risk of breast cancer, there are always things you can do to lower your risk of death in case you have the disease.	Although all women are at risk of breast cancer, there are always things you can do to increase your risk of death in case you have the disease.
For this reason, when you get a mammogram, you are taking advantage of the best method for early detection of breast cancer.	For this reason, when you fail to get a mammogram, you are missing on the best method for early detection of breast cancer.
If the cancer has not spread, it is less likely to be	If the cancer has spread, it is more likely to be fatal.
Another advantage of finding the tumour early on is that you will have more chances of opting for diverse treatment options and you may require fewer radical procedures.	Another disadvantage of finding the tumour late is that you will have less chances of finding treatment options and you may require more radical procedures.
In short, when you get mammograms regularly, you are doing your best to detect breast cancer in its early stages.	In short, when you do not get mammograms regularly, you are not doing your best to detect breast cancer in its early stages.

This simple framing change showed an increase of 12% in performed mammograms (after six months), and 15% (after twelve months) in the group in which mammograms were presented within a loss frame, compared to the group in which they were presented with a gain frame.

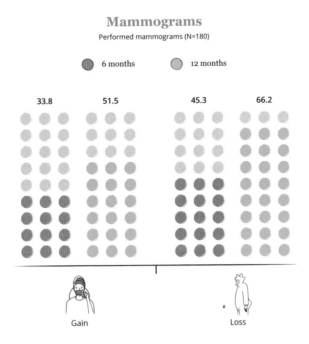

Data retrieved from: IDB, Behavioral Economics for Better Public Policies, edition 2

Allocation or labelling

Every time we spend money, we feel we have lost something. However, some-times spending money is a good thing. For example, when we are spending money for a carefree retirement. How can you tackle this monetary feeling of loss aversion? Research[277] shows that people don't experience loss aversion when spending money they have already allocated to specific purposes.

Money labelled differently is spent differently

So, if you are able to help people with this allocation, you can bypass people's aversion to spending money. This is why several banks now provide virtual saving buckets. You don't just put your money into your savings account; you allocate it to specific saving goals. By the way, this again has to do with fram-ing. This time, the gain-frame works better (saving up for a holiday) than a loss-frame (having less money in my checking account). So, another way to use framing to overcome loss aversion is to frame the outcome as a potential gain (the opposite of the previous insulation example).[278]

Imagining future self

We see a lot of loss-aversive behaviour at financial decisions. The way we spend and manage our money can have a tremendously positive or negative impact on our lives. This is a realm in which Behavioural Designers can help people make better decisions. Let me build upon the example of saving for a carefree retirement. If you want a 'happy-go-lucky future', you need to put money into pension plans right now. As a Behavioural Designer, it implies that we need to help people overcome a present bias. We as humans prefer immediate rewards (spending money during a shopping spree) to long-term benefits (saving for a carefree pension). If you make someone describe and imagine the ultimate last quarter of their life, the pain of not having a life is magnified, and loss aversion will kick in. Let me mentally paint a vivid picture of myself as a silver-haired golden girl (but mind you, oh so classy, with a magnetic je-ne-sais-quoi aura) whose only worry is sitting down and finally having time to read that stack of books that is so seductively tempting me in the corner of my room right now – and you've got me to a par. All you must do next is show me in which pension fund to cash my money is as to make this happen, and I'll do it. As you might have guessed already, appealing to someone's job-to-be-done is a very effective point-of-departure of this 'imagine'-tactic. But the behaviour doesn't have to be a 'biggie', such as entering a pension plan. If you wanted to sell me mascara, all you need to do is pitch me 'mascara that doesn't make you look like a worn-out panda by the end of the day', and you've got me too. Pandas belong in China, not on my face. Simple as that.

Giving perspective

Finally, we can help people to get some perspective. Sometimes our mind plays tricks on us, and feelings of fear and risk aversion can become too intense or get way out of proportion. Asking people to think about the worst that could happen, often helps them to put things in perspective. A trick by the way that you can use in stressful situations yourself. Force yourself to let your system 2-ratio override your system 1-emotional fears. It has helped me. Often, things aren't as bad as they seem when you take some deliberate time to think the consequences over.

Directing attention

We can also use loss aversion to draw people's attention. In Denver, the municipality wanted businesses to register as to an online tax payments-system, instead of paper filing. At the time, a letter was used to encourage companies to 'Go Green!' But this had plateaued. When they reframed the reminder letter emphasizing the time and money lost when not filing online, 'the number of Denver businesses that registered online increased to 76%, and the number that finally filed their taxes online by 42%'.[279] And to' stick to the US: in the Washington DC metropolitan area, they wanted to diminish the usage of plastic and paper bags. They tested two policies: a five-cent tax on disposable bags, and a five-cent bonus for re-usable bag use. Before the policies came into effect, 82% of customers used disposable bags. This declined to 40% after the tax was implemented in contrast to the bonus, which didn't have any effect whatsoever. In the first policy, you would lose out; in the second, you would gain something. In the San Francisco Bay Area, they imposed a tax on disposable plastic bags, which dropped the usage of plastic and paper bags by roughly 50%. However, something interesting was learnt in SFO airport also. They only taxed plastic bags, not paper bags. The effect? The usage of paper disposable bags increased. So, to see the most impact, you need to regulate all disposable bags usage. Otherwise, you might get unintended side-effects.[280]

W6. Can we make someone aware of their future self?
HYPERBOLIC DISCOUNTING

I already touched upon it briefly in the previous intervention, but we humans have a very strong bias that prevents us from engaging in a new behaviour. We have already touched upon the *present bias*, and perhaps you've heard of *hyperbolic discounting*. These are fancy words describing that we as humans prefer smaller rewards now to larger rewards in the future. It is not a straight line, it's indeed a hyperbole, but to avoid drowning you in theory, it is best for you to remember that:

Humans prefer present rewards to future ones. Once rewards are very distant in time, they lose their psychological value[281]

We, as humans, tend towards instant gratification. 'I want it all, and we want it now', to quote Queen. Again, this is our system 1 overruling our system 2. Our brain loves immediate stimulation and loves bypassing our system 2, which oversees our self-control. And this can become problematic, because a lot of instant gratification is linked to unhealthy behaviour. We eat poor quality processed foods that instantly satisfy our cravings, compromising our health in the long term. We overspend on our credit cards by seeing advertisements of products we want now, obstructing our financial health. We scroll for hours on the social media in order to catch the one video or picture that makes our brain light up – instead of spending quality time with friends and family. And we are addicted to dopamine. Therefore, hyperbolic discounting can lead to poor decision-making. Decisions that prioritise short-term gratification often neglect and detract from our long-term well-being. This occurs especially in addictive behaviour such as smoking.[282] While substance addiction often plays a role in people's decision to smoke, nicotine addiction itself has been linked to impulsivity and the undervaluation of long-term outcomes.[283] But overall: the more we overvalue instant gratification, the more likely it is that we will be distracted from longer-term, more meaningful goal

Hyperbolic discounting makes it difficult for us to maintain focus on actions creating long-term success and happiness. Over-reliance on instant gratification distracts us from pursuing more meaningful activities and leads to destructive financial, social and health results. It makes us blind to the benefits of long-term decision-making, which can sometimes include gains far greater than those of the more immediate decisions. The whole environmental collapse is a clear example of this short-term thinking. Only recently have more people started to realise that the way we consume, produce and travel at present, will have significant long-term damaging effects. And hyperbolic discounting can have system effects too. But also, at a personal level, it can cause us to be too short-term-minded. For example, if you've got some money to spare, it would be wise to put it in your pension fund, or make extra down payments on your mortgage. But as we overvalue instant gratification, you will probably prefer booking a holiday or buying new clothes or eating out – enjoying your money right now. Who knows what the future may bring, right? 'Live in the moment' is the mantra of today. Of course, we need to be mindful of how we can live life to the fullest on a day-to-day basis. But be careful that your system 2 is not post-rationalising your enjoyment of today's decisions. We must enjoy life, and we don't know what the future holds. But for most people, it would probably have been a better decision to put the (extra) money into their savings account, instead of spending it on instant gratifications. Then they would have their money compound interest for a future carefree retirement.

Don't get me wrong, I am not being judgmental. We must make decisions in everyday life that are not all that easy to compare. How do you reach something so attainable as enjoying a piece of cake now, to something possibly unattainable like looking ravishing in a bathing suit a few months from now? Our brain loves simplicity and is innately risk-averse – so we, by nature, opt for the sure or the within-reach decisions. This means that we are often willing to accept a small but certain reward over a larger gain that is less certain because there is a chance, we won't secure it.[284] Our system 1 rules us all. The capacity of our system 2 to manage our self-control is limited. Especially when confronted with cognitive overload. So, don't be too hard on yourself: We simply don't have the measure of self-control we probably all would love to have. We just need to be aware that we as humans suffer from this phenomenon, and so do the people we are trying to influence as well. It can stand in the way of better decision-making, and if we want to help people make better decisions, we must take hyperbolic discounting into account.

So, how can we aid people in getting away from this human tendency? There are several ways we can help them to overcome hyperbolic discounting and to make better decisions for their future selves. You can prime someone for future focus.[285] *Priming* is showing someone a stimulus (which could, for example, be a word or a picture or a sound) that will influence their reaction to a second stimulus. I prime myself with high-energetic music before working out (okay, if you want to know: the Soulwax remix of Marie Davidson's song *Work It* always does the trick for me[286]). It strongly influences how I experience doing my squats after listening to the song. I feel like a winner instead of a victim (you must listen to the song to get the 'winner thing', and it does contain explicit language). Researchers found that exposing someone to the words *long-term*, *future* and *self-control* tends to make people more likely to think that they are more in control of themselves and the future.[287] A friend of ours primed himself to abstain from instant gratification by reminding himself that 'I am someone who is on a disciplined regime to become fit'. A final example: a research team led by Richard Thaler (the co-author of the book *Nudge*) were looking for a solution to students dropping out of high school[288] in West Virginia. They changed the West Virginia Law that made students under 18, who choose to leave school prematurely, to also lose their driving licenses. The effect was auspicious: the high school dropout rates fell by one third. The research team explained this had to do with hyperbolic discounting. Previously, students probably underestimated (discounted) the future adverse effects of dropping out. But now that there was a clear short-term consequence, they instead stayed enrolled. In other words, they prioritised short term rewards (keeping their license) over long-term rewards (finishing their education). This is why it may also be more effective in getting people to buy more energy-efficient appliances, to give them immediate cash-back bonuses for upgrading appliances, rather than the month-to-month incentives after appliances have been upgraded. It satisfies our short-term reward-craving brain.

W7. Can we show progress in percentages or in abstract measurements? FEEDBACK

Another way to boost WANT is to satisfy our brain's need for control. One way to do this is to give people feedback on how much progress they have made as to specific behaviour. Research shows that providing people with progress indicators will ease their cognitive load – for they know where they are in the process, and how much work there is left to do. There are a lot of ways to show progress effectively. You might communicate to a user that they're on step 2 out of 5, that they're 65% done with a task, or that they only need to earn a certain number of points before claiming something. But one of the most effective ways is to use percentages or abstract measurements. Let me give you an example as to this right away.

Kiva[289] in the US and JustGiving[290] in the UK, both aim to raise money for microfinancing. They deliberately display the amount of money raised so far, and thus show how this relates to the desired target amount in percentages. This gives us humans a feeling of control, as by this intervention donors are put in the powerful position of tipping the balance. Can you imagine the satisfaction it must bring if you are the one who is able to help somebody get to the desired 100% target by giving that final push? Kiva also adds to this by featuring details about projects and loans close to meeting their target, e.g. showing that Josefina Del Carmen has already raised 75% of the money she needs to buy farming goods. This technique of focusing on percentages is based on Karlan and List.[291] They analysed whether showing a percentage of the raised funding could positively impact the total of the donations. Their results were impressive. For as the percentage of donations increased, the average donation amount was also boosted:

- At 10% of target achieved, the average donation was around $15
- At 33% of target achieved, the average donation was $26
- At 67% of target achieved, the average donation was almost $40

The increased percentage also led to improved response rates from 3.7% to 8.2% of the solicited individuals. Also, the increased percentage improved the response rates from 3.7% to 8.2% of the solicited individuals. To sum it up: showing the percentages made not only more individuals respond, but the size of donations increased as well. The cognitive bias we discussed earlier can explain this: hyperbolic discounting. Knowing that a donation today has an actual impact satisfies our preference for immediate rewards (instead of future gains). This is why showing progress in percentages can boost the willingness to donate money. So, if you need to raise money (or when you've got to raise the project budget), then think about showing how much of the budget you already have secured in percentages, and how close you are to the desired target amount. It may be far more effective than simply asking for a funding or a donation. Another example of a non-profit organisation – which indicated that setting goals in a fundraising campaign and showing progress has been very effective – is *Watsi*. Watsi provides healthcare to those in need. When Watsi first launched their campaigns, they realised that the campaigns with a set percentage goal performed better than the open-ended campaigns. Or, as Al-Qinneh of Watsi said: 'We've noticed that campaigns that have a goal associated with them do well. They reach the goal at a faster rate than ones that don't. Not only that, but campaigns with a set goal would typically exceed the goal, resulting in more donations than open-ended campaigns.'[292]

Apart from showing percentages, abstract measurements can also boost WANT. Abstract measurements could be things like dots, stars, stamps. This is linked to the *endowed progress effect*, the cognitive bias we discussed previously. Researchers studied wine buyers at a liquor store. Some were offered a complimentary bottle of wine after ten purchases; others were offered a complimentary bottle of wine after earning 100 points, with each purchase earning them 10 points. The wine enthusiasts who participated in the programme with dots showed more commitment to the programme.[293] I don't know if you are a gamer yourself, but you see abstract measurements cropping up quite often in gamification. Think about levels or dots. But the same concept can also be used in other applications. A good example is Todoist. Inspired by gamification, it uses dots to award productivity. In this case, they have translated into the abstract measurement of karma the dots that are to reach the karma levels appointed to you every time you complete a task. And it seems to work. As Todoist CEO Amir Salihefendic puts it: 'In the beginning, maybe you're just interested in leveling up. Later on, you get interested in hitting daily and weekly goals. For productivity apps in general, it's very hard for users to stick with a system, and there's a lot of hopping around. Karma is a way of getting people to stick with the system.'[294]

W8. Can we make the end-goal of the behaviour visual?
FEEDBACK

You are in for a treat because this will be the shortest read regarding any behavioural intervention. It builds upon the previous intervention question, but I felt this was still worth its behavioural intervention question. Apart from showing progress in percentages and abstract measurements, it can also be very effective to visualise the end-goal of the behaviour. We touched upon this in the last intervention, and you could see it in the examples I referred to regarding the circles and progress bars of Kiva and JustGiving. But make sure you don't just communicate in words how much progress has been made, but make it even more easily digestible for system 1 by using pictures. Another example of making progress visible is through the smart meters that can be installed in houses in order to preserve energy. In Queensland, Australia, 220 households that had replaced their old meters by smart meters were given feedback on their water usage. Some got general advice as to water conservation only, others received information using *social norms* ('Join southeast Queenslanders...'), and the final group was given a visual feedback as to their actual performance, and tips that could help to reduce water where they used water most.

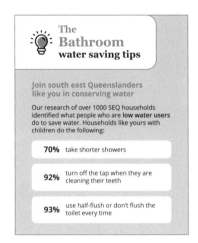

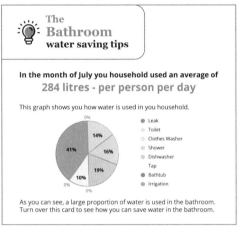

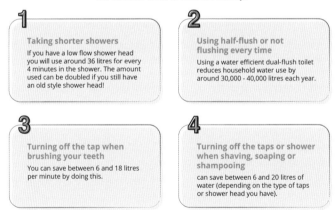

Data source: www.bhub.org – Descriptive norm & visual feedback on water usage & tips

The condition in which the feedback was made visual, using percentages and a circle diagram, had tips added with a view to doing better next month. The average water usage among all households dropped by 10.29 litres per person per day, and the median dropped by 7.6 litres – reductions of 7.3% and 6.2%

respectively. When they looked at the behaviour in the longer run, the information only and descriptive norm postcards resulted in immediate water savings. Still, these changes were lost over time, as households returned to their pre-intervention water-use levels. Among those receiving the *visual feedback*, water use declined more slowly, but the effect of this intervention was longer-lived.[295] I will now wrap this intervention question up and pack it away, but not without putting a nice bow on top first. It has to do with what researchers call the *goal gradient effect*.

The closer we get to a goal, the harder we work to reach it

In that sense, we are rather like lab rats. Researchers initially discovered this effect by putting rats in a maze with food. The closer the little rodents got to the food, the faster they started to run.[296] The cool thing is that this effect also kicks in with artificial progress towards a goal (hence the stars, points and level effectiveness). This again is linked to the endowed progress effect. In this one paragraph, you have become 10 points smarter already! How's that for upping your karma, and mastering 80% of the Behavioural Design intervention questions? Quickly do some brainwriting, and we'll progress towards the 100% – with just seven more intervention questions to go.

W9. Can we add meaning to a number or statistics?
ANCHORING

This subsequent intervention I want to introduce you to, demonstrates how our system 1 sometimes operates in mysterious ways when it comes to numbers. The fact is, most of us humans are pretty clueless when it comes to numbers. Is something expensive? Is something valuable? Is something a little or a lot? We don't know, so our system 1 uses short-cuts to getting a reference point for our decisions. This reference point is also called *an anchor*. We humans use anchors and base our further decisions upon them, and often we place far too much weight upon this initial piece of information. It therefore is just another one of our cognitive biases, which are also known as the *adjustment heuristic* or *anchoring-as-adjustment*. Two well-known studies in behavioural psychology illustrate how this anchoring works.

The first research was done by Kahneman and Tversky[297] (yes, here they are again to help us shed light on all things irrational). They ran an experiment with two groups of people. Both were shown a roulette wheel that they had to give a turn. Only the wheel was rigged – for one group, the wheel stopped at the number 10 and for the other at 65. They had to write the figure down, and asked an unrelated question: 'What is your best estimate of the number of African nations in the United Nations?' The results were fascinating. The group who observed the roulette wheel stop at number 10 guessed the number of African countries would be about 25%. The group who noticed the little roulette ball stopping at number 65 assumed far higher values; their average guestimate was 45% of African countries. What happened here? The anchoring bias was kicked into play (quite literally in this case). Both groups used the first number they were confronted with as an anchor, and started to valuing from this anchor point onwards. The first group probably thought something like: 'ten of the countries seems rather a bit too few, let's go up a bit', ending on average at 25%. The second group had the same thought process but ended somewhere completely different: '65 seems like a bit much, let's go a tad lower' – which ended at an average of 45%. The numbers and questions were completely unrelated, but that's the trick our mind plays on us.

The second example of the anchoring bias in action that I love comes from Dan Ariely,[298] one of our other favourite behavioural researchers on whom we can always count to do an experiment explaining human irrationality. He asked people to write down the last two digits of their social security number, and then asked people to bid in dollars for wine, chocolate, and computer equipment. I guess you can already imagine the outcome: those with social security numbers ending with high digits (think 70s, 80s, or 90s) were willing to pay more for the wine than those with social security numbers ending in the lower digits. The people with higher two-digit numbers would submit bids between 60% and 120% higher, than those with lower social security numbers. Again, the social security number served people as an anchor. When people were asked if they thought their social security numbers had influenced their valuation of the item, most of them said no.[299] So, we are genuinely not aware that we use anchors. It's another one of our subconscious decision-making processes in our brain. However, Kahneman and Tversky's theory proposed the anchoring effect as a *conscious adjustment from an anchor*, which goes against the subconscious theory. We can say that anchoring is a cognitive bias which is able to influence our decision-making. The anchoring effect has been replicated within very different contexts, such as 'probability estimates, legal judgments, forecasting and purchasing decisions'.[300] So, we need to give it our attention and to be aware of how often it is used to influence our decision-making.

Several studies have proven that anchoring is very hard to avoid. Even if you know anchors must be wrong. In one study,[301] students were asked to guess at what age Mahatma Gandhi had died. They were given the following anchors: before the age of 9 or after the age of 140. Both clearly incorrect answers. However, the anchors did influence their decision: the first group estimated that Ghandi had died at the age of 50, the other group thought it would be at 67. So, quite a difference. I do have to note that researchers criticized this experiment as they claimed the anchors to be unrealistic, and far beyond the range of acceptable answers. However, they stated that anchoring would not occur if anchors would be more realistic, so adjustment isn't necessary.[302]

Despite criticism, the anchoring effect has been replicated in many studies. Let me give you a few more examples, so that you can casually whip them out and make a lasting impression on someone when they ask you: 'Have you ever heard of the anchoring bias?' The following experiment kind of replicates Ariely's social security number-experiment. Participants were asked to write down the last three digits of their phone number, multiplied by one thousand (e.g. 548 = 548,000). They were then asked to estimate house prices. These were again influenced by the (irrelevant) anchor, even though at the beginning of the study[303] they gave a 10-minute presentation on facts and figures as to the housing market. This is an experiment that might be of use to in practice. If you ever want to buy a house, you need to know that the price of the first house your estate agent shows you will serve as an anchor. You are probably influenced by anchors in daily life far more often than you think. For example, anchoring effects have been ascertained in the consumer-packaged goods category. You can be deluded in many ways by anchors when buying these goods. A special kind of anchor called an *expansion anchor* is often used in advertising. For instance: '200 uses!' or 'Buy this 12-pack potato chips for your family'. Another kind of anchor is a *quantity anchor* mentioning purchasing limits: 'only 6 per person allowed'.[304] Both of them influence our consumption. Anchoring is hard to avoid, but someone forewarned is someone forearmed, right?

To recap, we have learnt that the anchoring heuristic can influence our rational decision-making in various realms. Buying more candy than you need is one thing, but we should pause for a minute to grasp how this anchoring effect can have a more severe impact. The following example illustrates this. It shows that at the same time, all humans, including those with higher education and expert jobs, are just as much influenced by this cognitive bias. You would think that judges are human beings who excel (or at least find themselves in the top tier) in arriving at rational decisions based on rational laws, right? If so, think again. Unfortunately, there is a lot of bias in the courtroom, and judges are also influenced by anchors. Even if those anchors are entirely irrelevant. In one study,[305] judges presented a case involving a shoplifter who had been caught in the act for the 12th time. The judges were asked to sentence the shoplifter, after the prosecutor voiced a sentencing demand. And here there is something I found shocking – the judges were informed that this demand was random and arbitrary. Therefore, rationally speaking, it was of no use to the judges. However, the demand's magnitude (length of the sentence) did influence the jurors' verdict. Judges who received the lower anchor (shorter sentence) arrived at a shorter average sentence than the judges with a higher anchor did.

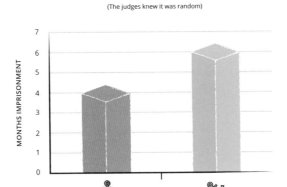

The Prosecutor's Random Anchor
(The judges knew it was random)

Data source: www.thelawproject.com.au/insights/anchoring-bias-in-the-courtroom

This is already worrying, isn't it? You wouldn't think jurisdiction was based on chance. But it is more than you would think (or like). The researchers turned it up a notch, creating the strangest experiment possible. Again, judges were presented with a case in which a defendant was charged with theft. Instead of giving the prosecutor's demand before deciding upon a verdict, the judges were told to throw a dice. I know, it sounds ridiculous, but wait and see what happened. The dice was rigged, and landed on predetermined numbers, just as the roulette wheel we discussed earlier. Indeed, high and low. Here's how the dice affected the number of years that someone was sentenced to prison by our honoured judges:

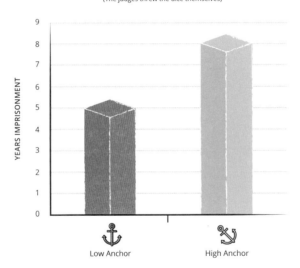

Judges Throwing Dice
(The judges threw the dice themselves)

Data source: www.thelawproject.com.au/insights/anchoring-bias-in-the-courtroom

But it is not just the judges that are biased. You probably know that in the United States, regular American citizens can be appointed to a jury in a trial. If the anchoring effect already influences judges, you can imagine how this influences humans without any prior legal knowledge. If you want to sue someone in court, the more you ask for, the more you get. In an experiment, 80 students were presented with a hypothetical legal case.[306] The prosecutor argued that a birth control pill caused ovarian cancer in a woman, and they sued the Health

Maintenance Organization (HMO) that prescribed the medicine to her. The students were divided into four groups, and each group heard a different demand for the damages: $100, $20,000, $5 million, and $1 billion. The students were then asked what compensation they would find suitable. Would the anchor influence the juror's perception as to the connection between the pill and the disease? What's your verdict, were they influenced? Yes, you are indeed correct: they were. And these were the results:

DEMAND	COMPENSATION (AVERAGE)
$100	$990
$20,000	$36,000
$5 million	$440,000
$1 billion	$490,000

The students in the low anchor condition were '26.4% confident that the HMO had caused the injury, whereas students in the high anchor condition were 43.9% confident that HMO caused the injury'.[307]

Influence of Monetary Anchor
on Causation

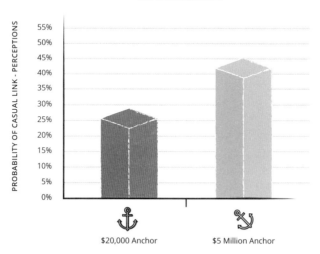

Data source: www.thelawproject.com.au/insights/anchoring-bias-in-the-courtroom

Luckily, we know that judges don't roll dice before sentencing, and hopefully prosecutors don't make crazy demands. However, don't be too sure of the last. In an actual courtroom, a woman named Stella Liebeck got awarded 2.9 million in damages, after having spilt hot McDonald's coffee on herself. Yes, you are reading it correctly: she herself was the one who spilt it. Liebeck initially demanded $20,000 in damages. So, how come this number went through the roof? First, the fast-food chain dismissed her initial demand and offered her $800 instead. When she got herself a lawyer, he knew of a prior case of a woman getting burned because of McDonald's coffee, spilt on her by a McDonald's employee. This was settled at $230,000. You would say that Liebeck should get less (after all, she was the spiller in this case). But her lawyer had learnt that high demands could lead to high rewards. So, he made an outrageous demand: thus, setting a ridiculously high anchor. And it worked like a charm on the jurors. They awarded her with a damage compensation of 2.9 million. Some jurors even wanted to grant her an absurd $9.6 million. Of course, McDonalds applied for a court appeal. In the end, Liebeck knew when she hit the jackpot, and agreed to settle at $600,000.[308] Not bad for a shaky hand when you need a caffeine kick, right? We do have to realise that: 'Even though judges typically do not throw dice before making sentencing decisions, they are still constantly exposed to potential sentences and anchors during sentencing decisions. The mass media, visitors to the court hearings, the private opinion of the judge's partner, family, or neighbours are all possible sources of sentencing demands that should not influence a given sentencing decision.'[309] There are far more experiments in the courtroom, but let's move on to the next exciting topic: How could you use anchoring? If you want to read about more judicial experiments, follow the link under the visuals, and you'll be in for a 'treat'.

Okay, how may anchoring help you to design for desired behaviours? Well, perhaps you are in the business of selling a product or service. Apart from pricing, anchoring also influences people's quality perception of a product, and whether they find it fair to pay (or be paid) for a specific product or service.[310] So, what does this mean in practice? If someone is considering to buy your product, you should know that they base their opinion based on a reference category of similar products or services. This category is their anchor. For instance, if you are buying a new pair of jeans, you remember the trousers you saw or purchased in the past, and in that way you estimate a price for the new pair of jeans that seems fair to you. In short:

Previous experiences as to goods serve as our anchor we use in deciding how similar new goods might be priced

If you want to make an impression at the next family get-together: this may be called *coherent arbitrariness*[311] in behavioural psychology. Of course, this process is entirely subjective. The danger is that your product or service could be over- or undervalued by your potential client or customer if the anchor they used doesn't represent the actual value of your product or service. So, a piece of advice, let's say you are launching an entirely new product or service onto the market. In this case, people don't have an arbitrary former price as an anchor point. You are the one who can determine the anchor. Set a high anchor first. Any discount or price reductions you make afterwards then 'feel like a bargain and will increase consumer demand'.[312] We will discuss some more price strategies in the next behavioural intervention. But for now, let's move on to another way you can make anchoring work for you by a very different approach. Maybe you are not in the business of selling things, but simply want people to be better informed or understand figures and numbers as these could be essential for them in understanding what is relevant to their wellbeing or welfare. One realm in which it is crucial for people to understand numbers and statistics consists of the media or news. We all know how influential headlines can be as to people's opinion formation or taking decisions. But the truth is, most of us find it very hard to interpret numbers mentioned in headlines or newspaper articles. To give you a few examples, here are some of the amounts mentioned in articles published in *The New York Times*.[313]

- 'The Ohio National Guard brought *33,000 gallons of drinking water* into the region, while volunteers handed out bottled water at distribution centers set up at local high schools.'
- 'The storm killed thousands of people in Honduras, left *one million homeless* and destroyed what was left of a declining Banana industry, once the country's lifeblood, as well as other vital crops.'
- 'The group says it has helped to preserve more than *120 million acres* around the world.'
- 'They also recommended safety programs for the nation's gun owners; Americans own almost *300 million firearms*.'

What do these numbers mean? Is it a lot? Is it bad? High? Low? Should I care? Am I in danger? Should I do something? Should I call the Mrs? As to this, we are basically clueless. A group of researchers at Brown University decided to tackle this problem. They took the numbers and statistics they encountered in the media & news, and crowdsourced for anchors using MTurk.[314] They came up with a set of anchors (which the researchers called 'perspectives') helping people to interpret the information a lot better. This is what it looked like:[315]

- 'The Ohio National Guard brought *33,000 gallons of drinking water* to the region, while volunteers handed out bottled water at distribution centers set up at local high schools. *To put this into perspective,* 33,000 gallons of water *is about equal to the amount of water it takes to fill 2 average swimming pools.*'
- 'The storm killed thousands of people in Honduras, left *one million homeless,* and destroyed what was left of a declining Banana industry, once the country's lifeblood, as well as other vital crops. *To put this into perspective,* one million people *is about 12% of the population of Honduras.*'

- 'The group says it has helped to preserve more than *120 million acres* around the world. *To put this into perspective,* 120 million acres of protected land *is about 1.15 times larger than the state of California.*'
- 'They also recommended safety programs for the nation's gun owners; Americans own almost *300 million firearms. To put this into perspective,* 300 million firearms *is about 1 firearm for every person in the United States.*'

The researchers discovered that *'like-for-like' anchors* worked best. An example is saying, 'Afghanistan is about the same size as Texas with about the same population'. In contrast, saying that Kenya has twice the population of Texas would be less effective. Then follow the number with the phrase: *'to put this into perspective'.* Also, personalised anchor turned out to be efficient. If your target audience doesn't live in Texas, for instance, they still don't grasp the size of Afghanistan. If you can, try to tailor an anchor as regards someone's location or culture. *The New York Times* already uses an automated plug-in that inserts relevant anchors based on your location.[316] What can we learn from this? If we must communicate a number, try putting it into perspective by finding an anchor, and, if you can, by making it personally relevant. And use the sentence 'to put this into perspective'.

By using anchors, you can make information far more understandable as it gives meaning to a number or statistic

And you can imagine that in many realms like health care, energy conservation, finance, and so on, people will need to understand the numbers and figures. An anchoring intervention might be just that little push they need to boost their willingness to do something, make betting decisions for themselves, their future, and their surroundings. Isn't that a happy note, after our trust in the legal system being bruised so badly?

How to undo the anchoring effect?
So, now that we're on the positive path of anchors, let's continue (and end this intervention) by investigating whether there is a way to fight anchors? Is there a possible antidote? These German researchers started with a 'traditional' anchoring experiment which proved that this cognitive bias can influence even experts. They took a battered car to sixty car mechanics in order to ask if it

was still worth having the car fixed by requesting their opinion as to the vehicle's current worth. These people mentioned they thought that the car would be worth either DM 2,800 (low anchor) or DM 5,000 (high anchor). So, what would the expert opinion be then? Again, the anchoring effect was significant. When given the high anchor, the car was valued 40% higher than at the low anchor (DM 3,563 vs DM 2,520). So, what is the remedy then? They came up with a clever idea: What if they asked the mechanics whether they could tell them why their estimate could be wrong. So, after a researcher had said: 'I think the car is worth DM 2,800/5,000, but when I mentioned this to a friend, he considered this estimate too low/high. So, what would you say argues against this price?' This is what happened: the mechanics were less impressed by the anchor. They estimated the value either at DM 3,130 (and not DM 3,563) or DM 2,783 (and not DM 2,520). Moreover, the more reasons a mechanic mentioned against the initial proposed value, the less they were influenced by the anchor. This is called the *consider the opposite*-approach, as a corrective strategy.[317] Then they replicated the same technique in a completely different realm. When they asked students to estimate a politician's chance of winning the next election, they again set an anchor. For instance, 'Do you think the current prime minister has more or less than 80% of a chance to win?' The usual anchoring effect kicked in again. Then they applied the same anti-dote. When they asked another group of students the same question, but requested them to name three reasons why the prime minister might lose, the anchoring effect diminished significantly.[318]

So, what happens here within our hidden psychology? Studies have shown that applying a consider-the-opposite-strategy makes us humbler; to be exact it reduces our overconfidence in the correctness of a chosen answer.[319] Overconfidence is often the effect of ignoring facts. By listing the counter-arguments, people can no longer neglect evidence that might contradict the anchor. It is also thought to diminish *hindsight bias*.[320] Again, a cognitive bias allows people to convince themselves after an event which they had accurately predicted before it happened. We as humans perceive past events as easier to predict than they actually were. This again boosts our overconfidence in the estimates we make in future. It is also known as the *'I-knew-this-along'*-phenomenon[321] (you probably know some people who are hindsight-biased gold-medallists. Now you know they are annoying and often wrong).

You activate system 2 to neutralise your system 1

So, there you have it. If someone is trying to sell you something or gives you a quote, hold your horses and first try to come up with reasons why the price (the anchor) is not correct, and thus you might escape the anchoring trap and score a better deal yourself. Let's throw out our anchors right now.

W10. Can we design a positive state-of-mind? PRIMING

We will now end with an intervention that has caused discussion among researchers: *priming*. Some say it works; others say it doesn't. But before I explain everything about priming, I would first like to give you a little assignment. Can you complete the next word: S _ _ P for me? Just fill in the blanks. Okay, before I answer, I will immediately get myself a quick snack to eat, and I'll be right back, okay? You just finish the word S _ _ P. So, what did you make of the word? A fair chance is you think the word is SOUP, am I right? The correct answer is SOAP. What happened just now is priming. I primed you with my remark I was going to get something to eat. Your system 1, aka your 'pattern-making machine', found it logical that the word I asked you to complete would be related to eating. Thus you came up with soup. If I had said I was first going to wash my hands, your guess would probably have been the word *soap*. This, in a nutshell, is priming. It is the phenomenon that when you are confronted with a particular stimulus (which, for instance, could be a word, image or sound), this influences how you react to a subsequent stimulus. It works in our brain because our system 1 again is trying to make sense of your world, and trying to find patterns. So, if I show you the word *coffee*, a moment later you will remember the word *tea* a lot better than the word *tree*. You were primed by the word *coffee*, and it became easier for your system 1 to make a connection with tea. Let me give you another example. Listening to an energetic happy song first thing in the morning, will affect how I respond to clothes scattered all over my bathroom floor. I feel okay about it. I would toss them, like some self-acclaimed twin of Michael Jordan, into the washing basket. Priming methods are used a lot in positive mental coaching.

Why is priming important? Well, primes can be pretty impactful as to how people communicate and behave. One famous study on priming comes from John Bargh. He asked students to rearrange the order of words to form a sentence.[322] However, one group had to rearrange positive words (such as patience, sensitive, honour, considerate, polite), the other negative words (aggressive, rude, annoying, intrude). With these words, the students were either primed as to rudeness or politeness. The students then had to wait until the professor had checked their answers. The students who rearranged the polite words patiently, waited on average 9.3 minutes before they interrupted. Whereas the ones using the rude words only waited for 5.5 minutes. The same researchers became famous for a priming study which reported that reading words related to 'elderliness' (e.g. *Florida*, *Bingo*) caused participants to walk slower when leaving the laboratory than the participants who had read words unrelated to the elderly.[323] What the research showed is that:

If you prime people in a certain way, they are more likely to act in that same way

But to tell the truth: Bargh and his team have been challenged quite a lot. Some researchers were unable to replicate the results of the two studies. To me, it is a fundamental crossroads at which you and I should take different directions. Someday, someone will undoubtedly challenge you that your behavioural interventions are not working upon everyone. And that is true. I think some people's obsession with proving that behavioural economics isn't an actual science is such a waste of effort. To me, behavioural economics isn't about replicability. It is about time and time again trying to find out how we can develop interventions that will work at a particular moment for a particular group of people, taking their subconscious decision-making and biases as a point of departure. We are after all dealing with humans. And we have noticed that humans are fickle. They are greatly influenced by their past experiences, social contexts and beliefs. Replicability is rather a myth. We may see patterns; we may learn from similar contexts and challenges, but please don't go out of your way to prove replication.

I believe that it could even potentially stand in the way of coming up with in-novative, more creative solutions. If you want to replicate, you might be able to all kinds of boundaries that could stifle divergent thinking. So, let us not go in that direction. Let us look at examples that worked and see if we can learn from them. And, then again, test if they work within your context for the humans you are trying to influence. Solomun's *Late Night* blasting out of the stereo works for me in order to get my happy energy up, but it might very well be your worst nightmare. While Johan Strauss Senior's *The Radetzky March* may just do the trick for you. Who knows? We are non-judgmental social anthropologists after all, utterly fascinated by human particularities. And I love to experiment upon myself with Behavioural Design, including priming. Just seeing if it works.

So, now we have got this out of the way, let's look at some priming interventions that have shown positive results. Researchers have found that the priming ef-fect can subconsciously help people to engage in a more healthy behaviour.[324] In this case, priming has helped students to become more active. Their exper-iment was similar to Bargh's experiment we discussed before. Some students were given sentences that promoted a healthy and active lifestyle, while others were given sentences that did not. The students primed by the sentences as to healthy lifestyles, were found to be more likely to take the stairs when going up to their class, whereas the other students were more likely to take the elevator. Another study[325] showed that priming could affect psychical endurance. People in this study were offered either a visual prime of a bottle of Polish spring water or of the sports drink Gatorade. After being primed, while sitting on a chair the participants had to raise their dominant foot 31 cm above the ground and keep it there. The participants primed with the water bottle kept their foot up for 87 seconds, while the participants primed with the sports drink topped that to 187 seconds on average. The researchers explain this because Gatorade is associat-ed with endurance, which primed participants as to 'grit'. So, they endured the demanding psychical task longer. And therefore:

Primes can be used to trigger the achieving of goals

Another study showed that priming can also promote honesty.[326] The experiment took place in a university cafeteria where people could get drinks, but had to pay for them by putting money into an 'honesty box'. The researchers examined the effect of the image of a pair of eyes when the contributions were being made to this honesty box. People paid nearly three times as much for their drinks if eyes were displayed instead of some control image.

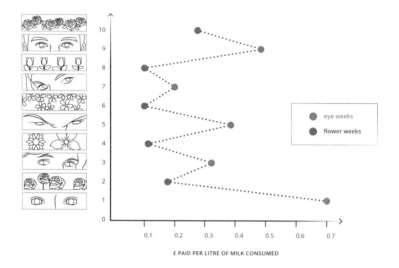

£ PAID PER LITRE OF MILK CONSUMED

Data source: Bateson, M., Nettle, D., & Roberts, G. (2006)

We can take from this that a priming cue of 'being watched' can make people change their behaviour. Showing someone the positive reviews of your product will prime them to believe that your product is good. And the first words you use to describe your offering may affect the appeal of your offering and also the price people are willing to pay for it, as this experiment as to mindless eating shows.[327]

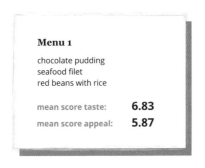

Menu 1

chocolate pudding
seafood filet
red beans with rice

mean score taste: **6.83**

mean score appeal: **5.87**

Menu 2

satin chocolate pudding
succulent Italian seafood filet
cajun red beans with rice

mean score taste: **7.31**   +7%

mean score appeal: **6.66**   +13%

Results from: Wansink, Brian & Sobal, Jeffery (2007)

Now that we are discussing product preferences, here's something that you might use as a prime if you have a store: for, a music prime can influence what people buy. As a study,[328] researchers played French or German music in a supermarket, while shoppers weren't told the music was French or German, but it was clear to depict it ('oh la la' versus 'hum-pa-pa'). The music turned out to be a prime for subsequent shopping behaviour. French music led to French wine outselling German wine by five bottles to one, whereas German music led to German wine outselling French by two bottles.

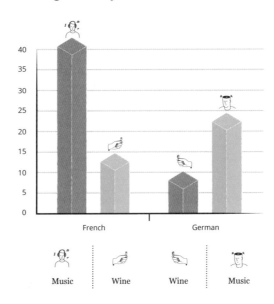

Data source: North, Hargreaves and McKendrick (1997)

Another study aimed to see if a music prime could also influence what people were prepared to pay for a bottle of wine.[329] The experiment took place in a wine cellar; one group of customers was primed with classical music, and the other with top-forty music. Classical music primed thoughts of sophistication and affluence. Consequently, classical music led to customers to buying more expensive wine than top-forty music did. So far for priming in order to influence product preference and price. However, can music also prime to influence taste perception? Yes, it can! Another research team asked people in return for a glass of wine to depict the taste of the wine.[330] For the study, four songs were picked, representing four different emotions:

- *Waltz of flowers* by Tchaikovsky (subtle and refined)
- *Just can't get enough* by Nouvelle Vague (zingy and refreshing)
- *Slow breakdown* by Michael Brook (mellow and soft)
- *Carmina Burana* by Orff (powerful and heavy)

Participants described the taste of the wines they drank differently, depending on what type of music was played. 'The specific taste of the wine was influenced in a manner consistent with the mood evoked by the music. If the background music was powerful and heavy, the wine was perceived as more powerful and heavy than when there was no background music played. If the background music was subtle and refined, then the wine was perceived as being more subtle and refined, than when no background music was played. If the background music was zingy and refreshing, then the wine was perceived as zingier and more refreshing than when no background music was played. If the background music was mellow and soft, the wine was perceived as mellower and softer than when no background music was played.' So, audio priming is able to influence and spark the willingness to prefer, buy and value your product.

Let's leave products behind, and see if priming can also be used to make people feel better. Yes, it can: Priming is related to (unaware) expectations. If we believe beforehand that something will be good, it generally tends to be good. And if we think it might be bad, it will be bad.[331]

Okay, what all this comes down to is that:

If we are able to design a positive state-of-mind, we can design positive behaviour

You can increase someone's (or your own) enjoyment by using primes to change expectations. So, go ahead – prime someone or yourself for good outsets. Play that happy song, say that positive mantra out loud, read something inspiring before you start doing whatever, spray on some lovely perfume, bake an apple pie (the smell is also a very effective prime, a study showed that students who were asked to do a task in a room that smelled of cleaning products were more likely to wash their hands afterwards, than students who were primed by the smell of cookies).[332] Try if it works and go ahead to scatter positive primes around in order to positively influence the mood and behaviour of those around you. You can be the bearer of happy things to come. On this positive note, we hereby leave the intervention questions.

Designing behaviour in practice: AGAIN Intervention Questions

Now that you have a stack of ideas for CAN- and WANT-interventions, it is time to see if you can add a SPARK and repetition to them. Below you will find the Magnificent 10 for designing repeat behaviour. To prevent an overflow of information (I must take care of your system 1, too), I have kept the explanation concise. This doesn't imply that SPARKs and AGAIN are unnecessary. However, the foundation of behavioural intervention is working on CAN and WANT. SPARK and AGAIN are rather the activators of CAN and WANT. So, they are essential, but the heart of thinking about behavioural change is thinking about capability and willingness. This is why I wanted to give you some more background on these. But don't forget: SWAC is only SWAC when a SPARK and AGAIN are added. Just one final remark: some of them could easily be considered a CAN- or WANT-intervention. They are indeed, but are especially useful also in designing for repeat behaviour. Use the same proven approach: do brainwriting rounds for every Moment that Matters.

THE MAGNIFICENT 10

AGAIN: How can you help someone continue with the desired behaviour?

A1.	Can we use a noun word to describe someone? Desired behaviour can help shape someone's identity. Try to label someone with a noun word, for instance, you are a voter. If someone can see him or herself as 'a voter' this not only builds their identity of a 'worthy' person acting in the accordance of the desirable social norms, but it also gives them a means to signal their personal qualities, making it worth the continue the desired behaviour.	SOCIAL IDENTITY/LABELLING
A2.	Can we give someone something they don't expect? If someone gives something to us, we feel obligated to give back. It is a social norm in which we respond to an action with an equivalent action. Most effective are variable rewards, the rewards people cannot see coming but makes them unproportionally happy.	RECIPROCITY
A3.	Can we give someone early positive feedback? New behaviour always comes with insecurity. If you can provide people with early positive feedback that shows that they are on the right track, it will help them continue the behaviour. Think about showing progress, giving (public) praise, etc.	POSITIVE FEEDBACK LOOP
A4.	Can we make sure someone experiences benefit quickly? Humans are motivated to sustain in the desired behaviour if they have an early success experience or notice the benefits of the desired behaviour rather quickly. We as humans value benefits that take immediate effect much more than those received later.	INSTANT GRATIFICATION
A5.	Can we show how much effort, time, money is already spent? If people have invested in the desired behaviour (time, money, effort) they are more likely to continue with the behaviour. If you can show people how much they have already invested in the desired behaviour, they are more likely to proceed.	ENDOWMENT EFFECT
A6.	Can we make the behaviour automatic? As humans are lazy (lowering our cognitive overload), we often don't switch from the choices that are already made for us. See if you can make the desired behaviour default, the automatic choice. People will sustain in the behaviour as changing the behaviour that is set as a default feels/is too much of an effort.	DEFAULT
A7.	Can we enhance someone's ego? Humans are attracted to behaviours that enhance their self-esteem. We act in ways that make us feel better about ourselves. If you can show that engaging in the desired behaviour has a positive effect on someone's ego or public image, this enhances their self-esteem and willingness to continue the behaviour.	SELF-ESTEEM
A8.	Can we help someone make a planning? If you can help people plan the actions to stick to the desired behaviour this will help them continue with the behaviour.	SCHEDULING
A9.	Can we make someone commit to the desired behaviour? Humans like to be consistent with the things they have previously said or done. If you started doing A, you are inclined to follow-through with A (and not B). This has to do with the fact that out brain is always looking to reduce our mental stress.	COMMITMENT/CONSISTENCY
A10.	Can we show the desired behaviour has meaning? We as humans want to contribute, we want to do things that have meaning. So, if you can show the desired behaviour has meaning and someone has a part to play in this, you can willingness to sustain in the desired behaviour.	EXPECTANCY THEORY

TOOL: DOWNLOAD THE 'MAGNIFICENT 10' AGAIN INTERVENTION QUESTIONS CHEAT CARD

 TO DO: DO A BRAINWRITING SESSION TO COME UP WITH AGAIN-IDEAS

Designing behaviour in practice: SPARK Intervention Questions

When thinking about SPARKs, life can become very simple all of a sudden. There are merely three kinds of SPARKs: *reminders, obstructions* and *interruptions.* I guess you will feel that there can be various executions for each type of SPARK. For example, reminders could be SMS reminders (for example, tomorrow you have a dentist appointment. It could be email prompts (you have left an item in your shopping basket, for instance) or it could be that you get a phone call from someone reminding you to do something. The same goes for the two other SPARK-types.

SPARK

How can we set someone into action towards the desired behaviour?

S1.	Reminders	Think how you can remind someone of the desired behaviour.
S2.	Obstructions	Think how you can pause the undesired behaviour.
S3.	Interruptions	Think how you can interfere with automatic behaviour.

 TO DO: DO A BRAINWRITING SESSION TO COME UP WITH SPARK-IDEAS

A little test: Can you spot the Behavioural Interventions?

Let us round off this Ideation building block with one last case, so that you get the hang of how to apply Behavioural Design in practice. In the United States, secondary education is a very costly matter, to say the least. College costs skyrocket, leaving the nation with over $1 trillion in student loan debt.[333] Fortunately, financial aid from the federal government is available for those in need. However, students (or parents) do have to apply for this, something that many students eligible for this kind of aid fail to do. National statistics show students leave more than 2.9 billion dollars in free federal grants on the table each year, simply because they do not apply for them.[334] Arizona State University observed that over 80% of eligible students applied for financial aid after passing the deadline, leading to lower aid packages. Therefore, they teamed up with a group of Behavioural Designers[335] to see if they could increase the number of applications before the deadline of March 1st. Usually, this is achieved by rather expensive methods such as personal guidance or one-on-one coaching. However, they did so by sending out weekly reminder emails, starting eight weeks before the deadline was to be met. Or, in other words, sparking AGAIN and AGAIN with emails. The emails themselves were filled full of behavioural interventions. This is a good moment for a bit of a quiz. Can you identify all the interventions indicated below? Under the visuals, I'll show you the answers. But let's activate some spaced learning for you here. There most probably was already some time in between your reading about the different interventions and now, so give it a try:

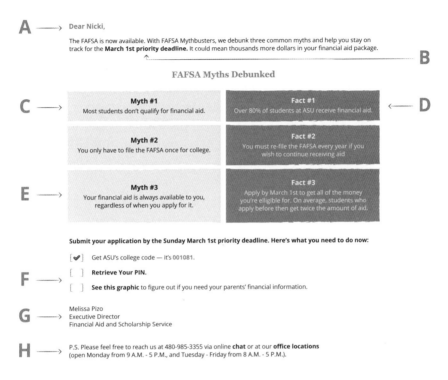

A ⟶ Dear Nicki,

The FAFSA is now available. With FAFSA Mythbusters, we debunk three common myths and help you stay on track for the **March 1st priority deadline.** It could mean thousands more dollars in your financial aid package.
⟶ **B**

FAFSA Myths Debunked

C ⟶

| Myth #1 | Fact #1 | ⟵ **D** |
| Most students don't qualify for financial aid. | Over 80% of students at ASU receive financial aid. | |

| Myth #2 | Fact #2 |
| You only have to file the FAFSA once for college. | You must re-file the FAFSA every year if you wish to continue receiving aid |

E ⟶

| Myth #3 | Fact #3 |
| Your financial aid is always available to you, regardless of when you apply for it. | Apply by March 1st to get all of the money you're elligible for. On average, students who apply before then get twice the amount of aid. |

Submit your application by the Sunday March 1st priority deadline. Here's what you need to do now:

[✔]   Get ASU's college code — it's 001081.

F ⟶ [ ]   **Retrieve Your PIN.**

[ ]   **See this graphic** to figure out if you need your parents' financial information.

G ⟶ Melissa Pizo
Executive Director
Financial Aid and Scholarship Service

H ⟶ P.S. Please feel free to reach us at 480-985-3355 via online **chat** or at our **office locations** (open Monday from 9 A.M. - 5 P.M., and Tuesday - Friday from 8 A.M. - 5 P.M.).

Data source: www.bhub.org/project/beating-the-deadline-reminders-to-apply-for-financial-aid-on-time/

- **A & G**: *Personalisation* encouraged readers to continue reading the email
- **B**: They worked with salience by presenting the deadline in bold and putting it at the email's beginning, which served as a forcing function
- **C**: They enhanced *clarity* by using easy-to-understand language to correct misperceptions about who qualifies for the aid
- **D**: *Social proof* was added to show the widespread use of financial aid
- **E**: *Loss aversion* was put in the mix, telling a student they might lose extra financial aid if they did not apply on time
- **F**: *Specificity* was added by showing what students had to do next, and *friction* was taken away by helping students to retrieve their PIN and getting insight into data they needed for the application
- **H**: *Assisting* was activated by making it very easy to contact someone, should they have any questions

This is a great case showing you how SWAC can come together. But I also wanted to show you this intervention because the results make it clear that *who* you spark also matters a lot. The emails were tested at 63,000 students and 22,000 parents. The results were astounding; submissions to apply for aid increased by 72%.[336] But can you see what was the most effective? Sparking both students *and* parents. So, always make sure that you have mapped out who influences your main 'target' when designing your intervention. What is their social network, and who is their social influence?

Number of Priority FAFSA Filers
By Treatment Condition
(Interventions 1 & 2)

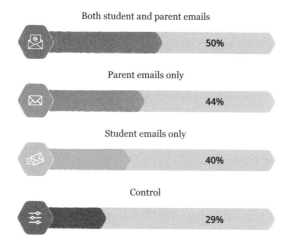

Both student and parent emails — 50%

Parent emails only — 44%

Student emails only — 40%

Control — 29%

Data source: ideas[42]

Oh, and just out of curiosity ... How did you do on this little quiz? Nailed it? Could be better? Don't worry, either way, you'll be fine. Remember, this isn't just a book; it is your toolbox. You can refer to it at any time, skipping to the parts you want to look into again. And don't forget to get your downloads on the book webpage. I've got some lovely cheat cards ready for you to keep close when designing your interventions.

CONCEPTING

– Turning ideas into interventions and influence strategies

Introduction

There is a big difference between an idea and an intervention. Look at it like this: The whole ideation process we just went through has given us many ingredients. High-quality ingredients that potentially can be cooked into a delicious dish that people will taste with pleasure, and will have them beg for more. But even a Michelin star cook needs to find the right combination of ingredients to make a dish that gets lifted to that magical level. What you and I must do now is to find the right combinations of ingredients. That is what we call concepting: Connecting the dots, putting things in the correct order, and making the right combinations. And you already know which combination to use that will see to a killer intervention: SPARK, CAN, WANT, AGAIN.

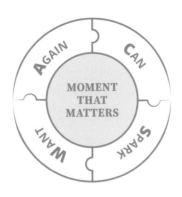

A behavioural intervention is sticking the four pieces of the
SWAC puzzle together

But that's a behavioural intervention. Though that isn't a behavioural intervention strategy just yet. Remember what we concluded earlier: Influence is never a one-off game. You will probably need more than one intervention to make someone engage in the desired behaviour. It is hard for people to do new things. The status quo feels so familiar. Why favour the known over the unknown? Why change an okay situation? Is the grass truly always greener on the other side? Better a monkey in your pocket than one underfoot, right? We have seen the biases and system 2-post-rationalisations that are at play in humans, which makes them heavily lean towards not changing behaviour. What it comes down to is that:

Every new behaviour comes along with feelings of uncertainty
for people

And we humans don't like that. At all. We love to be in control. Of course, with all the intervention ideas, we're gathered in our ideation building block. We deliberately came up with ideas to fuel people's system 1 with cues that will take off the heavy decision-making load – lowering the uncertainty. But we still need to be very aware of *how*, in which order, to feed all intervention ideas to people.

The perfect influence strategy: the SUE | 4C Influence Flow

There are different ways of looking at a strategy to influence someone. Fortunately, there is also a recipe to set up a behavioural intervention strategy. I don't know if you are in sales or CRM, but you often see the attract, convert, delight funnel in this realm. This can be a great approach to converting someone, but I want to introduce you to a 'conversion funnel' based on behavioural psychology. In other words, the last mental model in your Behavioural Design Toolbox: the *SUE | 4C Influence Flow*. When looking at humans and decoding their behaviour (and especially their non-behaviour), we need to consider roughly four steps (or 4Cs) when setting up an intervention strategy.

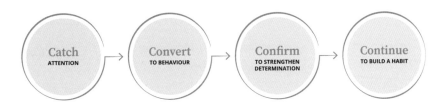

So, what is an intervention strategy? It is developing SWAC-interventions as to each influencing step. Together we will call this the SUE | 4C Influence Flow. It looks like this:

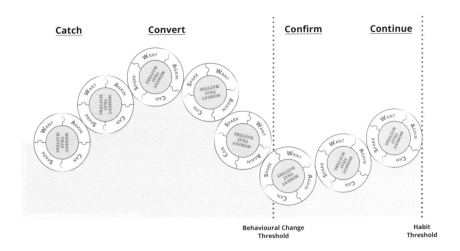

The strength of the SUE | 4C Influence Flow-approach lies in the fact that it is based on how human decision-making works. We have learnt that most of our decisions are based on system 1-shortcuts. Therefore:

For any influence strategy to have a chance of success, we need to make sure system 1 is open to change

In short:

- In the catch and convert step, we design for system 1
- In the confirm step, we design for system 2
- In the continue step, we continue this interplay process between system 1 and 2

This brings me to a question that I get asked quite often when we teach people that they have to design for system 1: 'Can I never give some system 2-information then?' Because sometimes you need to give information. For example, when someone is closing a mortgage, they simply need to be aware of the more rational side of things: The interest rates, the payment conditions, the terms of the contract. The answer is, yes, you can. Remember, we have learnt that our brain is a constant interplay between system 1- and system 2-thinking. Whereas our system 1 is expert at making (subconscious) choices, our system 2 is a champion in post-rationalisation. Our brain loves control. We hate uncertainty. So, if our system 1 has decided something, our system 2 finds all the arguments to justify it. It is a very powerful automatic process that we can hardly control, but which helps us to make sense of the world and the choices in it we arrive at. To give you an answer to the question whether you can never give information and give you insight in how the 4C Influence Flow works, I want to give you an example from my private life.

My husband drives an old Volvo, and he wanted to switch to driving electric. To be precise, a Tesla Model Y. He isn't a car fanatic, and was perfectly happy with his Volvo until his brain decided (system 1) he wanted that Tesla. Literally, the day after he made this decision, he went into the post-rationalisation mode, giving me all kinds of system 2-arguments why driving a Tesla was the way to go. Just to name a few, he bombarded me with: 'You see how many Teslas there are on the road already?' 'Look, that is the Model Y. Don't you love the design?' 'The new model Y got raving reviews.' 'It is so much easier to park in Amsterdam; there are so many special parking spots for electric cars.' 'Driving a fuel driven car is so not done anymore.' All CATCH elements. I didn't care; whatever he wanted to drive, I was fine with it. So, he booked a test drive (CONVERT)…. and he hated it. Within 5 minutes, his system 1 decided that he didn't like the car. It was so funny to see his system 2 almost immediately kick back into action again. 'The old Volvo is so safe and drives so comfortably.' 'The battery life will be so much better in the future; these electric cars are far from perfect yet.' 'We already live in a consumption economy – so why discard something that is still perfectly fine?' 'If I want to be more environmentally friendly, we'll keep the Volvo, and I'll take the train more often.' This change of opinion occurred all within a time span of two weeks. And don't get me wrong, I am okay with it – It is just an example of how our brain helps us come to terms with our decisions. And to us, this is essential to consider when designing an influence strategy. The truth is, Tesla forgot to CONFIRM my husband as to his initial decision. They should have given him a good feeling as soon as he arrived at the test drive. The truth was that he was given the keys, was assigned a car from a distance and had to set off without any further explanation. That iPad-like console alone caused him enormous stress while driving. Even after the drive, nothing was done to confirm his choice for Tesla, for example through social proof. A missed opportunity! To summarise: although we can attract someone's attention and convert it into behaviour by designing for system 1 (CATCH and CONVERT), in the confirmation step (CONFIRM) we can give someone a good feeling about performing the desired behaviour by providing system 2 arguments that confirm the decision to perform the desired behaviour. But there is a sequence to it:

You first must open someone's system 1 so as to make it receptive to system 2-information

This is often forgotten: we bombard people with system 2-information from the start (which they can't or won't process as well as it should be) and forget that we are designing for humans, who are ruled by their system 1. What makes the SUE | 4C Influence Flow so powerful is that it takes the interplay between the systems 1 and 2 into account. You see, certain things I keep repeating. Not because I underestimate your mental capabilities. Not at all. But because I know from practice that there are some things we must unlearn – we have to rewire our brain in order to look at humans – and not just clients, citizens or employees. Even we at SUE must remind ourselves constantly that designing for system 1 is the pinnacle of our work.

The SUE | 4C Influence Flow in action

Now that we've learnt something about the foundation of the SUE | 4C Influence Flow, let's talk a bit more about the four steps in an influence strategy. The best is to consider the four Cs as hurdles that you need to jump. I named them 'hurdles' on purpose. Remember we discussed that Behavioural Design actually is primarily the game of taking away barriers? No behaviour will happen if you don't clear out the behavioural bottlenecks. And at each step of your influence strategy, there could be potential behavioural bottlenecks you need to solve, using a suitable SWAC intervention. If, for instance, someone has a pre-existing belief about something, this person won't be receptive to any message or intervention that doesn't fit in with this belief. Let's say that someone genuinely believes his vote won't matter at the results of elections – they probably cannot be convinced to go voting no matter what. If you genuinely don't believe that regular exercise will get you in shape, why bother taking action with a view to any form of active movement then? So, in order to make an intervention work, we need to work from a fertile ground; we need to lay a foundation. In other words:

We need to open system 1 by defining what keeps it closed

If you have done the interviews and have plotted out all your human insights on an Influence Framework, you have probably already uncorked those bottlenecks. Again, keep going back to the work you did before. Your Influence Framework is a treasure box of insights, that will help you to develop the right SWAC interventions in the right place. As to all 4Cs of your influence strategy, humans tend to: 1) make mental mistakes. Or intuitively back away from the desired behaviour; because of: 2) past experiences. or: 3) the social context in which they find themselves. On the download page, you can find templates and videos that teach you more about identifying the possible behavioural bottlenecks in all 4Cs. Still, most probably, you have already identified them at the Insight step. For now, the most important thing to remember is that:

1. A behavioural intervention is all about having SWAC
2. A behavioural intervention strategy is putting multiple SWAC interventions in a 4C Influence Flow

Putting the pieces of the SWAC puzzle together:
Turning ideas into interventions

Now that you have got the theory down to the difference between an intervention and an idea - and to what turns a single intervention into an intervention strategy - it is time to get going. I want to make it very practical at this point; so, concepting is a four-step process.

1. Again, we start with the Moments that Matter. Your task is to build a complete SWAC around each Moment that Matters. Remember, you don't have to increase both CAN and WANT at every moment. Sometimes there is already enough willingness or capability and you actually have that part of the puzzle. There is always a SPARK and AGAIN to be added to the CAN and/or WANT. It is possible, however, to combine CAN, WANT, SPARK and AGAIN at a specific Moment that Matters.

2. Now take the individual ideas you developed in the ideation building block. If you have done your brainwriting, you will have several CAN, WANT, AGAIN and SPARK ideas for each Moment that Matters. You may have worked in a team. In that case, it is always good to share the different ideas with each other first. Often you can find synergies. You thought of this, what if we add this that I thought of? This is an inspiring, creative process, where you build on each other. Make connections. Crack the puzzle together. Which combination of CAN, WANT, AGAIN and SPARK ideas makes the most sense at a specific Moment that Matters? Ask yourself: Are your ideas still useful for the specific Moment that Matters? Or are they more appropriate for another Moment that Matters? That is fine. You are now in the combination game. You can move ideas around. That's the beauty of working with loose post-its. You can move them around. For now, your job is to look at each Moment that Matters and attach a CAN and/or, WANT, AGAIN and SPARK to it. You turn it from loose ideas into a complete intervention.

3. The next step is to combine your behavioural interventions into an intervention strategy. Now all you have to do is check whether you have filled in all the necessary steps in your 4C Influence Flow. Sometimes I literally print out four A4 sheets with the words catch, convert, confirm, continue

and hang them on the wall. By sticking the post-its with my SWAC interventions under those words, I immediately get visual feedback about whether I have made SWAC interventions for each step in the 4C Influence Flow or whether some are missing. Remember, not all behavioural challenges require all four Cs. Do you need to get someone's attention first? Or is it mainly about getting them to behave? And so on. Find out what you need in your 4C Influence Flow. The beauty of the 4C Influence Flow is that it has AGAIN in its DNA. Thinking in the four steps of influence automatically forces you to think about more than one intervention.

This is the approach where you plot your interventions on the specific step of the 4C Influence Flow. But a second approach is also possible. You can also start your ideation with the 4C Influence Flow in mind. This always has my preference. In your ideation you try to develop ideas with 'catch', 'convert', 'confirm' and 'continue' in mind. For example, ask yourself which WANT intervention question will help you to develop ideas that will attract attention? Which CAN intervention question will help you come up with an idea to convert someone to behaviour? And so on. Both approaches can work perfectly. Sometimes it depends on the behavioural challenge. Sometimes it depends on your preference.

4. Finally, review all the SWAC interventions and your 4C Influence Flow. Are the individual SWAC interventions logically linked? Do they have the right order? You may also find that you can use the same SPARK for more than one intervention. For example, you could send a reminder SMS in both the CONVERT step and the CONTINUE step. Your job here is to keep things flowing. Again, put yourself in the end user's shoes. First they see this, then that. Does this make sense? Are we missing a step?

This is the process of concepting. In summary, concepting is about turning your loose ideas into complete SWAC interventions. And we will then strategically use those SWAC interventions in a 4C Influence Flow to design an intervention strategy.

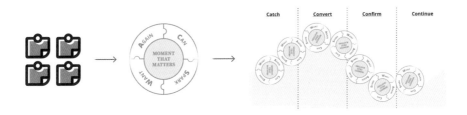

Some extra concepting advice for designing habits

This isn't a book specifically about habits. However, sometimes it is this specific behaviour we are asked to crack our brains on at the 'continue' step. Therefore, I want to briefly tell you what I have learnt over the years when it comes to habit building. As we discussed earlier, we all must deal with the fact that our willingness to change tends to fade. My experience is that, only making a behaviour small and creating a stable context, often isn't enough.

To get a desired behaviour to LAST, we need to add forcing functions

Forcing functions are all about keeping us on the right track, using principles from behavioural science. So, without any pretences to have an all-encompassing know-how on habit building, I want to end with an acronym that I developed as a memory aid and that helps me combine a set of proven behavioural principles into a recipe for habit success. As said, habits should last. To me, this is what LAST stands for:

- L = Loss aversion
- A = Accountability
- S = Social
- T = Tiny

Next to making the new behaviour tiny or dividing it into smaller units, I have added three forcing functions that work wonders:

1. Add **loss aversion** to the mix. Making someone put something at stake that they really wouldn't like losing drives the willingness to change. Could you, for example, make someone commit to donating money to a charity they don't like? Or, taking their least-loved family member out to dinner, or doing the dishes alone for a month? As long as it is something someone dislikes, you are activating loss aversion.
2. Add **accountability**. Telling someone you want to build up a specific habit, and asking them to hold you accountable (for example, by checking in once a week) does help. The actual thought of social pressure makes us want to stick to a habit. Also, by adding accountability, you can lose face by not living up to your intentions.
3. Make it **social**. The first way to do this is to have people express their desired new behaviour in public. Better still, make them write the new habit down on paper. Our mind loves consistency. If someone has made a written commitment to do something, their mind likes to be consistent with this. It's a mind trick that can work wonders, especially when making it social. The second way to make it more social is making sure you design for positive feedback. Engage someone's social network in order to give them compliments and cheers. This will trigger positive emotions that help stick to the new behaviour. If something feels good, you are inclined to keep on doing it.
4. Start small, **tiny** steps will build up exponentially and make it smaller by connecting the new behaviour to existing behaviour. Our brain reprogrammes more quickly if we are building upon a current routine. So, for example, say you'll drink a glass of water every time you have washed your hands after a toilet visit.

If you top this with a varied mix of rewards, you will have your ducks in a row in order to create habits. Rewards can be both psychological (e.g. a runner's high after running), immediate (e.g. a pleasant scent of our hands after washing them) or longer-term (e.g. a nice dinner after a month of exercising), or social (e.g. social approval of peers). A mix works best. And a special kind of reward that is very effective is to design for a quick success experience. Just like Instagram has added filters to make even your most crappy photos look good, it helps to kick in a habit if we don't have to wait too long for success.

Some examples of shaping SWAC interventions

To make things more vivid, let me give you a few examples of SWAC interventions that could arise from concepting.

Example 1: Finishing online forms

- <u>Behavioural challenge</u>: Suppose you have a website, and you want someone to buy a product online or subscribe to a training or an event.
- <u>Human Insight/opportunity</u>: We all take care of many things online, but we often don't finish the processes as we are constantly interrupted.
- <u>Behavioural Statement</u>: How might we aid our *website users* (SPECIFIC TARGET GROUP) to *get more done in less time* (JTBD) by helping to *complete an online form* (SPECIFIC BEHAVIOUR) and by getting rid of *as many distractions as possible* (ANXIETY)?
- <u>Moment that Matters</u>: Moment that someone has to fill in a form.
- <u>4C Influence Flow</u>: We need to CATCH someone's attention and CONVERT them to filling in the form; we need to CONFIRM that they are on the right track. And make sure they CONTINUE to complete the form.
- <u>SWAC</u>: You could avail yourself of a CAN-idea of using to PREFILLING in as many fields as possible. Someone gives their apartment number, and postal code and the address prefills. You could also add a WANT-idea by using FEEDBACK by showing their progress in percentages, using the CAN-intervention SALIENCE by making the form itself more salient. You can help someone fight distractions by making sure the form you want them to complete is on a separate webpage where the top-menu disappears; we do so at SUE. As soon as you wish to enrol in our Behavioural Design Academy, we help you experience as little obstruction as possible. The top-menu disappears, we provide you with easy to reach contact details should you require help, and we prefill where ever we can. You can add a SPARK by sending an email reminder to someone when they do not finish the form. You can add AGAIN by making this spark email very personal.

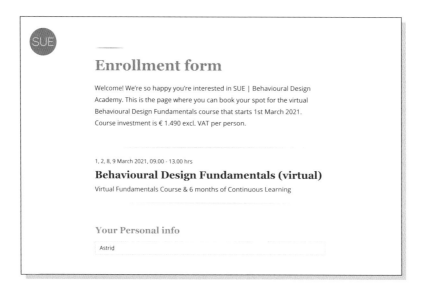

Example 2: Voting behaviour

- Behavioural challenge: We want people to go to the ballot.
- Human Insight/opportunity: People strongly believe that their vote does not affect the outcome of the general elections.
- Behavioural Statement: How might we help *eligible voters* (SPECIFIC TARGET GROUP) who want to *take care of their family* (JTBD) to *cast their vote* (SPECIFIC BEHAVIOUR) by taking away *the feeling that their vote doesn't matter (ANXIETY)*?
- Moment that Matters: The week before the elections.
- 4C Influence Flow: We need to CATCH someone's attention that voting is important and CONVERT them to vote; we need to CONFIRM that they made the right decision to vote. They only must vote once, so CONTINUE is not required.
- SWAC: one CAN-idea might be to use QUESTION SUBSTITUTION. Don't ask someone to go and vote but ask a different question: 'Do you consider yourself to be someone who cares for the future of your family?', 'Yes?', 'Please, go and vote; it matters.' A WANT-idea could be to use the SOCIAL PROOF by showing people how many of their neighbours have voted during the last elections. A SPARK could be to give people who have voted a visible 'I voted button', also activating SOCIAL IDENTITY.

Example 3: Electric driving

- <u>Behavioural challenge</u>: Imagine you work for a local city council, and you want to promote electric driving.
- <u>Human Insight/opportunity</u>: People don't want to get out of their cars. Most of them need these to commute and are used to the comfort of having their own means of transport. They feel electric driving involves a lot of hassle: charging, running out of power.
- <u>Behavioural Statement</u>: How might we help *car drivers who want to use their own car* (SPECIFIC TARGET GROUP) and *want to get from A to B quickly* (JTBD) to *switch over to electric driving* (SPECIFIC BEHAVIOUR) while making sure they *don't lose the comforts of driving their car* (COMFORT)?
- <u>Moments that Matter</u>: On the road, tool booths (commuters) and moment they need to park.
- <u>4C Influence Flow</u>: We need to CATCH someone's attention that electric driving can provide many comforts as they drive their own car to and from work, so CONVERT them to switch to electric driving during the commute but also when they have to park the car, we need to CONFIRM them that they have made the right decision as to drive electric by giving them instant benefits, for we want them CONTINUE doing so.
- <u>SWAC</u>: You could have had the CAN-idea to take away FRICTION by making parking in the city free for electric cars. It could also be that you concluded that electric cars don't have to pay the toll to get into the city and you assign an extra driving lane for cars activating INSTANT GRATIFICATION for the electric car drivers who don't have to wait in line for the toll boots, adding a WANT-idea. The tool boots and parking meters are perfect SPARK-moments. The fact that electric car drivers are immediately rewarded with special driving lanes and free parking confirms their decision to switch to electric driving and offers them long-term benefits, triggering AGAIN. This, in fact, is an actual case. In Norway, 60% of all newly bought cars are electric due to exactly this Behavioural Design intervention.[337]

Example 4: Exercising in a gym.

- Behavioural challenge: We want people to come to the gym to work out.
- Human Insight/opportunity: Someone has started going to the gym, but you noticed that many people do not stick to their exercising behaviour. After talking to people, you have come across an anxiety. When people go on holiday, this breaks their exercise routine, resulting in dropping out of the desired behaviour.
- Behavioural Statement: How might we help *gym members* (SPECIFIC TARGET GROUP) who want to *thrive by being more energised* (JTBD) to *stick to their exercising routine* (SPECIFIC BEHAVIOUR) by taking away *the hurdle of not being close to the gym* (ANXIETY)?
- Moments that Matter: A moment that matters is right before a vacation, and every morning of the vacation itself.
- 4C Influence Flow: We need to CATCH the gym-goer 2 weeks before their holidays, and CONVERT them to keep exercising once a day even when they are on holiday. I.e.: we need to CONFIRM that they can still make fitness progress when they're not at the gym. They will have to bridge the entire vacation: so, we need the behaviour to CONTINUE.
- SWAC: A CAN-idea may be based on ASSISTING. You could come up with the idea to make a series of online training videos that show you how to stay in shape by only using your body weight for just 10-minutes. A WANT-idea could be based on RECIPROCITY. You offer someone a *'coach-in-their-pocket'* for free as soon as you hear that they are going on holiday. REFRAMING the videos into a portable coach, and giving them exclusive access to your online gym-channel. You could SPARK the behaviour by every day sending them to their inbox both an SMS-reminder and a link. You build in AGAIN by making sure you're doing a video-series that will help people to bridge their holidays and will provide them with FEEDBACK on the progress they are still making as to their fitness level.

Three final pieces of advice as to 'concepting'

I'd just like to end with three pieces of advice in order to make your 'concepting life' easier and more successful. I stated this previous to starting on the ideation building block.

1. First of all, don't work on all of the intervention questions at once. To start pick about five CAN- and five WANT-intervention questions. You can always go back to ideation if, at this stage, if you feel you cannot come up with strong SWAC-interventions just yet. My experience is that most of the time, you need not start all over again, but are simply missing one final piece of the SWAC-puzzle. For instance, it could be that you have found your SPARK-, your WANT-, but you don't consider your CAN-ideas as befitting enough. Then go back to the CAN-intervention questions, and work on another CAN-intervention question to gather more CAN-ideas. Often, selecting that extra intervention-question becomes relatively easy when you are searching for an element to complete your intervention, and you have a far clearer idea as to where to look for it.

2. Secondly, without A, there's no SWAC. We overestimate how quickly people are to pick up or catch on. I often see people think: 'Well, I showed them how to do it, so why don't they do it?' For, we are humans in a world filled with distractions! So, don't fall into the trap of switching to new solutions too soon. Or of concluding that this doesn't work. It takes time to change someone's behaviour. Take someone along step-by-step. Repeat steps when necessary. Approach the challenge from different angles by using various SWAC interventions.

3. Thirdly, you might feel that concepting is a tad overwhelming. Don't worry; keeping the following in mind will make things much more manageable. First of all, you don't need to develop new or extra intervention ideas during the concepting step. The ideas you have come up with in the ideation building block, you will use to make SWAC-combinations that we will then divide over the different 4C-steps. You need not come up with new ideas, except for the sparks. So, you have already done the bulk of the work. We just need to combine your separate ideas into the complete SWAC-interventions and place them at the right spot in the intervention strategy. That's it. Secondly, you need not always include all of 4Cs in your influence strategy.

It could very well be that you already have someone's attention. Or that you need not design what already is habitual behaviour. Or maybe someone doesn't need that much confirmation. To help you identify what building blocks you need in your intervention strategy, I have created a tool called 'Decoding Humans'. To make your life even easier, the tool consists of simple questions that help you to decide whether you are dealing with a specific C-hurdle or not. You can download the tool again at website-download page. In fact, I would advise you to fill in this tool right after your Insight interviews. Often, it is easy to pinpoint hurdles right away after talking to someone. It hardly takes any extra time then.

 TOOL: DOWNLOAD THE DECODING HUMANS TOOL

 TO DO: COMBINE YOUR SEPARATE IDEAS SWAC-INTERVENTIONS

 TO DO: PUT YOUR SWAC-INTERVENTIONS IN A 4C INFLUENCE FLOW

Recap Intervention Strategy

What is important to know about 4C Influence Flow©?

To shape someone's behaviour we need to jump four hurdles:

Catch = We need to catch their attention

Convert = We need to convert them to the desired behaviour

Confirm = We need to give them confirmation they did the right thing

Continue = We need to continue if we want to design repeat behaviour

How does the 4C Influence Flow© help us come up with an influence strategy?

It is firmly rooted in how people make decisions and how behaviour is shaped. It helps us direct the needed interplay between system 1 and system 2. It helps you first catch intention and convert to behaviour with system 1 interventions, which we make system 2 interventions confirm.

What is improtant to know about the 4C Influence Flow©?

Not every flow step needs to be included every time you design behaviour. For instance, sometimes you already have someone's attention. The order of the flow is essential, though. It is a linear process.

How can you create a 4C Influence Flow©?

By plotting the Moments that Matter underneath every stage of the 4C Influence Flow© and ensuring that every Moment that Matters has a SWAC intervention, combining CAN and/or WANT with AGAIN, and a SPARK. The beauty is, by thinking in a 4C Influence Flow©, you automatically think about AGAIN.

BUILDING BLOCK 6

SELECTION

– Spotting the ideas with most test-proof potential

Introduction

One of the essential characteristics of the SUE | Behavioural Design Method is humility. Ehm, being humble is part of a method, you might think? But yes, it is. We have followed an intelligent step-by-step process in order to come up with interventions, and into these we put our intelligence, creativity and behavioural science-know-how, but who says they will work? We need to test-proof them in our real-target group. And we need to do it before we finalise our ideas (or get through our budget, for that matter). But I bet you are now at a stage that you have so many interventions which you like. And that's great, that was the whole meaning of diverging: To find as many angles, perspectives and solutions as possible. However, not everything can be tested. We have used individual brainwriting to come up with the ideas, but selecting the best interventions is something a group of people can be far more talented at.

How to pick the interventions to test-proof on real people

When dealing with a group of people, we must try to eliminate some psychological phenomenons within groups, and make the desired behaviour (in order to select the best ideas) as easy as possible. First, we should take social compliance into account. We have learnt that it is very challenging for an individual to go against the norm, break rules, think differently. Social deviance is a problematic behaviour to show, as it triggers another psychological principle we have discussed: *loss aversion*. We humans have a preference for eliminating the risks of loss to increasing the odds of winning. And the most significant loss in a group process is getting on the wrong side of the highest-ranking person in the group, and dealing with the personal retributions. But it's precisely that kind of social deviance of going against a group's top-ranked person that helps to select the best ideas. A simple technique to eliminate this pressure and to fight compliance is to use a technique called *dotmocracy*.

This technique is simple: Everyone gets three similar-coloured sticker dots – and everyone groups around the paper with all the interventions. You decide for yourself which interventions you think should be tested (no discussion with one another now); and when you have all decided, you say 'go' – and simultaneously stick your dots onto your three favourite interventions. It could be three dots on the same intervention, dots on your own intervention, or dots on two different interventions. Just pick the interventions you think have the most potential. Nobody can follow the lead of others, and it instantly gives you an overview of which interventions the group prefers. Usually, as a group, you discuss the selected interventions with two or more dots on which people are asked to elaborate as to the reason for picking the intervention. After the explanation, a second round of dotmocracy is possible, in which dots are placed on the interventions that came out best in the first round. You can now discuss with one another and elaborate on your selection as a conclusion, but this is it. Although occasionally sticking dots simultaneously is sometimes impossible (the best group-size therefore is five or six people), the process shows people that authority is not an issue. Everyone's vote has the same impact. There are no larger dots, and no different coloured dots. And there's no order for placing the dots. One last thing: When you're deciding where to stick your dots, you can take as a overview criterion which intervention you think may have the most impact upon behaviour. And if you see an intervention you believe to be unfeasible (budget-, staff-, timing-wise or any other way), well, just don't pick it. This is the point we are now at in the SUE | Behavioural Design Method – we are converging, so some ideas simply must go. In the end, it tends to look like this:

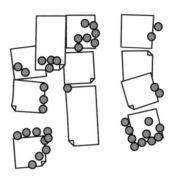

By the way, we are now using a digital tool in order to create post-its, and doing voting sessions with a dotmocracy called Mural. To save some trees in the process. To make the selection process more manageable, it is advisable to put your interventions on paper on the wall at the 4C Influence Flow. So that you have them in a logical order. Simply take a piece of paper, write down the Moment that Matters, and stick your post-its with your CAN-, WANT-, SPARK-, AGAIN-idea around it. This gives you a good overview of the interventions. The ideas on the post-its you didn't use at this point, you can put aside for now. They are now unnecessary distractions. However, please don't throw them away! It could be that after testing your interventions, you need to go back to the drawing board, and you might need them.

The question remains: how many ideas are there to select as prototype? I wish I could give you a golden rule, but unfortunately, there isn't one. When making your selection, you can keep these criteria in mind:

- Put your dots on the interventions you would like to test
- One dot = important, two dots = very important, three dots = essential, no dot = not important for now
- Consider the feasibility – if you see insurmountable barriers, don't select that intervention
- Consider ethics; I will show you how to do so in the following chapters

Just one remark: this is not about convincing your team members at this stage. You don't present or defend interventions before you start voting. Seeing potential in an idea as an individual is a very system 1-activity. You have gone through the whole process of insight and ideation; at this point, you will have a clear feeling where you think the need to intervene is most relevant. Furthermore, during ideation, your system 1 will have had moments of energy or excitement that indicate which interventions you think will be most effective. We are also all humans; in the way we use emotions at the insight step in order to pinpoint if someone is getting closer to achieving their job-to-be-done, you can also use your emotions to lead you to the way. After everyone is done voting, you'll end up with a so-called 'heatmap' – an overview of where you as a group see the most potential. So, then the wisdom of the crowd comes in. Together, you can make a valid conclusion on which interventions to prototype and to test. How to do this, I will show you in the next chapter.

 TO DO: STICK ALL YOUR INTERVENTIONS UNDER THE RIGHT STEP OF THE 4C INFLUENCE FLOW

 TO DO: DO DOTMOCRACY TO SELECT THE INTERVENTIONS AND MAKE A FINAL SELECTION

 TO DO: REMOVE THE INTERVENTIONS YOU DID NOT SELECT (BUT KEEP THEM FOR A LATER STAGE)

STEP III

IMPACT

How to turn ideas into a success
SUE | Behavioural Design Method©

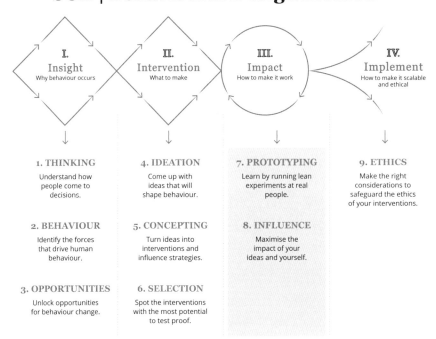

I. Insight Why behaviour occurs	II. Intervention What to make	III. Impact How to make it work	IV. Implement How to make it scalable and ethical
1. THINKING Understand how people come to decisions.	**4. IDEATION** Come up with ideas that will shape behaviour.	**7. PROTOTYPING** Learn by running lean experiments at real people.	**9. ETHICS** Make the right considerations to safeguard the ethics of your interventions.
2. BEHAVIOUR Identify the forces that drive human behaviour.	**5. CONCEPTING** Turn ideas into interventions and influence strategies.	**8. INFLUENCE** Maximise the impact of your ideas and yourself.	
3. OPPORTUNITIES Unlock opportunities for behaviour change.	**6. SELECTION** Spot the interventions with the most potential to test proof.		

BUILDING
BLOCK 7

PROTOTYPING

– Learning by presenting lean experiments to real people

Introduction

So here we are. You have your interventions based on the human insights unlocked by the SUE | Influence Framework, you've used the SWAC Tool to come up with these interventions, and you've designed an influence strategy using the 4C Influence Flow. Now it is time to prototype. Prototyping is so much fun!

Prototyping is all about embracing your eagerness to learn and cultivating your curiosity

The most important reason you should prototype is that you can use behavioural science to get insights and develop interventions. Still, if there is no evidence that these will trigger the desired behaviour, they are no more than assumptions. Almost anyone can develop interventions, but choosing and implementing the right interventions is where most things go wrong. Implementing to create change is where real innovation lies.

Creativity is thinking about things, innovation is about doing things

We are often surprised by what we expect to test the best, and what is considered most convincing by real people. Also, sometimes small details in our interventions turn out to be true influence gems, having a far more significant impact than we could have imagined beforehand.

The importance of prototyping

To illustrate how vital prototyping can be, and how it can increase the successful outcomes of your interventions, let me start by giving you an example from our practice. We were asked to develop a value proposition for a medical device to help patients with type I diabetes to manage their insulin levels. Most patients must check their insulin levels by drawing blood and measuring, which is both invasive and painful. Our client developed a technology that made blood sampling unnecessary; an app could now warn patients whether their insulin levels needed attention. We tested these four prototypes of value propositions:

Your device always knows what your insulin levels are, but you only hear about it whent it's necessary.	Your device always knows what your insulin levels are and lets you know when something's up. That way, you only have to focus on diabetes when it's really necessary.	You know that your insulin levels are stable, because otherwise you would have heard about it.	Tackle your unstable insulin levels with a simple message from your device.

Our client expected the third to be the preferred one by the actual target group. It makes sense: it is not too long, and it is quite a reassuring message. However, the prototyping test revealed a completely different result. The message our client thought to have the most positive impact was described by real diabetes patients as 'short and unclear' and 'I don't understand this'. The 'winner' from the prototype test was the second value proposition. Indeed, the most extended message. People described this one as: 'This is nice because it is so clear'. And there you see that we all are used to doing things in a certain way (advertising should be short and snappy), and we all have assumptions – and, most of the time, no evidence. The prototyping practice often proved us wrong or framed us more positively: it sent us in the right direction.

To add on to these findings of the prototype test, we found a big little detail that changed the business success of this device. Our client was used to market this device *b-to-b*, as a medical specialist. This value proposition we created was to market b-to-c, the end-user. Our client used the word *patient* in every communication – on their website, brochures and packaging. It turned out that people who had to use the device hate the word *patient*. Their job-to-be-done is to lead an everyday life. The term 'patient' makes them feel bad: This is how their medical advisor sees them and even their loved ones – but they want to be regarded as 'normal' people who need to monitor their insulin levels. Finally, prototyping brought another significant insight. When we were initially briefed on the project, our client warned us: 'There is quite a loud signal in the app when the insulin levels are alarming; we will fix this later.' However, our interviewees declared that they found the signal brilliant. Now they really could live a normal life, as they could trust the app to give them a clear warning when action from their side was needed. This changed their life: instead of being confronted with their disease many times a day when drawing blood, they could now live and rely on the device to alarm them when necessary. The 'annoying alarm' was a game-changer that helped them to do their job-to-be-done far more easily.

We took the teachings from this prototype test and ventured into a second prototyping round. We wanted to see if people who need to manage their insulin levels would order the device. As it requires an intrusive physical intervention (an under-skin sensor must be implanted in the arm), our client was hesitant about this. We built a simple webpage on which people could order a test device for free, using the preferred value proposition and discarding the word *patient*. We had to close the webpage as the number of test devices were quickly claimed. We then prototyped if people would be willing to pay for a test device (in reality, that would also be the case). It hardly impacted the number of test devices claimed.

How to prototype?

Most people immediately think about what prototype to make. But in prototyping that's not the first step. The first step is to sit down – whether you are on your own or working within a team – and think about what answers you're looking for in order to understand how your intervention is going to work in real life. An intervention is never a one-off. You've learnt about the flow of an intervention. You know that you must work on catching, converting, confirming and continuing. So, more than one question needs to be answered in relation to these steps in your influence strategy. Some examples: 'How will people learn about your policy?' 'What will the first experience with your product be like?' 'Do people understand how they can join?' 'Do people understand what to do when seeing your landing page?' 'Are people willing to share your service?' 'Are people willing to pay for your offer?' As you can see, these are all questions related to different stages of the 4C Influence Flow.

A pitfall in prototyping is making a prototype too big. Let's say you have an idea for a patient-activity centre in a children's hospital. You could make a prototype that is a sketched drawing of the centre. You might learn more about what colours the kids would like on the walls or which furniture they would prefer. But it won't help you to answer any specific questions. How will parents learn about the centre? How can a doctor sign up a patient? How do parents get feedback on how their child is experiencing the centre? How can they rate the centre? These all require different ideas and prototypes. To make it very practical, I'll guide you through the prototyping in four steps:

	WHAT		HOW		HOW		HOW
	do I want to learn?		can I learn?		can I make prototypes?		can I get the best feedback?

Step 1 in prototyping: What to learn?

This is the step in which you break down your intervention into bite-sized pieces that can be easily made and tested. So, what actions do you have to take in order to decide what to prototype:

1. First, use your 4C Influence Flow to look at the different bite-sized pieces of your intervention.
2. Then visualise the experience – or journey – based on the 4C Influence Flow. This can be done very roughly, using post-its and simple stick drawings. It's just for you to get a sense of what your target will experience when seeing your intervention. Draw every step of the journey on a separate piece of paper/post-it so you can rearrange them when needed.
3. Each step in the user's experience brings questions that you need to answer so as to understand how your intervention works in practice. Identify what you need to learn. And come up with the very specific questions that will get you there.

You need a few simple materials to take these three steps. This is what we use: Post-its to map out your user's journey, a couple of A3 papers to stick your post-its on, sharpies or permanent markers to write with on the post-its, your 4C Influence Flow to check the stages of your strategy/intervention, tape to stick your A3 papers onto the wall. After taking these three steps, you are more than ready for the second step of prototyping them to transform you into a Prototyping Powerhouse.

 TO DO: VISUALISE THE EXPERIENCE OF YOUR INTERVENTION

 TO DO: COME UP WITH PROTOTYPING QUESTIONS: WHAT DO YOU WANT TO LEARN ABOUT A SPECIFIC STEP?

Step 2 in prototyping: How to learn?

The second step is short but essential. You cannot learn everything, so you must decide what has priority. You can prototype almost anything, so you need to make a selection. How? There are two actions needed:

1. First, prioritise the questions you've written down in the first step. Which answers do you want and need? If you work in a team, use the dotmocracy technique to make the selection.
2. Second, decide what kind of prototype can help you to answer those questions. Is it an app? Is it an ad? Is it a written pitch on an A4? Is it a storyboard? What is the medium you will use?

Everything can be prototyped

 TO DO: DECIDE WHICH KIND OF PROTOTYPES YOU WANT TO MAKE

Step 3 in prototyping: How to make?

This is the part where we are going to make your prototypes. Remember your primary goal of prototyping is getting feedback. It is meant to learn, so you can adapt quickly (or on time even). Maybe you have occasionally heard of the concept 'MVP' or 'minimal viable product'. It is a concept coined by Eric Ries, author of the *Lean Start-Up*.[338] The purpose of an MVP, similar to the purpose of the prototype you are about to make, is to test our assumptions as to using the smallest amount of effort and development-time possible.

Or, as it states in the book, and here I paraphrase this: 'You must learn what works before the money runs out. So, we are at an early stage right now. Trying to make a minimally viable product; our system 1 has difficulty in judging crappy prototypes. However, don't try to make perfect prototypes.' I love this quote by Reid Hoffman, who founded LinkedIn and is a successful online entrepreneur and venture capitalist: 'If you are not embarrassed by the first version of your product, you've launched too late. (...) You lose out by delaying the onset of the customer feedback loop: If you'd launched sooner, you would have started learning sooner.'[339] The word *embarrassed* plays a key role here. You shouldn't be stupid and get yourself into lawsuits (read the ethics chapter, it will help you come up with the right considerations). As to me, the 'launching' part isn't what

I want you to remember from this quote. What I would love you to remember is that:

Prototyping is all about learning sooner and activating the customer feedback loop

So, don't get scared of the thought of indeed having to draw, write or build. You don't have to be an artist to do a prototype. You did it as a kid already! Prototyping is fun. Prototyping is where you learn and take one step closer to success. But of course, we need a plan – a proper way of approaching things. There are ways to make building a prototype a lot easier for yourself.

1. Start by considering the setting. Decide where you want to share your intervention. Is it in your offices or the 'war room' that you have been cracking your brain on the intervention? Or do you want to see your prototype in action within the context where it will be used in real-life? Knowing your context can be helpful before you start building. Some things cannot be transported or must be made on 'site'.
2. Assemble a prototyping kit: This is simply a box with materials you can use if you are doing physical or paper prototyping. This is a one-time action. Once you have your kit ready, you must check supplies now and then. I've given you pointers below as to what to stick in your kit.

✎ MATERIALS NEEDED FOR PROTOTYPING KIT

○ Tape	○ Glue	○ Coloured paper
○ Post-its	○ Rope	○ Cardboard cutter
○ Scissors	○ Ruler	○ Push pins & paper clips
○ Play-Doh	○ Lego blocks	○ Plain white paper (A4 & A3)
○ Cardboard	○ Elastic bands	○ Felt tips in different colours
○ Whiteboard markers	○ Foam material	○ Permanent markers black & red

3.   Or subscribe to a digital tool: There are a few good, free to use digital sources that can help you make a digital prototype reasonably quickly and easily. You don't have to be a UX-specialist or digital designer to work with them. These are perfect for testing screens or web pages. Here are some tips as to digital sources we use; I have now affiliate deals with any of those, so please check out which ones you like. Good things to look for when choosing a digital prototyping tool are the ease of learning the tool, the ease of sharing, the ease of usage, the costs, and the fidelity.[340] (Here's a tip within a tip: If you follow the endnote, there is a link to a handy article giving an overview of good digital prototyping tools. Below are the ones we have used before, but there is more out there).

4.   And then, start building. The prototype needs to be a minimally viable product, not perfect, but realistic enough to convince your user. Don't put too much money into your prototype. You can also use sources such as Keynote or your friends or colleagues as actors. After all, your prototype could be rejected and end up in the 'square archive' (also known as the recycling bin). Well, the paper ones, hopefully not your friends. But you get my drift: It should be simple and focused on what you want tested.

5.   Make different varieties of the same intervention, depending on what you want to learn (it could be the pitch, the button, the wireframe, etc.). It could look like this:

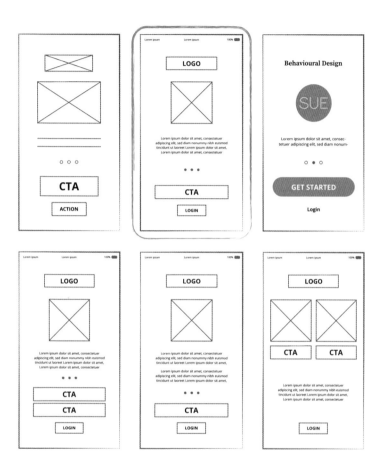

We always number the variations, so it is easier to organise feedback – the final step in prototyping we are approaching now: Gathering valuable feedback.

TO DO: MAKE THE PROTOTYPES

Step 4 in prototyping: How to get valuable feedback

This is the most exciting part of the process: You'll get to learn what your user thinks of your intervention, and you will receive input on how to make your plan better than that of your actual end-user.

Prototyping will help you see what truly matters to people, and what parts of your intervention needs some improvement

You'll be amazed by what you'll learn. The 'I didn't see that one coming'-experience will also happen to you. And if that occurs, stand still for a moment, and think what would have happened if you didn't have that experience and just went along with your idea – blowing away your budget (or killing your reputation or self-esteem when failure hits you hard). To quote IDEO.[341]

If a picture is worth a thousand words, a prototype is worth a 1,000 meetings

This is what it was all about all along, right from the start when you began revealing all of the human truths in your Influence Framework up to this: Aligning your efforts with what people want or need. Prototyping is making sure your efforts weren't in vain, and will lead you to the success you are hoping to find. The truth is, you need not worry too much at this stage. If you have built your interventions on insights from your Influence Framework, and your interventions are likely to change behaviour for the better. You are now on the verge of discovering the tweaks you still need it to make so as to realise this. Or to make a timely 'pivot' when your interventions did not have the expected effect – holding on to the insights, but going back to the drawing board. Not based on assumptions but based on proper, real-people feedback. To give you one more reason for L.O.V.I.N.G.-prototyping. You get actual end-user responses. So, if you have to pitch your idea to your manager, investor, wife or whomever – you're not pitching an idea *you* want, but an idea the *end-user* wants. And you have the quotes or footage to prove it. Believe me – this changes the manager/client/boss-convincing game forever! You'll have plenty of user arguments as to any doubts the person may have you're pitching. You have tested the idea. To give you an example – as for instance, we have heard so many times: Our target group only prefers advertising in positive phrasing. Positivity is rooted in our corporate values, so using words with a 'negative' association is an absolute no-no. And adds using the pains of the end-user you've uncovered in your SUE | Influence Framework are dismissed just like that. You might answer: 'That's what we also thought, just like you.' But the truth is: the value proposition that showcased a pain was preferred by 82% of the users – the one with the gains just by 12%. Here are some quotes of your users that show their genuine reactions to both versions. You have made a solid case; it is no longer your opinion against theirs. It is the opinion of the people who truly matter: the ones who must buy, promote, visit, comply. Can you see how it can work for you? By the way, the feedback of the real users when seeing using pains within communication is often something in the direction of: 'Someone finally understands me'. For users, their pains have little to do with a sender's negativity, but far more with their reality. It is again a case of inside-out versus outside-in thinking. So, valuable feedback, that's what we are looking for. How do you go about it? What action steps are needed?

1. *Define what kind of feedback you're looking for.*
   Do you want feedback at the first impression of an idea? Are you wondering what people will think of the name? Make a list of your feedback goals to keep with you during the testing.
2. *Invite five or six new people to interview, and make a script to ensuring that you'll test what you want to test.*
   Use your skills learnt in the Insight building block so as to make the most out of the interviewing. If necessary, reread parts of that chapter. Make sure these are different people than those you interviewed to gather insights. These interviews can be a bit shorter: 30/45 minutes each.
3. *Design for openness, stay neutral and adapt on the fly.*
   Explain to participants that you are just here to learn, and it's all a work in progress. Don't defend or sell. Encourage participants to build on the idea. Add parts during the test, or kill your darlings.
4. *Capture the feedback.*
   We like to video- or at least audiotape our tests. But we do make sure that there are not too many people in the test room. You can install a webcam, and let other people watch in the room next to it.

5. *Next, share and analyse your impressions.*

    What did the test person like best? What got them enthusiastic? What would convince them of the idea? What needs improvement? What failed? What do you need to test more extensively?

And remember: Your unhappy customers (or users) are your greatest source of learning. That's not me saying this; it was Bill Gates.[342]

Before you start: Privacy matters

Ethics matter a lot in Behavioural Design, and an essential part of ethics is the protection of privacy. You've probably all heard of the new GDPR (General Data Protection Regulation)-legislation. And rightfully so, things got more restrictive concerning privacy. The GDPR provides the following rights as to individuals:

- The right to be informed
- The right of access
- The right to rectification
- The right to erasure
- The right to restrict processing
- The right to data portability
- The right to object
- Rights in relation to automated decision-making and profiling

The main point I want to get across is to not get sloppy with personal data. Don't use people's real names, don't make recognisable photos, erase data after use. You only need a rough description of someone (age, family situation, education, work situation) and the real gold mine is: *their precise quotes*. So, restrict yourself to those. Just make sure to write down the exact words people are using. There you want to get as personal as possible. Before the interview, we inform every respondent about privacy and have them sign a form that we explain to them. Our clients also must sign privacy forms. We do not share footage, personal data or photos without written permission. I think it goes without saying that we use the same procedure at the Insight interviews.

TO DO: INVITE 5/6 PEOPLE FROM YOUR REAL TARGET GROUP FOR THE PROTOTYPING TEST

 TO DO: MAKE SURE YOU HAVE YOUR PRIVACY STATEMENTS READY FOR READING AND SIGNING

 TO DO: DO THE PROTOTYPING INTERVIEWS AND NOTE DOWN EXACT ANSWERS AND QUOTES

 TOOL: DOWNLOAD THE PROTOYPING BIBLE

BUILDING
BLOCK 8

INFLUENCE

– Maximising the impact of your interventions and yourself

Introduction

I genuinely hope you enjoyed the prototyping process as much as I always do. If you're the last in line to give your intervention the go-ahead, well, then you've crossed the finish line. In reality, most of us must first convince our stake-holders of our plans. This could be your manager, boss, colleague or partner. Who-ever. And they have not been part of this process; they haven't added *The Missing Layer* to their thinking, they haven't seen how Behavioural Design could shine a bright light on every challenge. So, now it is time to show you how to use Behavioural Design in order to give yourself more impact. I'd like to give you some tips as regards using behavioural economics in order to get that well-earned *'yes'* you worked so hard for.

Tip 1: Using Behavioural Design to boost your personal influence

The two tools you now have in your Behavioural Design-toolbox (Influence Framework and SWAC Tool) are real *power tools*. They are multi-usable. Do not only use them to solve your challenge or improve your product, service, policy, or business. Use them on persons as well. Influence is always a people's game. You don't have to convince an institution, you need to convince a human be-ing, and there's always that *Hippo* (highest paid person's opinion) in the room.

We always do a quick SUE | Influence Framework of the key stakeholder(s). What are their jobs-to-be-done? What could be the anxieties of that person in approving our approach? What would make them comfortable when sticking to the status quo, instead of moving in our direction? What could be the gains of our approach that will help them to achieve their job-to-be-done? Do you remember I talked about getting the exposure hours as to knowing your target group? My tip is to do the same regarding your key stakeholders, such as your manager. Make sure you talk to them regularly. Not to pitch your idea, plan or budget, but to get to know the human being behind your stakeholder. Again, it starts by unlocking their jobs-to-be-done. They could be functional, emotional and social. They might be work-related but also personal. So, many of us see management as different from us, but this no less is true. They also need recognition, security, and all other things we are seeking for ourselves. They also have their managers they must report to. So, sit down with them. It could be a planned meeting (a lunch) or an informal talk at the coffee machine. Just have your 'human anthropology'-radar wide open all the time. You don't need to do an in-depth interview. I have a blank Influence Framework for my key stakeholders, and I've built and updated it piece by piece. So, it is a living document. It helps me get more insight into how to predictably influence the behaviour of my stakeholder. Still, it also allows me to be more empathic and understand your stakeholder's context. I read this quote from Chike Ozah, and I couldn't agree more: 'Context can make you have empathy for a bad decision. I can empathize with somebody who did something that I didn't necessarily agree with, but it makes me understand their decision better.'[343]

But next to understanding your key decision-making better, and having more empathy for their context and the decisions triggered by this context, using the SUE | Influence Framework on individuals also helps you to set up your presentation or proposal. It forces you to think outside-in. Please don't write it with yourself in mind, but with the person you are trying to convince. Tackle every anxiety or comfort one by one, and show them how your plan can help achieve their job-to-be-done. Highlight the gains it will have for them, and so on. Make sure it is about them and you, and your chances of getting a 'yes' will increase significantly.

The same goes for the SWAC Tool. Find out what the hot and cold spark-moments are of the person you are trying to influence. Isn't your decision-maker a morning person? Make sure you don't get booked into a morning meeting. Often, we accept a meeting request instead of directing it. Take control! Also, think about how you CAN make the desired behaviour (of giving it a go) as easy as possible for your decision-maker. For instance, instead of asking for the whole budget at once, can you ask for a small start. Often, we forget to end our meeting with what we need from someone. What do you want? A week's extra work? Extra staff? Budget? If yes: how much and when? Also, think about adding WANT. Can you add social proof by first getting feedback from the significant peers of your decision-maker, and showing their reactions? Can you reframe the meeting? For instance, don't end with: 'I would love your feedback', but end with: 'What would this concept need to get your approval?' It helps you design an entirely different meeting. Use your *behavioural intervention-lenses* to steer the decisions.

Tip 2: Using prototyping results to get a go-ahead

It would be best if you always remembered that your manager, client, or whoever you are trying to convince, has to decide to give you the go-ahead. Sounds logical but focus on the word *decision* for a moment. You might think you are in a challenging position as dependable on that decision, but don't forget that all humans are looking for a sense of control – your manager, client, or a life partner. Arriving at a decision is inevitably tied up with insecurity. No matter how confident someone might look or come across, system 1 is also looking for ways to arrive at an informed decision. Of course, their past experiences will help, but you can also have a role in lowering their cognitive load of decision-making. If you can assist in reaching an evidence-based decision, this may help a lot. Fact is, you have this evidence: you prototyped! Traditionally, we tend to present our final solution. That seems logical because it was what we learnt in the process, and this is what we believe in. However, the person you are trying to influence was not part of this process.

I advise you to showcase the actual prototypes in your presentation. If you take someone along with your choices and why, it will be much easier for them to understand why you ended up with the final solution. Tell them: 'We first developed this solution; this is what the prototypes looked like. We showed this to our end-users, and this is what they told us, and you present the exact quotes of the end-users. Based on this feedback, we decided to discard this part of the solution, but we were able to pinpoint what was the killer feature. We then optimized the ideas and tested them again. So, now we had these positive results.' This way, your final solution is presented as the logical and only way to go. It is still the same solution as it would have been if you hadn't showcased the prototypes, but now you have shown your decision-maker what considerations you made, at what stage and why – providing insight into the changes you made and why. This resolves many questions that might have influenced your decision-maker's opinion.

By the way, we nowadays add quantitative testing to our prototyping. Once we have the winning idea(s) of our prototyping test, we test if the concept will impact a larger population. We do a quick panel test, and gather more evidence that the solution will scale. Of course, this is optional, but you can imagine that adding this will help your decision-maker to gain more confidence as to arriving at the right decision. Something else important happens when you use your prototypes and the end-user quotes. You design the meeting in a way it is not 'our opinion against yours'. Also, don't be afraid to show failed prototypes. If you take someone along the path you have gone in order to develop the solution you are presenting today, they can see what didn't work or what you tried. You will showcase your intelligent decision-making process. How you tested, learnt and optimised – this way, you are building trust into your presentation. In the end, we humans love a sense of control. Your job is to give your decision-maker a feeling of control as much as possible. This is exactly what showing how you went about it and what led to the final solution exactly does.

Tip 3: Making system 1 work for you

Indeed in everything you do from this moment on, you'll have to remember that you are dealing with humans whom are led by their system 1. So, if you have ever felt your client, manager or partner is irrational, you now have scientific proof that you are indeed correct there. This also means you can have system 1 working for you. And I'd like to show you a couple of ways in which this works.

Liking/similarity effect
People are more inclined to say 'yes' to people they like. But how can you make people like you? The science of influence comes up with three apparent answers to this. People tend to like you more if:

1. You are similar to them
2. You give people compliments
3. If you cooperate with them towards a mutual goal

Therefore, it pays if you spend some time researching who your decision-maker is. What do they like? What is their family situation? Religion? Hobbies? Place of residence? Former careers or employers? See if you yourself can find any similarities to them. Again, be genuine here. If you cannot hit a ball even if it was thrown at you from 30 centimetres at turtle speed, don't brag about your tennis accomplishments when if you see that your manager loves to play tennis. Be sincere with compliments. However, often higher-ranking people aren't given any compliments. They are expected to coach, inspire and get their teams to grow, and it is often forgotten that recognition is also a human need for them. Cooperating towards a mutual goal also refers to jobs-to-be-done. What can you yourself and they accomplish together at a deeper motivational level? What can you help them to achieve in life? I don't know if you ever watched TED talks[344] – to give you one more example. But if you do so, perhaps you have noticed something. Most of the talks start out with a personal story: 'When I grew up in that tiny village in India', 'My parents were middle-class farmers', 'After my burn-out, divorce, accident, and so on...'. This is a way to activate 'the liking effect'. It makes you human; it adds that personal touch. It creates a recognisable situation for your audience. Admitting that you are nervous is another way (if this is true, of course). We are constantly trained to deliver the perfect pitch, but some find it hard to do so. Admitting this activates liking as even the experienced presenters or speakers have been there. No one's first attempts were stressless. In short, try to 'humanify' your presentation. And last but not least, dress to the part. Don't scare away your decision-maker by a completely different attire than they are wearing. Of course, you can have your style, but don't show up as the hottest festival chick or guy in town, if you're in a corporate environment. Try to blend in a bit, but have one distinctive feature, so they will indeed remember you. Margaret Thatcher always carried her handbag; our Prime Minister is well-dressed but always rides his bike to work; Richard Branson always has this long, wavy hair, and so on. However, there is another way to activate similarity. I'll explain this in the next paragraph.

The chameleon effect

Maybe you have heard of this effect before, but in other terms: *mirroring.* When your mimic someone's behaviour, it also creates similarities. This can get awkward, though. So, don't overdo it. Behavioural researchers discovered that we as humans already have the *subconscious* tendency to mimic others' behaviour, manners and facial expressions.[345] Chartrand and Bargh found the chameleon effect after observing people subconsciously mimic confederates. People had to perform a task in which they had to work closely with a confederate trained to repeatedly engage in one of two behaviours: Rubbing their face or shaking a knee. The researchers noticed that the people tended to mimic the confederate's behaviour, both when the confederate made eye-contact and frequently smiled at the subject, and when the confederate did not make eye-contact and was not smiling. This research showed that there is a link between perception and behaviour. Or, as the researchers put it: 'The mere perception of another's behavior automatically increases the likelihood of engaging in that behavior oneself.'[346] What we can take away from this is that there is consensus among researchers that 'behavior matching is related to greater liking and rapport between the interactants, and mimicry increases liking and fosters smooth, harmonious interactions.'[347] Well, this is precisely what we are looking for, right? Maybe you are asking yourself right now: 'why does this mimicking work?' It is commonly thought that the chameleon effect serves the basic human need to belong. Automatically behaving similarly to other group members, including having similar facial reactions to things that happen, does help to prevent an individual member from standing out as different. So, it helps us prevent social distance from other group members.[348] Oh, one last thing – research has shown that mimicking also enhances the mood of the 'recipient'. So, go ahead and elevate this mood of your decision-maker. Get them into that *I want to belong to your in-group state-of-mind*. But please don't turn into a mime-player, copying their every move. That is simply annoying. Trust upon your automatic brain to do the right amount of mimicking for you; just make sure to make eye contact and be an active listener, instead of starting a monologue with only eye for yourself. And the rest will follow.

Personal bias/stereotyping

As you know, our system 1 uses short-cuts to base our decisions upon. Stereotypes are typical system 1-short-cuts. Is someone wearing glasses? They must be smart. Is someone wearing a suit? Must be working in an office. Take this example from politics; a candidate's appearance can influence the votes they will get. We maybe think we vote for someone's competence, but our system 1 tricks us again. Researchers did an experiment in which participants were presented with the faces of the winner and the runner-up for 89 political races and were asked to judge how competent they thought the candidates were. However, they only showed them photographs with the candidate's forehead. The researchers found that the level of candidate competence was judged by their face.[349] Having a prominent forehead is such a characteristic we link to competence. So far for our rational judgment again. By the way, George Washington already knew it.[350] He consciously grew his hair long and 'then he'd pull it firmly back, broadening the forehead to give him', as Chernow writes in his biography, 'an air of martial nobility'.[351] The more forehead, the better. Nowadays, we notice chins. But not at that time. Foreheads conveyed power.

In short, stereotypes are everywhere and they massively influence our perceptions, opinions, and behaviours. And this can have serious adverse effects. A Starbucks manager in Philadelphia once called the police to report two black men sitting without ordering anything. The men were arrested on suspicion of trespassing, and were handcuffed. Then they were released without charge. Starbucks has since apologised and said that in response, it would close more than 8,000 US stores to give 175,000 employees bias training.[352] There are things we can do to try to decrease personal bias. However, diversity training programmes have limited success, and individual effort alone often invites backlash. Again, Behavioural Design can offer a solution – by thinking in systems. Or as Iris Bohnet states: 'What works is gender equality by design. We should be de-biasing organisations instead of individuals.'[353] One way to do this is to get rid of names, zip codes and demographic information from job applications to help recruiters fight their racial or gender biases. Also, more social contact with people who are different from us can reduce prejudice.[354] For example, designing mentor programmes can increase managers' on-the-job contact with the female and minority workers lower down in the organisation.[355]

Now that we know this of stereotypes, we can also make them work for us. Take a long and hard look at yourself. In this split-second, what kind of first impression do you make? Which stereotypes about you could be present in the mind of your decision-maker? And can you anticipate them? Make them work for you instead of against you. One way to do this is to, again, dress the part. But you can also try to debunk a stereotype. To tell you about a personal experience. I am a woman (already stereotype galore), but I am also very light-weighted. I always have been, something I am not complaining about, is great – 99% of the time. But when I am in Board Meetings, especially when I was younger and the age stereotype also kicked in, they didn't take me seriously; they mistook my weight for the fact that I couldn't bring intellectual weight into the meeting. I learnt to debunk that simply by saying: 'I know you see this slim woman in front of you, you must be thinking she cannot handle this project, she will be blown away, but I assure you I can handle a lot of pressure just let me show you what I want to do' and then I would start my presentation. It worked like a charm. So, instead of stepping on the 'they have to accept me as I am' train, board the 'I'll make sure a play their system 1 without them even knowing it' ship. Who is in the power position then?

Peak-end rule or the primacy/recency effect
I could only end this paragraph with the peak-end rule. The name already says it all: We remember the first and last things we are told or see, best. It's how you can turn your impression into a lasting memory. It looks something like this.

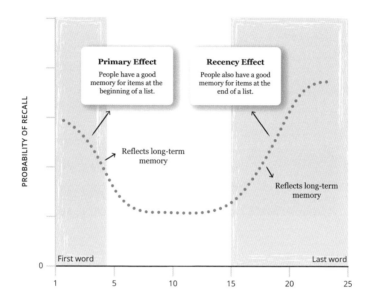

There are two ways how to use it. First of all, in building up your storyline, make sure the most important thing you want to convey isn't somewhere stuck in the middle. Put it either at the beginning or the end. But this also goes for the design of your physical spaces. Ensure you receive someone in your office with something nice, and end your meeting with a bang. We once did a project for Rotterdam, The Hague airport. They were amid constructions. This caused a bit of a mess. Combine this with the fact that many passengers find air travel already stressful, and you are potentially in for many discontents. We couldn't change the whole situation; construction had to be done. But we very consciously designed for the primacy and recency effect. Already in the parking lot, we made sure travellers were received with the most incredible hospitality, and just before they embarked onto the plane, they were surprised with a little act of kindness. We activated the peak-end rule, and it worked. Complaints were minimal. It goes without saying that we also did several other behavioural interventions in the terminal. Still, when we had to choose which interventions to apply, this one proved to be very effective. You also know why Ikea has that ultra-cheap hotdog- and ice cream-offer behind the registers: It creates 'the recency effect'. If you look at the Ikea in-store experience, it looks like this:

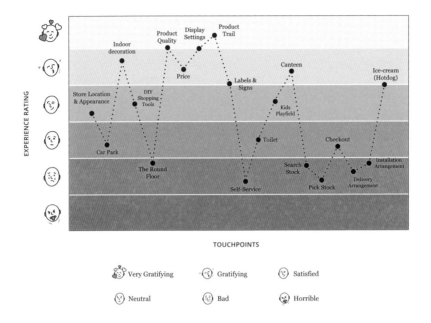

EXPERIENCE RATING

TOUCHPOINTS

Very Gratifying   Gratifying   Satisfied

Neutral   Bad   Horrible

Do you notice that enormous gap between the product trial in-store and the self-service? The experience rating drops from very gratifying to bad. And that's what the ice cream and hotdog do: they put you back to the gratify level. The level you will remember best. I warned you the world would never look the same again. It, by the way, again is a plea for making a human journey and linking this to both positive and negative emotions. It helps you to identify the Moments that Matter. The second thing you can do is, if you find yourself in a competitive situation in which you must go head-to-head with competitors to win a project or budget, to make sure you are either the first or the last to present. Again, take control of your meeting. Don't let it control you. Make sure you design for that lasting impression. I must end this paragraph with research involving Kahneman because this researched such a unique subject: A colonoscopy.[356] This is an uncomfortable, even painful procedure. You would think someone would want the procedure to be over as quickly as possible. But still, the researchers found that this may be rationally true, but psychologically it is not the case. The researchers found that patients consistently evaluated the discomfort of the experience based on the intensity of pain at the worst (peak) and final (end) moments. So, when the procedure was made less painful at the end but lasted longer, it was perceived as being less uncomfortable. So far, for time efficiency in all realms.

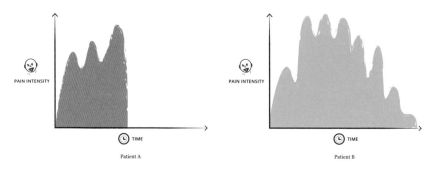

Data source: Redelmeier, Katz, Kahneman (2003)

There is another study that involved Kahneman providing evidence for the peak-end rule. Participants were subjected to two different versions of a single unpleasant experience: Putting your hand in ice-cold water. In the first trial, people had to put their hand in 14 °C water for one minute. The second trial had people stick the other hand in 14 °C water for a minute, but then had to keep their hand in the water for an extra 30 seconds, during which they raised the temperature to 15 °C. Everyone was then asked which trial they were willing to repeat. All opted for the second trial, despite the more prolonged exposure to uncomfortable temperatures. The researchers concluded that 'subjects chose the long trial simply because they liked the memory of it better than the alternative (or disliked it less).'[357] So, go ahead and design for that happy ending. Not the Bangkok kind, that might get you into trouble, but the kind that makes an experience with you pleasant to remember.

Tip 4: Use the intervention questions to make an irresistible request

Every time you write something, make sure that you pack it with behavioural interventions in the future. When the separate intervention questions have become system 1, you will do this automatically as soon as you start writing. When they are still somewhat system 2, you can first write a text and then add behavioural interventions. I want to show you an example. Let's say you would love to join our Behavioural Design Fundamentals Course and you must convince your manager to do so. This could be a way to convince her/him from:

Loss Aversion: Every organisation is nowadays transforming into becoming radically customer-centric. We don't want to miss out as an organisation on the competitive advantage of having a certified Behavioural Designer on the team who understands human decision-making, and has mastered a practical method to transform this knowledge into our everyday work practice.

Framing: SUE Behavioural Design had bundled together ten years of research, dozens of books, and hundreds of research papers and slide decks into just two days of masterclasses. They did all the exploration and shifting for us on what matters and what doesn't. Instead of you having to invest in long-term educational programmes, I can get it done in just two days. It will save me and you two years of delving into the subject, not even to mention the additional educational course investments you'll need not make. But foremost, this is not just a training. This subject interests me a lot and is something that keeps me developing and growing. Adding this to my expertise will keep me motivated.

Authority: SUE | Behavioural Design Academy is an official educational institute registered by the International Education Quality Assessment Commission (EQAC), the Dutch Council for Training and Education (NRTO). It is also one of the highest accredited courses of the Dutch Marketing Association (NIMA). 100% practitioners teach the course with over 20 years of work experience who are among others – known from TED and Erasmus University Business School.

Social Proof: SUE | Behavioural Design Academy has trained over 2,500 professionals in more than 45 countries from organisations such as UNHCR, Rabobank, ING, ABN Amro, Dutch Liberal Party, Adidas, Randstad, T-Mobile, BBDO, DDB, eBay, and many more. They score an average satisfaction rating of 9.2 out of 10. On their website you can find dozens of testimonials, also of people like me. Such as:

'I wasn't disappointed. During the training, my eyes opened. Theoretical and interactive sessions on human behaviour created a new way of thinking, and created a feeling that the possibilities of this knowledge are unlimited. Don't expect me to be an expert. But you'll feel and see the potential. We're now three weeks after the training, and I'm still learning new things, but more importantly: How to effectively change behaviour. Instead of thinking I cannot do it, I now do the research myself, which previously I rarely did. And I use the Behavioural Design Method to influence behaviour.'

Scarcity: The training is exclusive and only open to experienced professionals. Only 16 spots per edition are available for application. The group is kept small on purpose to ensure a maximum learning curve and ensure participants get extra value from the interaction with high-quality peers in the course. Spots run out fast. After one week of opening an edition, 80% of the spots are already taken.

Anchoring: We can pay the fee over five months. You only must invest 298 euros for just five months to make us a frontrunner in your business. On top of this, the fee includes exclusive FREE access to a six-month Continuous Learning Programme with weekly digital training.

Reciprocity: SUE | Behavioural Design Academy comes with a lot of bonuses. They believe skills aren't acquired in just two days, but ought to be internalised and trained further. By enrolling in the Fundamentals training, I will be granted FREE access to this 'Continuous Learning Programme' with six months of weekly digital masterclasses. Next to this, complementary *Refreshment Days* are organised. Graduates are also part of an exclusive alumni group to keep the conversation and education going and stimulate peer-to-peer learning. To top things off, alumni get substantial reductions on the Behavioural Design Academy events. So, you don't invest the fee for just two days, but for a 'lifetime of learning'.

A letter or email to your boss may look like this:

Subject: Behavioural Design Academy, and why I should join

Hi [insert name manager],
I know that you're very busy and get a lot of emails, so I will not take up too much of your time. I would love to enrol in the Behavioural Design Academy. We've put so much energy into trying to influence the behaviour of our [clients/employees/citizens/other]. To get them to [buy/click/try/recommend/embrace] our [products/services/policies/other].

In this training, I will learn how to shape minds and influence behaviour, revealing the scientifically proven methods of behavioural psychology. Still, first of all I will learn how to apply this to our projects. In short, it will help us make our strategies and ideas to a success. And it will help to get our customer-centred thinking going. The principal subject of this training is INFLUENCE seen from a behavioural science point of view. I genuinely believe the science of influence is a missing layer within our work. We could have far more control as to outcomes we want, if we knew how people arrive at decisions and how to influence them. And isn't that in the end our primary task: To steer the decisions and behaviour of our target group into the desired direction?

A few things worth considering:
- They will teach their ground-breaking know-how as to behavioural science, but make it very practical. I will learn to master a method and the tools that I can start applying right away when I get back.
- Senior practitioners teach the training. 'The Behavioural Design Method is not the only thing the training institution (SUE) teaches. They also use it themselves at organisations like UNHCR, Adidas, eBay, ABN Amro, BBDO, Amnesty International and Orange. To name but a few. They practice what they preach and also the other way round.
- They've trained over 2,500 professionals from over 45 countries, and got a 9.2 rating out of 10. There are enthusiastic testimonials online which you can find on their website (also as to our line of work!).
- It is our chance to learn from the frontrunners in the business, and to master the knowledge our competition already has. Or still lacks, which gives us a competitive advantage.

- It's just two days in Amsterdam, so it won't take up too much of my time.
- I can then share the learnt knowledge and tools with my colleagues. More insight into the workings of influence can help us get a grip upon successful outcomes. And we will understand how to become genuinely client-focused.

To summarise I think that sending me to the Behavioural Design Academy could really benefit our organisation. I would love to hear what you think as to this. Perhaps you even want to join me?

Love to hear from you! [insert your name]

Do you see that having a Behavioural Design mindset and your Behavioural Design toolbox can help you turn argumentation and writing into persuasive powerhouses? I know it is a skill, but practise will make perfect. And it will always be better than just taking a leap of faith and hoping for the best outcome. With this, we put back control into your hands too.

Tip 5: Unlocking the power of storytelling

Our brain is continuously trying to make sense of the world around us. The person you want to convince is probably busy, has only limited time for you and has tons of other decisions to make that very same day. Killing them with a boring PowerPoint is not the way to make an impression or to even get attention in the first place. You need to make sure your decision-making system 1 is pampered and prepared as to the things you want to get across. Remember that we talked about how our brain makes sense of the world by looking for patterns? One of the ways our brain forms patterns is through stories. According to Mary Catherine Bateson: 'The human species thinks in metaphors and learns through stories',[358] or as Jean-Luc Godard puts it: 'Sometimes reality is too complex. Stories give it form.'[359] So, using powerful storytelling can help your subject of influence to make sense of things. I feel storytelling is a skill everyone should have who needs to influence someone, which is often overlooked or underestimated. But not by you. You want to learn how to do this, don't you now? That leaves us with one final question. What is in fact powerful storytelling? There is more than one approach out there, but I prefer the concept of *the five-slide pitch* created by Martha Kagan of Ace the Pitch.[360] Or, as I like to call it, the five-step pitch (sometimes you don't have slides, but this approach will still work). This is what it looks like:

Source: Martha Kagan on Twitter

You first describe the situation, including the end-users you have researched at the Insight step. Who are they? Then you take plenty of time to sketch the problem. What are they facing? This is where the insights from your SUE | Influence Framework come in. What behavioural barriers did you discover? Followed by the opportunity (link this to your decision-maker's job-at-hand). It is not until this moment that you tell them about your solution. What you do in compelling storytelling is that you design with the aim of creating curiosity.

First make your listener fall in love with the problem, don't make them fall in love with your solution

If your problem is interesting enough, they'll want to learn about your solution. As a matter of fact, even if they might not agree wholly with your solution just yet, chances are you will still not be entirely dismissed. If they find your problem fascinating, you will most probably get the opportunity to refine your solution. As you have designed a context in which also your decision-maker is very keen to see the problem solved. Often, we are so in love with our solution that we start by giving the bulk of the attention in our presentation, but that's a habit we must attempt to reprogramme in our brain. Create anticipation first. Then make it clear that your thinking contains psychological intelligence. Thus a showcase results. Also, taking too much time in the beginning to recap the challenge, disclosing your strategy and process, and cramping this with an overload of information on your slides, is another trap. Be fast and smooth. See if you can do your pitch in 5 to 10 minutes or 15 minutes maximum. Make it simple, only use one-liners on pages, prevent choice overload, and use visual representations to make your point. All the things you've learnt by the intervention questions, you should use here also. Finally, end with a clear call to action. Most of us don't. We finish our argumentation or presentation and then wait for the feedback. At the same time, it is a capability intervention to make it easier for your decision-maker to respond by ending with a clear CTA to get what you need from them. What is your end goal? Do you need extra time to work on the intervention? Do you need additional staff or a budget? Do you want to run a test pilot? Be clear on what you want and need. So, this is how compelling story-telling can help to persuade someone.

Just one last thing. If you look at the five steps, you might have already seen a re-semblance with the entertainment industry. Almost every story plot of a movie or series is constructed this way. Movies always start with the situation: who are the main characters? We usually come in either in NYC or Providence, and before you know it our lead character to whom we have grown attached runs into a problem. Life is never a breeze for our leading man or women: Love lives crash, relatives disappear, or Armageddon hits town. But then all ends well – there is a solution. Brad Pitt saves the day, steamy sex fogs up our screens and children say: 'I love you mum'. And sometimes, even fatal diseases have a magical turn-around. The CTA is often the cliff-hanger that makes us binge-watch or watch the sequels I, II and III. But on a more serious note, you can learn a lot from how entertainment designs the attention spans. They manage to get us glued to the screen. All we've got to do is (quite literally) watch and learn. And hey, is there a better excuse to see more movies and series? It's a dirty job, but someone has to do it.

So, that's it. After many pages, our story ends here. We have tackled all three building blocks of the SUE | Behavioural Design Method together. We have linked Insight, Intervention, and Impact together. They conceived effective interventions, and now they will live happily ever after. So, it leaves me nothing left to say:

The End.

Okay, fairy tales usually end here, but we will take a sneak-peak at what happens next. What considerations do we need to make in order to ensure our Behavioural Design interventions have a positive impact? What can you do to become better at Behavioural Design? One last chapter on the final building block of any Behavioural Design Intervention: Implement. Not all of it would wear you out, but the essential part of it is Behavioural Design ethics. In order to make sure that *you* will also live happily ever after.

STEP IV

IMPLEMENT

How to turn ideas into a success
SUE | Behavioural Design Method©

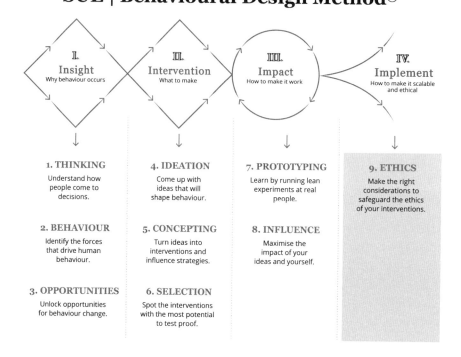

I.
Insight
Why behaviour occurs

II.
Intervention
What to make

III.
Impact
How to make it work

IV.
Implement
How to make it scalable
and ethical

1. THINKING
Understand how
people come to
decisions.

4. IDEATION
Come up with
ideas that will
shape behaviour.

7. PROTOTYPING
Learn by running lean
experiments at real
people.

9. ETHICS
Make the right
considerations to
safeguard the ethics
of your interventions.

2. BEHAVIOUR
Identify the forces
that drive human
behaviour.

5. CONCEPTING
Turn ideas into
interventions and
influence strategies.

8. INFLUENCE
Maximise the
impact of your
ideas and yourself.

3. OPPORTUNITIES
Unlock opportunities
for behaviour change.

6. SELECTION
Spot the interventions
with the most potential
to test proof.

BUILDING BLOCK 9

ETHICS

– Making the right considerations to safeguard the ethics of your interventions

Introduction

You know what they say: save the best for last. Well, perhaps it's not the best but, in this case the indispensable. I have referred to ethics in Behavioural Design several times in this book. It is not just a relevant but a fundamental and critical topic to think about and act upon. The know-how of behavioural psychology can be a powerful tool for shaping choices and behaviour. At SUE, we have created a toolkit for Behavioural Design Ethics to make sure we can leverage this power to do good. This chapter will give insight into how we incorporate ethics in our way of working. It will also provide you with practical tools to help you pinpoint the considerations *you* need to make so as to safeguard the ethics in your future Behavioural Design. It is our take on things. It isn't perfect yet. It is an ever-evolving work in progress, but it is also a solid start.

Manipulation versus influence

But before we come to the different levels at which we should apply Behavioural Design ethics, we first must address the one question that will always loom over us: is Behavioural Design manipulation? I have already addressed this question in the ideation building block, but you can never have enough repetition as to some subjects. And I am sure you'll be asked that same question more than once in the future, or maybe it's a question you're asking yourself right now. First, I would like to reframe the question: Are we in the manipulation business, or are we designing positive influence? To me, there is a great difference between manipulation and influence. A significant difference too. As said, and I will repeat quite literally what I told you in the ideation building block: the know-how of behavioural science can be a potent tool for influencing choice and shaping decisions. Thus, this may be a very dark wisdom. It can be (and is) used to get people hooked to phones or unhealthy foods, to manipulate voting behaviours or create separation in society – to name but a few. We cannot deny it, and people can easily use it to exploit fears and anxieties in others. However, we may also apply this same wisdom to help people engage in healthier habits such as exercising, eating healthy food, or creating a better world by supporting people to recycle, act against climate change, or helping those in need. Therefore, Behavioural Design isn't as such 'dark wisdom'; it's what you do with it. It all boils down to intention.

If your intention is to help people make better decisions that will improve their lives, their work or living environment – then that's a positive influence. If your intention is not the progress or improvement of the person(s), then you are manipulating

At SUE | Behavioural Design, we are very much concerned with the ethics of applied behavioural science, and you should be so too. Does this sound commanding? I can sugar-coat it, but not building ethical awareness and balance into your projects is simply not an option. We need you to do it. The world needs you to do it. For we've got to form a countermovement. Unfortunately, the people now using behavioural science often don't have good intentions – using behavioural science solely for personal advancement or for benefiting a lucky (privileged) few. They are the manipulators. You, my friend – I think now that we've spent many pages together, we are on a friend basis, don't you agree? So, you, my friend, are a positive influencer. And how are you going about it? Knowing you already a bit, you've probably already taken the first concrete steps by defining a personal or company mission that has progress in its DNA. That's a great start. But now you must make sure you are proving your mission by your daily actions. Perhaps you still remember our mission:

Unlocking the power of behavioural psychology to help people make better decisions in work, life and living environment

So, now that we're both in the business of coming up with interventions that will influence choice and shape behaviour, we need to prove we are worthy of our mission. We should walk the talk. This takes two things: a clear vision of the ethics of Behavioural Design, and a code of conduct. Unfortunately, there isn't already a commonly accepted code of conduct in the behavioural science field. In this chapter, I want to provide you with insights and tools in order to use as our ethical compass. This can be applied at three levels:

- Organisational Level
- Personal and Team Level
- Project Level

All of these come with tools that you can download at the book *bonus webpage*. Please feel free to use them and adapt them to your mission. I hope it will give you some practical guidelines as to using Behavioural Design from a positive point of view. Still, it isn't perfect yet. We are prototyping it and learning every day. It is a constant work-in-progress we will keep sharing with you through our website and content. Our goal is to be very open and transparent about how we try to safeguard the ethics of Behavioural Design, and how we sometimes struggle with it. Now that you are in this for progress, improvement, better decision-making, and positive behaviour, I invite you to embrace our tools and best practices. Let's create a positive countermovement together, applying Behavioural Design for the good, and for counterbalancing and exposing those who use it with evil or selfish intentions. But let me start by taking you to the organisational level.

The Organisational Level

At an organisation level, it all starts with this *actionable mission* that has progress in its DNA, and is backed by the willingness and capability within the organisation in order to act upon it. Acting upon a company mission requires a mandate from management, as well as a *company culture* that attracts talent and clients who fit into and believe in this mission, and to reject those who don't. It also requires a company culture that is open to discussion. We live by our Behavioural Ethics principles, which are:

Guiding Ethical Principles

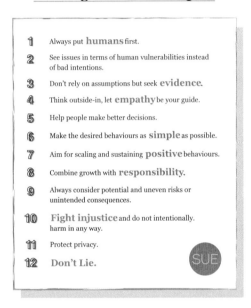

1   Always put **humans** first.

2   See issues in terms of human vulnerabilities instead of bad intentions.

3   Don't rely on assumptions but seek **evidence.**

4   Think outside-in, let **empathy** be your guide.

5   Help people make better decisions.

6   Make the desired behaviours as **simple** as possible.

7   Aim for scaling and sustaining **positive** behaviours.

8   Combine growth with **responsibility.**

9   Always consider potential and uneven risks or unintended consequences.

10 **Fight injustice** and do not intentionally. harm in any way.

11 Protect privacy.

12 **Don't Lie.**

Next to the mission and its principles, we also safeguard our Behavioural Design ethics by carefully selecting the projects we engage in and the people we work with. Both at SUE and our Academy, we aren't one-size-fits-all. Even in the days when we were still a small-scale company with little money in the bank, we decided always to put our mission first, and be selective as to who we work for and who can enrol in our training. We will never work for or train people working in industries that harm people, animals, the planet, or that neglect social and equal rights (if you want to find out more, check out our Terms & Conditions on our website). We are not selling our souls to the devil, not for a million. Or more. However, occasionally the world isn't just black-and-white, and we find ourselves in shades of grey. This sometimes results in difficult decisions. We always genuinely try to base our decisions upon our moral compass, so that they still remain open to discussion by anyone within our company.

That being said, we do have ongoing conversations within our team about the projects we work on. Not working for the fur-, tobacco- or weapon-industry is an easy decision. But should you work for an alcoholic beer brand or only for their 0% beers? And what about milk? Or for the oil industry if they want you to work on their transition to sustainable energy? There aren't always clear-cut answers to this, and can lead to different point-of-views. This is one way we try to safeguard our ethics: by actively and purposely keeping the ethics discussion alive within our team. This code of ethics you are reading right now, and the tools that come with it, can help us to define the boundaries. But sometimes boundaries change because we've learnt things. And there are, of course, always loopholes. We had someone who 'slipped' into our Academy by applying via a Gmail-address, and faking his employer details. And we failed to do a sufficient background check. He turned out to work for a cigarette brand. Not one of our finest moments; still, our background checks are far more thorough now, trust me. But we don't have and will never have a complete sense of control over who reads our blogs, sees our keynotes, uses our tools, watches our videos, or will buy this book. We know that, and we are aware of it.

I don't want to live my life with a negative perspective on human nature. I genuinely believe that the intentions of the majority of people are not bad – and I hope everything we do at SUE | Behavioural Design and the SUE | Behavioural Design Academy will spread massively. I refuse to believe people are intrinsically selfish or of bad will. We as people are just sometimes clumsy, too emotional, or merely incapable. If you look at people as humans who are trying their best, they can do so within the context they find themselves in. Heavily influenced by biases, past experiences, and short-cuts - this does reduce your pessimism as to human nature. Try judging people through the lens of 'good people, bad circumstances',[361] and I assure you it will take the edge of your annoyances and foster empathy and belief that most people mean well. This is why we, as SUE, want to provide more tools for these masses in order to help them make better decisions. Will we also reach the 2% 'asshole population'? Maybe. But we will also reach the 98% of people looking to make a difference, or eager to learn how to realise the progress that goes beyond selfish motivations.

But it's not only the way you look at things; it is also how you act. Whether Behavioural Design is a pearl of dark or enlightened wisdom all starts at intent. Is your intention to harm or do good? Is it about shareholder value alone? Or are you genuinely trying to add human value? Which can also make you good money, by the way. That's why we have developed the SUE | Influence Framework, which itself is all about progress: we resolve pains, enhance gains, take away anxieties, create better comforts, and help people help to better achieve their jobs-to-be-done. It is your power tool to turn human insights into tangible interventions that will spark positive action. It is a systematic approach to think outside-in instead of inside-out. You will put humans first and not yourself. I would love for every organisation to start using the SUE | Influence Framework. Still, the more important point I want to make here is that embedding a workable method in your organisation which genuinely puts humans first is a key to designing for the good. Of course, the SUE | Influence Framework is the best way to do this without any doubt. But on a more serious note: it helps the clients we work for grasp human decision-making truly, and us too. It reveals that often people have the best intentions, but stumble upon behavioural barriers and bottlenecks that prevent them from doing the better or right thing. So apart from the framework helping you to become radically human-centred, and discovering the human behind your client, employee, citizen or whoever you are trying to influence, it also is a revelation, as it shows that having a positive perspective on human nature is indeed not just 'touchy-feely' but a valid conclusion to make.

Work in progress for us is making the shift from a more individualistic (or a small group) of behavioural interventions to influencing collective behaviour. To have a genuinely positive impact, we need to reach a certain point of adoption. We can design for ever on a larger scale by coming up with system of interventions and creating network effects. We are working on this by adding quantitative research to our SUE | Behavioural Design Method in order to substantiate our behavioural insights, and find evidence for the weight of the behaviour drivers of a problem. Another way is that we are looking to run pilot projects after our prototyping tests to discover that we can scale the behavioural interventions and test their positive impact on a larger scale. We believe the future lies in connecting behavioural science with network science and systems thinking. We still haven't gotten 'all our ducks in a row', but we are working on it.

The Personal and Team Level

Let's move on to the personal and team level. I combine these two because a team is made up of individuals. You cannot separate one from the other. The interplay of these individuals makes up an okay or great team. When it comes down to you, you also have a significant role to play. The most important is always to be honest with yourself and have a learning mindset. I mean by this is that you have to accept that sometimes you engage in activities that may feel right at the moment, but which you might not be that happy about anymore afterwards. And sometimes it is the other way round. That's okay. The most important thing is that you learn from your experiences. We are firm believers of habits, automatic behaviours that will help you to shape your choices and behaviour without this taking too much cognitive effort. We have installed the ethical retrospective habit to activate this ethical learning effect. Try to make it a routine after every project, to ask yourself these five questions[362] (or do this as a team):

- What happened during the project that triggered emotions within yourself?
- How did I feel (positive or negative), and what were my reactions?
- What insights or conclusions can I draw from the experience? What did I learn?
- How can I (or we as a team) apply what I learnt in order to improve the future experience?
- What actions can I (or we as a team) take on the basis of what I learnt?

We often do project evaluations or retrospectives, but you can also add an ethical assessment by adding these five questions above. If you want to do some more self-exploration, check out the *Little Book of Me* by Alistair Sommerville.[363] It helps you pinpoint your values, and enables you to get the conversation going within your team. This is very important when it comes to ethics. You need to understand what effect you have on other people. It would be best if you also learnt how to express your opinions within a group. Shared understanding, empathy and self-awareness are the driving forces of making an ethical culture come to life. A helpful tool is the *Johari Window*,[364] I also made a download to explain the Johari Window you can again find on the book website download page.

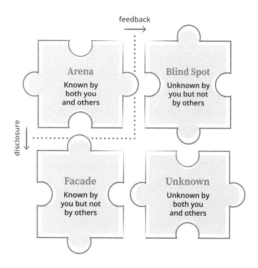

It provides insight into your blind spots, what facades you build up, and what is usually either out in the open or unknown to both you and others. It can be a handy team exercise to create mutual understanding and apply outside-in thinking within your team discussions. See if you find this a useful tool (or parts of it).

By considering Behavioural Design–ethics you're trying to lower the risk of unintended consequences

You and I genuinely have good intentions, and we are both stirred by our personal or company mission to use Behavioural Design in order to improve human decision-making. But sometimes we don't see the complete project picture at the start of a project. And we are all influenced by our biases and mental misunderstandings. So, we try to design behavioural interventions within projects in order to solve these challenges. Although we know that 100% perfection might be an illusion, you should always have the ambition to lead your projects as ethically as possible.

The Project Level

You can add three behavioural interventions to safeguard the ethics relevant to your project at a project level. First of all, we work with our *Behavioural Design Ethics Checklist* and our *Behavioural Design Ethics Cards*.[365] These help us to ask the right questions at the right moment during three project stages: The Project Intake, the Project Preparation, and the Intervention Evaluation. These questions help us to become aware of the ethical considerations we need to keep in mind before starting a project. But they also allow us to address the (unintentional) side-effects of our behavioural interventions. Feel free to use these tools and to adjust them to your mission statement; you can find them on our website (suebehaviouraldesign.com). If your mission is to design for good, we are perfectly fine with that! The second way we safeguard our Behavioural Design ethics, is to be aware of our cognitive biases. We all are a slave to our system 1, and we make (subconscious) mental mistakes or judgments of error based on the short-cuts our brain takes. However, no one can always wholly override their thinking and decision-making process. Kahneman once stated that people could improve their decision-making by forcing themselves to think more deeply. So, even your initial reactions will be modified.[366] I have created such a forcing function by making a short Cognitive Biases Checklist that we keep at hand during projects, and which you can download on The Missing Layer download page. It does help to force yourself to think more deeply about any possible mental mistakes, by literally reading the checklist with the most common cognitive biases.

For example, before you start a meeting, do an interview, or even as the first thing you do at the start of your workday. It helps us to address the cognitive bias we as a project team are dealing with and the biases that the people may have for whom we are designing a behavioural intervention (and that we need to consider). By searching for biases (even as organisations or institutions), you can try to reduce the impact biases have upon decisions. Kahneman calls this a process of *self-criticism* or of *quality control* with a view to decisions, which is feasible within reason. But you don't want too much of it. What Kahneman calls *paralysis by analysis*; but then within reason, shows there's room to improve what you as a team do by quality control within a project. As to making your 'reading-the-checklist behaviour' easier to perform, just print the checklist and keep it in a spot where you can easily see it. Just stick it on your wall, or make a blow-up to hang up in your team-meeting room.

Just one more remark: This is by no means a complete overview of cognitive biases – far from it. If you want to know more about cognitive biases, we can warmly recommend reading the blog post of Buster Benson on cognitive biases I referred to in the Insight Chapter. Safeguarding ethics in Behavioural Design is (unfortunately) never 100% foolproof. I always say: just get your moral compass to show you the way. Using our SUE | Influence Framework will already point you in the right direction, as this is all about creating progress. But I have also created a straightforward tool that can help you to decide relatively 'slipshod' whether we are on the right track with our behavioural intervention. I have called it the *Human Value Compass*, and at a fast check it gets you to ask yourself three questions:

- Will it deliver human value?
- Is it true: no lying, window dressing or sugar-coating?
- Is it feasible?

If not all of these questions can be answered by 'yes', it is time to abort the mission. The intervention is leading you into the wrong direction. So, back to the drawing table. As said, this is a 'quick check'. And we may use our *Behavioural Ethics Checklist & Cards* for more thorough ethical considerations.

So, there you go. You are now well-equipped to not just come up with the behavioural interventions that will turn your ideas into a success; and you now also have all the tools at hand to make sure you are able to direct the positive impact they will have. This leaves us with one final chapter. Or it isn't even an actual chapter – it's an afterword, and for you especially.

 TOOL: DOWNLOAD BEHAVIOURAL DESIGN ETHICS CARDS

 TOOL: DOWNLOAD GUIDING ETHICAL PRINCIPLES

 TO DO: USE THE ETHICS CARDS TO INTEGRATE ETHICS INTO YOUR BEHAVIOURAL DESIGN

BECOMING A BEHAVIOURAL DESIGNER

So, that's it then. You have stepped into my world. I hope you are both fascinated and excited about the powers of Behavioural Design, and how it can help you achieve personal and professional success. But also how it can put you in the immensely satisfying position of helping people to take better decisions, which then will create progress in their work, life and living environments. You can arrive at such a change. And together we can do great things. The truth is, every other positive cliché or slogan will apply here. And now that we are 'cranked way up' by this positive vibe, I want to end with a story of hope. I hope *you will use* this book. I hope it has earned a place on your desk, and that it won't be tucked away in your bookcase (ability intervention, keep it in sight ;-)). I hope you will fill it with your notes in the side-line, marking it with underlinings and exclamation marks. And that it will have earmarks all over the place, and first ideas enthusiastically scribbled next to passages. I finally hope you will consult it time and again, skipping to a part as regards which you need some refreshment .

Behavioural Design is a skill. And a new skill requires practice. It needs doing and re-doing, falling down and getting back up. Failing and learning. It is learning how to ride a bike without bleeding knees. Still, you must take the ride. So, I've taken you along the printed ride. However, reading about behavioural economics is hugely fascinating, but may not bring you the success you may ambition instantly. I do realise that applying Behavioural Design can be challenging – frustratingly hard. Especially when you are pioneering within your organisation or team, and must deal with people who haven't 'seen the Light' of

Behavioural Design (yet). At SUE, we can help you join forces with a Behavioural Design expert to help you inject your projects with behavioural intelligence, or we can teach you how to become a Behavioural Design expert yourself. And to fit both needs, we've created our unique combination of an innovation consultancy and academy specialised in Behavioural Design. To provide you with an environment filled with forward-thinking professionals, who want to unlock for you the power of Behavioural Design.

I invite you to check out our curriculum and consider joining our Behavioural Design Fundamentals Course. I know some of you already have done so, and I genuinely love you for it. I hope you will use this book as a reference tool, deepening your learning experience with us. If you are still hungry for more, check out our Advanced Course or Speciality Masterclasses. We will keep on adding new courses to help you progress further. To help you further on your mastery curve, I have created a *SWAC Interventions Card Deck©* and a *SWAC Interventions Playbook©*, giving you all that's needed to power up your products, services, campaigns, policies or teams with Behavioural Design. You can order them on our website. My goal for you is to reach the level of *Behavioural Design mastery*. Maybe you have read this book in chronological order this time. And now know that you don't need to do so in the future. Of course, you can, but I hope reality will show that it will now be your reference guide or your almost trusted colleague helping you to unlock the power of Behavioural Design. I hope this book, the tools, the videos, and downloads that come with it, become your sparring partner when we, as SUE, are not by your side. But don't forget we are around! And so please, don't be a stranger. I would love it if you shared your Behavioural Design successes with me, so that I can share them with other Behavioural Design enthusiasts, and we can help one another to steepen our mutual learning curve. You'll find my email address below. Also, don't hesitate to share the things you need to help you apply the SUE | Behavioural Design Method, or the training you would love to have. We are immensely thankful for any outside-in input, and we genuinely use it to create better products and learning experiences. May your success be great, your positive impact impressive, and your life be filled with joy – and with better decisions for you and those surrounding you. The world needs your talent, and I'd love for you to become part of my 'army' of fellow crusaders whom have set out to design better lives, workplaces and living environments by unlocking the power of Behavioural Design. May the force of good be with you!

Astrid Groenewegen, astrid@suebehaviouraldesign.com

 TO DO: DOWNLOAD THE BEHAVIOURAL DESIGN FUNDAMENTALS COURSE BROCHURE

 TO DO: DOWNLOAD THE ADVANCED BEHAVIOURAL DESIGN BROCHURE

 TO DO: SUBSCRIBE TO THE FREE BEHAVIOURAL DESIGN DIGEST MAILING LIST WITH TIPS & TRICKS

 VIDEO: WATCH MY YOUTUBE VIDEO SERIES ' BEHAVIOURAL DESIGN FOR DAILY LIFE'

THANK YOU

You would never have had this book lying in front of you, without the ongoing support, advice and input of the beautiful team of SUE | Behavioural Design, the SUE | Behavioural Design Academy and SUE & The Alchemists. Every day I am still deeply impressed by how they solve the most wicked Behavioural Design problems, with interventions that make me glow with pride. I couldn't be happier than having such a bunch of talented people taking on our mission to unlock the power of behavioural psychology for the sake of good. Special thanks to Tom, my partner, my co-founder, my husband, the love of my life – who stood by me in this process from beginning to end, and is the smartest person I know out there (despite everything ;-). Thanks to my parents who always said I should write. Here you have it! And thanks to my sweet, beautiful Lou. You were the number one distractor, but what great laughs I had. And hearing you sing 'Let it Go' as Elsa sure helped to take off the edge of things. Thanks to Friedrichshain and Kreuzberg Berlin, my endless place of inspiration, thanks Michelberger for being my home-away-from-home; Solomun for the techno that made me smile and do desk dances while typing away these words at 125 beats per minute. (I am a groupie, so know, I will embarrass myself by taking a picture with you, should I ever bump into you. Oh, and by the way: I am that girl doing the crazy dance moves at your live sets with a big smile on my face). Thank you, Thijs, whose great editing enabled me turn a well-intended brain dump into a readable book. And thank you Paul for taking over from Thijs and making sure this book is now available in both English and Dutch. Thanks to Demmy for the fantastic illustrations that show SUE's Knalldrang so well. And last but certainly not least, thanks to all our SUE clients and academy participants. Your questions, input and enthusiasm have been a driving force in writing this book. I hope you'll use it and create wonderful interventions that will help you to gain the success you're looking for, and help other people to make better decisions.

APPENDIX

All tools, downloads and videos in this book are available online, in English and Dutch:

I have introduced you to the 'Magnificent Ten' of the CAN- and WANT-intervention questions in this book. This is the complete set of *SWAC Intervention Questions* to boost capabality in order to change behaviour (CAN), and to make someone WANT to switch over to the desired behaviour. The lists are growing every day. Please, visit the website if you want to learn more about all the *SWAC Intervention Questions* and to learn how to apply them in different circumstances, like a half-day workshop or a two-hour brainwriting session. I have created a special *SWAC Interventions Card Deck* and a *SWAC Interventions Playbook* for this.

SWAC CAN Questions©

(capability)

CAN we make the desired behaviour(s) easier (or undersired behaviours harder) to do?

C01.	Can we make the behaviour automatic?	Default option
C02.	Can we give less options to choose from?	Option reduction
C03.	Can we ask an easier question?	Question substitution
C04.	Can we add repitition?	Mere exposure effect
C05.	Can we make it more distinctive?	Sailence
C06.	Can we add or take away hurdles?	Friction
C07.	Can we decide upon the single step someone has to take first?	Dominance
C08.	Can we use easier words?	Clarity
C09.	Can we break-down the behaviour into smaller steps?	Chunking
C10.	Can we limit the number of steps someone has to take?	Simplicity

Behavioural Design

SWAC Intervention Questions©

(capability)

CAN we make the desired behaviour(s) easier (or undersired behaviours harder) to do?

C11.	Can we break-up the costs or monetary amounts?	Simplicity
C12.	Can we limit the number of decisions by bundling?	Simplicity
C13.	Can we give someone a head-start?	Endowed effect
C14.	Can put the focus on the completed instead of the uncompleted tasks?	Zeigarnik effect
C15.	Can we show what people have to do next?	Specificity
C16.	Can we make a goal more specific?	Earmarking
C17.	Can we (visually) divide money for people?	Partitioning
C18.	Can we add a schedule?	Habit
C19.	Can we add small differences to similar choices?	Similarity
C20.	Can we show that even small behaviours add up?	Legitimising effect

Behavioural Design

SWAC Intervention Questions©

(capability)

CAN we make the desired behaviour(s) easier (or undersired behaviours harder) to do?

C21.	Can we provide personal guidance?	Assisting
C22.	Can we use pre-filled-in forms (or simplify them)?	Pre-filling
C23.	Can we add a deadline?	Forcing function
C24.	Can we put the desired behaviour within reach?	Proximity
C25.	Can we take a lift upon the existing behaviour?	Piggybacking
C26.	Can we limit the size of tableware?	Downsizing
C27.	Can we stop subsiding the old behaviour?	Costs of inertia
C28.	Can we make it reversible, give people a try first or offer a freemium?	Switching costs
C29.	Can we help people to envision the benefits of the new behaviour?	Concretisation
C30.	Can we make someone pause their behaviour?	Decision Points

Behavioural Design

SWAC Want Questions©

(willingness)

WANT how might we make someone willing to show the desired behaviour(s)
or unwilling to show the desired behaviours?

W01.	Can we show the behaviour of others?	Social proof/ bandwagon effect
W02.	Can we compare behaviour to others who are close?	Social Norm
W03.	Can we remind someone of their social image/identity?	Social identity/signalling
W04.	Can we use noun words to describe someone?	Labelling
W05.	Can we activate someone's social connections & social influence?	Network effects
W06.	Can we give someone a sense of belonging?	Social inclusion
W07.	Can we create an out-group?	Social exclusion
W08.	Can we make it personal?	Personalisation
W09.	Can we deliver the message by a trusted messenger?	Authority
W10.	Can we explain where people buy?	Context effects

Behavioural Design

SWAC Want Questions©

(willingness)

WANT how might we make someone willing to show the desired behaviour(s)
or unwilling to show the desired behaviours?

W11.	Can we present information in a different way?	Framing
W12.	Can we sell time instead of money?	Framing
W13.	Can we give people a limited offer?	Scarcity
W14.	Can we make people feel they are losing out on something?	Loss aversion
W15.	Can we show the time, money or effort already spent?	Endowment effect
W16.	Can we give them something they don't expect?	Reciprocity
W17.	Can we show the behaviour has meaning?	Expectancy theory
W18.	Can we explain what the desired behaviour leads up to?	Goal setting
W19.	Can we make someone commit to the desired behaviour?	Commitment/consistency
W20.	Can we make someone aware of their future self?	Hyperbolic discounting
W21.	Can we use words that describe fast rewards?	Instant gratification

Behavioural Design

SWAC Want Questions©

(willingness)

*WANT how might we make someone willing to show the desired behaviour(s)
or unwilling to show the desired behaviours?*

W22.	Can we give someone (immediate) non-monetary rewards?	Rewarding
W23.	Can we show progress in percentages or in abstract measurements?	Feedback
W24.	Can we make the end-goal of the behaviour visual?	Feedback
W25.	Can we give public praise or recognition?	Feedback
W26.	Can we add meaning to a number or statistics?	Anchoring
W27.	Can we present three options?	Extremeness aversion
W28.	Can we add a higher priced item?	Decoy effect
W29.	Can we make the (un)desired behaviour more visible?	Salience
W30.	Can we match the behaviour?	Behaviour matching
W31.	Can we design a positive state-of-mind?	Priming
W32.	Can we create a feeling of autonomy?	Reactance

Behavioural Design

REFERENCES

1   Wherever I write 'we', I mean our company SUE | Behavioural Design, which I co-founded with my part-
    ner Tom De Bruyne. The SUE | Behavioural Design Method$^{©}$ was developed by us both, and optimised
    by our team on basis of the learnings of real behavioural

2   Cialdini, R. (2009). *Influence: Science and Practice.* Boston, MA: Pearson Education.

3   www.suebehaviouraldesign.com

4   https://en.wikipedia.org/wiki/Synaptic_pruning

5   Rohwedder, S. & Willis, R. (2010). Mental Retirement. *Journal of Economic Perspectives* 24(1):119-38.
    NIHMS.

6   Barry, TE. (1987). *The development of the hierarchy of effects: an historical perspective,* USA.

7   Wikipedia, *Consistency (negotiation).*

8   Cialdini, R. (2009). *Influence: Science and Practice.* Boston, MA: Pearson Education.

9   Simon, H. (1969). *The Sciences of the Artificial.* Cambridge: MIT Press.

10 https://dschool.stanford.edu/

11 Brown, T. (2008). *Design Thinking.* Harvard Business Review, pp. 85–92.

12 Brown, T. & Kätz, B. (2009). *Change by Design: How Design Thinking Transforms Organizations and Inspires
    Innovation.* New York: Harper Business.

13 Osterwalder, A., Pigneur, Y. & Smith, A. (2010). *Business Model Generation,* Wiley.

14 Ries, E. (2011). *The Lean Startup.* USA: Crown Business.

15 Ries, E. (2011). *The Lean Startup.* USA: Crown Business.

16 Doneva, R. (2017). *Behavioural archetypes instead of personas.* https://medium.com/common-good/behav-
    ioural-archetypes-instead-of-personas-c7ccc5b8b998

17 Doneva, R. (2017). *Behavioural personas at Design Manchester.* https://medium.com/servicedesignjam-
    days17/behavioural-personas-at-design-manchester-8e14da002f40

18 https://www.meatlessmonday.com/

19 Goodwin, T. (2015). *The Battle is for the customer interface.* Techcrunch.

20 Kahneman, D. (2012). *Thinking, Fast and Slow,* Macmillan.

21 Thaler, R.H. & Sunstein, C.R. (2008). *Nudge: Improving Decisions about Health, Wealth, and Happiness.* Yale
    University Press.

22 Cialdini, R. (2009). *Influence: Science and Practice.* Boston, MA: Pearson Education.

23 Cialdini, R. (2016). *Pre-Suasion: A Revolutionary Way to Influence and Persuade.* New York: Simon & Schuster.

24 Ariely, D. (2008). *Predictably Irrational,* HarperCollins.

25 Ariely, D. (2011). *The Upside of Irrationality: The Unexpected Benefits of Defying Logic.* New York; Toronto:
    Harper Perennial.

26   Munger, C. (2014). *A Lesson on Elementary, Worldly Wisdom As It Relates To Investment Management & Business.* USC lecture.

27   Fogg, B.J. (2009). A Behavior Model for Persuasive Design. *Proceedings of the 4th International Conference on Persuasive Technology.* Persuasive '09. New York, NY, US: ACM. pp. 40:1–40:7.

28   Cialdini, R. (2009). *Influence: Science and Practice.* Boston, MA: Pearson Education.

29   The double diamond phases as described by the Design Council: https://www.designcouncil.org.uk/news-opinion/design-process-what-double-diamond

30   http://science.unctv.org/content/reportersblog/choices

31   Gazzaniga, M.S. (2011). *Who is in charge? Free Will and the Science of the Brain.* Ecco.

32   Parrish, S. (2019). *Interview with Daniel Kahneman.* FS Blog, Farnham Street Media Inc.

33   Webb, C. (2016). *How to have a good day. Harness the power of behavioural science to transform your working life.* London: Pan Macmillan.

34   https://www.dailymail.co.uk/news/article-9017489/Guests-Brussels-daddy-orgy-thought-cops-act-host-claims.html

35   Frieder, R.E., van Iddekinge, C.H. & Raymark, P.H. (2015). How quickly do interviewers reach decisions? An examination of interviewers' decision-making time across applicants. *Journal of Occupational and Organizational Psychology.*

36   Lakoff, G. & Johnson M. (1999). *Philosophy in the Flesh: The Embodied Mind and its Challenge to Western Thought.* Basic Books.

37   Gross, J.J., & Muñoz, R.F. (1995). Emotion regulation and mental health. *Clinical Psychology: Science and Practice,* 2, 151164.

38   Sapolsky, R.M. (2007). Stress, stress-related disease, and emotional regulation. In: *J. J. Gross(Ed.), Handbook of emotion regulation.* New York: Guilford Press.

39   Diefendorff, J.M., Hall, R J., Lord, R. G. & Strean, M.L. (2000). Action-state orientation: Construct validity of a revised measure and its relationship to work-related variables. *Journal of Applied Psychology,* 85, 250263.

40   Murray, S.L. (2005). Regulating the risks of closeness: A relationship-specific sense of felt security. *Psychological Science,*14, 7478.

41   Simon, H.A. (1982). *Models of bounded rationality.* Cambridge, MA: MIT Press.

42   Gopher, D., Armony, L. & Greenspan, Y. (2000). Switching tasks and attention policies. *Journal of Experimental Psychology: General, 129,* 308-229.

43   Sunstein, C (2020). *Three questions about behavioural economics.* Retrieved from IDB, www.iadb.org/behavioral.

44   Güth, W., Schmittberger, R. & Schwarze, B. (1982). An Experimental Analysis of Ultimatum Bargaining. *Journal of Economic Behavior & Organization,* 3, 367-388.

45   Parrish, S. (2019). *Interview with Daniel Kahneman.* FS Blog, Farnham Street Media Inc.

46   Lakoff, G. (2002), *Moral Politics: How Liberals and Conservatives Think, Third Edition.* University of Chicago Press.

47   Lakoff, G. (2004). *Don't think of an elephant! Know your values and frame your debate: The essential guide for progressives.* Chelsea Green Publishing.

48   Lakoff, G. & Turner, M. (1989). *More than cool reason: a field guide to poetic methaphor.* University of Chicago Press.

49   Benson, B.r (2016/2019 update). Cognitive bias cheat sheet. https://medium.com/better-humans/cognitive-bias-cheat-sheet-55a472476b18

50   Benson, B. (2016/2019 update). Cognitive bias cheat sheet. https://medium.com/better-humans/cognitive-bias-cheat-sheet-55a472476b18

51   https://www.beforetheflood.com/

52   http://www.jamiesfoodrevolution.org/

53   https://kahneman.socialpsychology.org/

54   Kahneman, Daniel (2011). *We're blind to our blindness. We have very little idea of what we know. We're not designed to.* Independent Press.

55   Christensen, C.M. (1997., *The innovator's dilemma: when new technologies cause great firms to fail,* Boston, Massachusetts, USA: Harvard Business School Press.

56   Christensen, C.M., Dilion, K., Hall, T., Duncan, D. (2016). *Know your customer's Job To Be Done,* Harvard Business Review.

57   Christensen, C.M., Dilion, K., Hall, T., Duncan, D. (2016). *Know your customer's Job To Be Done,* Harvard Business Review.

58   Christensen, C.M., Dilion, K., Hall, T., Duncan, D. (2016). *Know your customer's Job To Be Done,* Harvard Business Review.

59   https://hbswk.hbs.edu/item/clay-christensens-milkshake-marketing

60   Lewin, K. (1948). *Resolving Social Conflicts.* New York: Harper and Row Publishers.

61   Parrish, S. (2019). Interview with Daniel Kahneman. FS Blog, Farnham Street Media Inc.

62   Lewin, K. (1948). *Resolving Social Conflicts.* New York: Harper and Row Publishers, page 47.

63   https://conversionxl.com/

64   Benartzi, S., Lewin, R. & Iyengar, S. (2012). *Save more tomorrow. Practical behavioural finance solutions to improve 401(K) plans.* Penguin Publishers.

65   Iyengar, S. (2011). *How to make choosing easier.* TEDSalonNY, 10.50 min.

66   Wetenschappelijke Raad voor het Regeringsbeleid (2017). *Weten is nog geen doen. Een realistisch perspectief of redzaamheid.*

67   https://www.ycombinator.com/

68   https://en.wikipedia.org/wiki/Habit

69   https://www.helpscout.com/blog/customer-interview/

70   https://innovationbubble.eu/clients-customer/

71   Camerer, C., Babcock, L., Loewenstein, G. & Thaler, R. (1997). Labor supply of New York City Cabdrivers: 'One Day at the Time'. *The Quarterly Journal of Economics*. May 1997.

72   Kelley, T.E. (2008). *Innovation with fresh eyes.* Stanford Technology Ventures Program, https://ecorner.stanford.edu/video/field-observations-with-fresh-eyes/

73   https://www.youtube.com/watch?v=TaUlBYqGuiE&t=2s

74   https://www.edge.org/conversation/rory_sutherland-things-to-hang-on-your-mental-mug-tree

75   Bock, L. (2017). *Work Rules. That will transform how you live and lead.* John Murray Press.

76   Ariely, D., Bareket-Bojmel, L. & Hochman, G. (2014). Its (not) all about the Jacksons: Testing different types of short-term bonuses in the field. *Journal of Management*, Volume: 43 issue: 2, page(s): 534-554.

77   https://hbr.org/2012/09/the-secret-phrase-top-innovato

78   https://www.slideshare.net/aipmm/70-26633757

79   https://busterbenson.com/blog/2013/08-24-live-like-a-hydra/

80   https://www.bankofamerica.com/deposits/keep-the-change/

81   https://www.designbetter.co/design-thinking/empathize

82   https://www.behaviormodel.org/b-map

83   Thaler, R. H. (2018). *Nudge, not sludge.* Science, 361(6401), 431.

84   Berger, J. (2020). *The Catalyst: How to change anyone's mind.* Simon & Schuster.

85   Rogers, E.M. (2003). *Diffusion of innovations* (5th ed.). New York: Free Press.

86   Kahneman, D. (2012). *Thinking, Fast and Slow*, Macmillan.

87   https://articles.uie.com/three_hund_million_button/

88   Ly, K.; Nina, M., Zhao, M., Soman, D. (2013). *A practitioner's guide to nudging.* Rotman School of Management, University of Toronto.

89   Bettinger, Long, Oreopoulos, & Sanbonmatsu. (2009).

90   Waterpebble – your little water saver. (n.d.). http:// www.waterpebble.com. Retrieved February 6, 2013.

91   http://littlelonger.nl/92   https://www.businessinsider.com/good-habits-even-when-youre-lazy-2017-1?op=1

93   https://en.wikipedia.org/wiki/Fundamental_attribution_error

94   Parrish, S. (2019). *Interview with Daniel Kahneman.* FS Blog, Farnham Street Media Inc.

95   https://www.behaviormodel.org/

96   https://www.nrc.nl/nieuws/1991/12/16/vlieg-in-de-pot-6990663-a969231

97   Research of the Hogeschool van Amsterdam.

98   https://www.autoremarketing.com/subprime/commentary-simple-effective-behavio-ral-based-move-reduce-default-rates?

99   https://www.autoremarketing.com/subprime/commentary-simple-effective-behavio-ral-based-move-reduce-default-rates?

100   https://www.today.com/parents/girl-scout-sells-300-boxes-cookies-outside-marijuana-dispensary-6-t122455

101   Taylor, K.K., Gibbs, A.S. & Slate, J.R. (2000). Preschool attendance and kindergarten readiness. *Early Childhood Education Journal*, 27(3), 191-195.

102   Ansari, A. & Purtell, K. (2018). School absenteeism through the transition to kindergarten. *Journal of Education for Students Placed at Risk* (JESPAR) 24–38.

103   Mateo-Berganza Díaz, M.M, Becerra, L., Hernández Agramonte, J.M., López Bóo, F. & Pérez Alfaro, M., Vasquez Echeverria, A. (2020). *Nudging Parents to Increase Preschool Attendance in Uruguay.* Inter - American Development Bank Education Division Social Protection and Health Division.

104   Retrieved at: https://www.bhub.org/project/nudging-parents-to-improve-preschool-attendance/

105   Pop-Eleches, C. Thirumurthy, H., Habyarimana J.P., et al. (2000). *Mobile phone technologies improve adherence to antiretroviral treatment in a resource-limited setting: a randomized controlled trial of text message reminders.* AIDS. 2011;25(6):825-834.

106   Ideas42 (2017). *Encouraging Diabetics to Use Statins: Nudging for Long-Term Health.* Retrieved by: http://www.ideas42.org/wp-content/uploads/2015/08/Project-Brief_Statins.pdf

107   https://byronsharp.wordpress.com/2011/03/26/mental-availability-is-not-awareness-brand-salience-is-not-awareness/

108   Lally P, Chipperfield, A. & Wardle, J. (2008), Healthy habits: efficacy of simple advice on weight control based on a habit-formation model. *International Journal of Obesity*, 32 (4). and McGowan L., Cooke L.J., Croker H., et al. (2012). Habit-formation as a novel theoretical framework for dietary change in pre-schoolers. *Psychological Health,* 27:89.

109   Lally P., Wardle J. & Gardner B (2011). Experiences of habit formation: a qualitative study. *Psychological Health Medicine*, Aug; 16(4):484-9.

110   https://jamesclear.com/procrastination

111   Hidi, S. & Boscolo, P. (2007). *Writing and motivation.* Emerald Group Publishing Limited, Bingley.

112   Currey, M. (2013). *Daily rituals: how artists work.* Picador, Main Market Edition.

113   Clear, J. (2018). *Atomic Habits. An Easy & Proven Way to Build Good Habits & Break Bad Ones.* Random House.

114   Clear, J. (2018). *Atomic Habits. An Easy & Proven Way to Build Good Habits & Break Bad Ones.* Avery.

115   Neal, D.T., Wood, W., Labrecque, J.S. & Lally, P. (2012). How do habits guide behavior? Perceived and actual triggers of habits in daily life. *Journal of Experimental Social Psychology* 48:492–498.

116   Booth, J.N., Chesham, R.A., Brooks, N.E., Gorely, T. & Moran, C.N. (2020). A citizen science study of short physical activity breaks at school : improvements in cognition and wellbeing with self-paced activity. *BMC Med. 2020*;18(62).

117   Booth, J.N., Chesham, R.A., Brooks, N.E., Gorely, T. & Moran, C.N. (2020). A citizen science study of short physical activity breaks at school : improvements in cognition and wellbeing with self-paced activity. *BMC Med. 2020*;18(62).

118   Marchant, E., Todd, C., Stratton, G. & Brophy, S. (2020). The Daily Mile: Whole-school recommendations for implementation and sustainability. A mixed-methods study. *Visram S, ed. PLoS One.* 2020;15(2).

119   Hanckel, B., Ruta, D., Scott, G., Peacock, J.L. & Green, J. (2019). The Daily Mile as a public health interven-
       tion: a rapid ethnographic assessment of uptake and implementation in South London, UK. *BMC Public
       Health*. 2019;19(1).

120   De Jonge, M., Slot-Heijs, J.J., Prins, R.G. & Singh, A.S. (2020). The effect of The Daily Mile on primary
       school children's aerobic fitness levels after 12 weeks: A controlled trial. *Int J Environ Res Public Health*.
       2020;17(7).

121   Slot-Heijs, J.J. & Singh A.S. (2019). *The Daily Mile.*, Mulier Instituut.

122   Marchant, E., Todd, C., Stratton, G. & Brophy, S. (2020). The Daily Mile: Whole-school recommendations
       for implementation and sustainability. A mixed-methods study. Visram S, ed. *PLoS One*. 2020;15(2).

123   Marchant, E., Todd, C., Stratton, G. & Brophy, S. (2020). The Daily Mile: Whole-school recommendations
       for implementation and sustainability. A mixed-methods study. Visram S, ed. *PLoS One*. 2020;15(2).

124   Harris, J., Milnes, L.J. & Mountain, G. (2019). How 'The Daily Mile' works in practice: A process evalua-
       tion in a UK primary school. *Journal of Child Health Care*.

125   Chesham, R.A., Booth, J.N., Sweeney, E.L., et al. (2018). The Daily Mile makes primary school children
       more active, less sedentary and improves their fitness and body composition: A quasi-experimental pilot
       study. *BMC Med*. 2018;16.

126   Morris, J.L., Daly-Smith, A., Archbold, V.S., Wilkins E.L. & McKenna J. (2019). The Daily Mile™ initiative:
       Exploring physical activity and the acute effects on executive function and academic performance in
       primary school children. *Psychol Sport Exerc*. 2019;45.

127   Breheny, K., Passmore, S., Adab, P. et al. (2020). Effectiveness and cost-effectiveness of The Daily Mile on
       childhood weight outcomes and wellbeing: a cluster randomised controlled trial. *International Journal of
       Obesity*.

128   https://thedailymile.co.uk/

129   Lally, P., van Jaarsveld, C.H.M., Potts, H.W.W. & Wardle, J. (2009). How are habits formed: Modelling
       habit formation in the real world. *European Journal of Social Psychology*, volume 40, issue 6, October 2010,
       pages 998-1009.

130   Lally, P., van Jaarsveld, C.H.M., Potts, H.W.W. & Wardle, J. (2009). How are habits formed: Modelling
       habit formation in the real world. *European Journal of Social Psychology*, volume 40, issue 6, October 2010,
       pages 998-1009.

131   https://hbr.org/2002/09/pricing-and-the-psychology-of-consumption.

132   https://hbswk.hbs.edu/item/use-the-psychology-of-pricing-to-keep-customers-returning

133   https://hbr.org/2002/09/pricing-and-the-psychology-of-consumption.

134   https://hbr.org/2002/09/pricing-and-the-psychology-of-consumption.

135   https://hbr.org/2002/09/pricing-and-the-psychology-of-consumption.

136   Cialdini, R.B. (2007). *Influence: the psychology of persuasion*. Harper Business.

137   Schwartz, B. (2004). *The Paradox of Choice: Why More Is Less*. New York: Ecco.

138   Iyengar, S., & Lepper, M. (2000). When choice is demotivating: Can one desire too much of a good thing? *Journal of Personality and Social Psychology*, 79, 995-1006.

139   Brewer, N. T., DeFrank, J. T. & Gilkey, M. B. (2016). Anticipated regret and health behavior: A meta-analysis. *Health Psychology*, 35(11), 1264-1275.

140   Johnson, E. J., Shu, S. B., Dellaert, B. G.C., Fox, C. R., Goldstein, D. G., Häubl, G., Larrick, R. P., Payne, J. W., Peters, E., Schkade, D., Wansink, B. & Weber, E. U. (2012). Beyond nudges: Tools of a choice architecture. *Marketing Letters*, 23, 487-504.

141   Soman D. (2021). *Behavioural Economics in action*. University of Toronto, on EdX.

142   Soman D. (2021). *Behavioural Economics in action*. University of Toronto, on EdX.

143   Soman D. (2021). *Behavioural Economics in action*. University of Toronto, on EdX.

144   Iyengar, S. (2010). *The Art of Choosing: The Decisions We Make Every day - What They Say About Us and How We Can Improve Them*. Hachette UK.

145   Schwartz, B. (2004). *The paradox of choice: Why more is less*. New York: Ecco.

146   Iyengar, S.S. & Lepper, M.M. (2000). When choice is demotivating: can one desire too much of a good thing? *Journal of Social Psychology*, 995-1006.

147   Chernev, A., Böckenholt, U. & Goodman, J. (2016). Corrigendum to choice overload: A conceptual review and meta-analysis. *Journal of Consumer Psychology*, Volume 26, Issue 2, April 2016, Pages 333-358.

148   Thaler, R. H., & Sunstein, C. R. (2008). *Nudge: Improving decisions about health, wealth, and happiness*. Yale University Press.

149   https://www.ted.com/talks/sheena_iyengar_how_to_make_choosing_easier

150   Kahneman, D. (2012). *Thinking, Fast and Slow*, Macmillan.

151   Kahneman, D. (2012). *Thinking, Fast and Slow*, Macmillan.

152   https://fairfuneralscampaign.org.uk/content/what-funeral-poverty

153   https://content.govdelivery.com/accounts/NVLASVEGAS/bulletins/24c4a39

154   http://www.howtogetyourownway.com/effects/rhyme_as_reason_effect.html

155   https://www.abc.net.au/education/learn-english/rhyming-expressions-in-everyday-english/10509964

156   McGlone, M. S., & Tofighbakhsh, J. (2000). Birds of a Feather Flock Conjointly (?): Rhyme as Reason in Aphorisms. *Psychological Science*, 11(5), 424-428.

157   Trudel, R., Murray, K. B., Kim, S., & Chen, S. (2015). The impact of traffic light color-coding on food health perceptions and choice. *Journal Of Experimental Psychology: Applied*, 21(3), 255-275.

158   Schuldt, J.P. (2013) Does green mean healthy? Nutrition label color affects perceptions of healthfulness. *Health Commun.* 2013;28(8):814-821. doi:10.1080/10410236.2012.725270.

159   Borgmeier, I. & Westenhoefer, J. (2009). Impact of different food label formats on healthiness evaluation and food choice of consumers: a randomized-controlled study. *BMC Public Health.* 2009;9:184. Published 2009 Jun 12. doi:10.1186/1471-2458-9-[184] United Nations Environment Programme, GRIDArendal and Behavioural Insights Team (2020). *The Little Book of Green Nudges: 40 Nudges to Spark Sustainable Behaviour on Campus*. Nairobi and Arendal: UNEP and GRID-Arendal.

160   Geier, A., Wansink, B., & Rozin, P., 'Red potato chips: Segmentation cues can substantially decrease food intake.' *Health Psychol.* 2012 May; 31(3):398-401.

161   Stanford Medicine (2018), special report 'Soundwaves, the art and science of hearing'.

162   Goldhill, O. (2019, July 31). *Politicians love nudge theory. But beware its doppelgänger "sludge"*. Quartz.

163   Gunnell, D., Murray, V. & Hawton, K. (2000). Use of paracetamol (acetaminophen) for suicide and non-fatal poisoning: Worldwide patterns of use and misuse. *Suicide and Life-Threatening Behavior*, 2000; 30(4): 313–26.

164   Hawton, K., Ware, C., Mistry, H., Hewitt, J., Kingsbury, S., Roberts, D. & Weitzel, H. (1996). Paracetamol self-poisoning: Characteristics, prevention and harm reduction. *The British Journal of Psychiatry*, 1996; 168(1): 43–8.

165   Hawton, K., Bergen, H., Simkin, S., Dodd, S., Pocock, P., Bernal, W. & Kapur, N. (2013). Long term effect of reduced pack sizes of paracetamol on poisoning deaths and liver transplant activity in England and Wales: Interrupted time series analyses. *BMJ*, 2013; 346: f403.

166   Hallsworth, M., Snijders, V., Burd, H. et al. (2016). Applying behavioural insights. Simple ways to improve health outcomes. Report of the WISH (world innovation summit for health) Behavioral Insights Forum 2016.

167   Yip, P.S., Caine, E., Yousuf, S., Chang, S.S., Wu, K.C.C. & Chen, Y.Y., Means restriction for suicide prevention. *The Lancet*, 2012; 379(9834): 2393–9.

168   https://www.hetkanwel.nl/2019/04/27/containertuintjes-zorgen-voor-minder-afval-rondom-containers/?fbclid=IwAR2ZyHkypmFx_WuieENaQVsb7_8YSIUFbjlC4rvoi6aUeqEMOsC4pXmwZ5c

169   https://www.deingenieur.nl/artikel/3d-zebrapad-remt-auto-s-af

170   Caird. S., Roy, R. & Herring, H. (2008). Improving the energy performance of UK households: results from surveys of consumer adoption and use of low- and zero carbon technologies. *Energy Efficiency*, 1(2): 149–66.

171   Behavioural Insights Team, cabinet office. *Behaviour change and energy use*, page 12.

172   https://greencampus.ucc.ie/

173   United Nations Environment Programme, GRIDArendal and Behavioural Insights Team (2020). *The Little Book of Green Nudges: 40 Nudges to Spark Sustainable Behaviour on Campus*. Nairobi and Arendal: UNEP and GRID-Arendal.

174   Retrieved by: https://www.aalto.fi/en/services/campus-bikes-and-cycling

175   www.fanpop.com, Disney Aqua.

176   Ariely, D. (2008). *Predictably Irrational*, HarperCollins.

177   Cialdini, R. (2009). *Influence: Science and Practice.* Boston, MA: Pearson Education.

178   Winterowd, W.R. (1985). 'Kenneth Burke: An Annotated Glossary of His Terministic Screen and a "Statistical" Survey of His Major Concepts'. *Rhetoric Society Quarterly*, Vol. 15, No. 3/4 (Summer - Autumn, 1985), pp. 145-177.

179   Luntz, F. (2008). *Words that work: It's not what you say, it's what people hear.* Hachette Books.

180   https://lotta.se/mission-statement-generator/

181   https://quitnow.smokefree.nhs.uk/

182   https://ghost.org/changelog/ghost-onboarding

183   www.mixergy.com, Andrew Warner "Interview: HelloWallet: 0 to 300,000 Paid Subscribers In 5 Months – with Matt Fellowes", 29th November 2011; http://hrpost.hellowallet.com/engagement/webinar-recording-tips-for-effective-employee-emails/

184   Mathy, F. & Feldman, J. (2012). What's magic about magic numbers? Chunking and data compression in short-term memory. *Cognition*, 122(3), 346-362.

185   Miller, G. A. (1956). The magical number seven, plus or minus two: some limits on our capacity for processing information. *Psychological Review*, 63(2), 81-97.

186   Mathy, F. & Feldman, J. (2012). What's magic about magic numbers? Chunking and data compression in short-term memory. *Cognition*, 122(3), 346-362.

187   Leventhal, H., & Singer, R, & Jones, S. (1965). Effects of fear and specificity of recommendation upon attitudes and behavior. *Journal of personality and social psychology*. 34. 20-9.

188   Wee, Z.Q.C. & Dillon D. Increasing Physical Exercise through Action and Coping Planning. *Int J Environ Res Public Health*. 2022 Mar 24;19(7)

189   https://thebikeproject.co.uk/pages/cycle-training-for-refugee-women

190   https://cdn.shopify.com/s/files/1/0815/1355/files/2019_Pedal_Power_Report_FINAL.pdf?v=1586953467

191   https://thebikeproject.co.uk/

192   https://readingpartners.org/

193   https://www.nursefamilypartnership.org/

194   http://danariely.com/2010/08/30/back-to-school-2/

195   Martin, S.J., Bassi, S. & Dunbar-Rees, R. (2012). Commitment, Norms, and custard creams. A social influence approach to reducing did not attends (DNAs). *Journal of the Royal Society of Medicine*, Mar; 105(3): 101-104.

196   https://www.ncbi.nlm.nih.gov/pmc/articles/PMC3308641/

197   https://www.ncbi.nlm.nih.gov/pmc/articles/PMC3308641/

198   https://advanced-hindsight.com/

199   https://blogs.scientificamerican.com/mind-guest-blog/the-deadline-made-me-do-it/

200   Shu, S. & Gneezy, A. (2009). *Procrastination of Enjoyable Experiences*. Journal of Marketing Research. 47.

201   Shu, S. & Gneezy, A. (2009). *Procrastination of Enjoyable Experiences*. Journal of Marketing Research. 47.

202   Solman, D. (2021). *Behavioural economics in action*. Module 1.4. EdX course.

203   Soman, D. & Cheema, A. (2011). Earmarking and Partitioning: Increasing Saving by Low-Income Households. *Journal of Marketing Research*, 48(SPL), S14–S22.

204   Soman, D. & Cheema, A. (2011). Earmarking and Partitioning: Increasing Saving by Low-Income Households. *Journal of Marketing Research*, 48(SPL), S14–S22.

205   Soman, D. & Cheema, A. (2011). Earmarking and Partitioning: Increasing Saving by Low-Income House-
       holds. *Journal of Marketing Research*, 48(SPL), S14–S22.

206   Cheema, A & Soman, D. (2008). The Effect of Partitions on Controlling Consumption. *Journal of Marketing
       Research*. 2008;45(6):665-675.

207   https://en.wikipedia.org/wiki/Social_proof

208   Bond, R. & Smith, P.B. (1996). Culture and conformity: a meta-analysis of studies using Asch's (1952b,
       1956) line judgment task. *Psychological Bulletin*, 119(1): 111–37; Latané, B. (1981). The psychology of social
       impact. *American Psychologist*, 36(4): 343–56; Zaki, J., Schirmer, J. & Mitchell, J.P. (2011). Social influence
       modulates the neural computation of value. *Psychological Science*, in press.

209   https://thedecisionlab.com/biases/bandwagon-effect/

210   Tetlock & Lerner (2002) in *Schneider, ed. by Sandra L.; Shanteau, James (2003). Emerging perspectives on
       judgment and decision research. Cambridge [u.a.]: Cambridge Univ. Press. pp. 438–9.*

211   Cherry, K. (2020, April 28). The Bandwagon Effect Is Why People Fall for Trends. Retrieved July 05,
       2020, from https://www.verywellmind.com/what-is-the-bandwagon-effect-2795895

212   Kiss, Á. & Simonovits, G. (1996). Identifying the bandwagon effect in two-round elections. *Public Choice*.
       2013;160(3-4):327-344.

213   Morwitz, V.G. & Pluzinski, C. (1996). Do polls reflect opinions or do opinions reflect polls? The impact
       of political polling on voters' expectations, preferences, and behavior. *Journal of Consumer Research*.
       1996;23(1):53–67.

214   Benecke, O. & DeYoung, S.E. (2019). Anti-vaccine decision-making and measles resurgence in the United
       States. *Global Pediatric Health*.

215   https://thedecisionlab.com/biases/bandwagon-effect/

216   https://brainworldmagazine.com/mob-mentality-the-madness-of-the-crowd/

217   https://www.influenceatwork.com/principles-of-persuasion/

218   The Behavioral Insights Team. (2013). *Applying behavioural insights to charitable giving*. Retrieved from:
       https://www.gov.uk/government/uploads/system/uploads/attachment_data/file/203286/BIT_Charita-
       ble_Giving_Paper.pdf

219   https://www.brightlocal.com/research/local-consumer-review-survey/.

220   Goldstein, N.J., Cialdini, R.B. & Griskevicius, V. (2018). A Room with a Viewpoint: Using Social Norms to
       Motivate Environmental Conservation in Hotels. *Journal of Consumer Research*, 35(3), 472-482.

221   Platow, M.J. Haslam, S.A., Both, A., Chew, I. Cuddon, M. Goharpey, N., Maurer, J., Rosini, S., Tsekouras, A.
       & Grace, D.M. (2005). It's not funny if they're laughing: Self-categorization, social influence, and respons-
       es to canned laughter. *Journal of Experimental Social Psychology*, Volume 41, Issue 5, 2005, Pages 542-550.

222   Provine, R.R. (1996). Laughter. *American Scientist*, 84, 38–45.

223   Cialdini, R.B. (1993). *Social influence: Science and practice* (3rd ed.). New York: Harper Collins.

224   Turner, J.C. & Oakes, P. J. (1989). Self-categorization theory and social influence. *In P. B. Paulus (Ed.), The
       psychology of group influence* (2nd ed., pp. 233–275). Hillsdale, NJ: Erlbaum.

225   Platow, M.J. Haslam, S.A., Both, A., Chew, I. Cuddon, M. Goharpey, N., Maurer, J., Rosini, S., Tsekouras, A. & Grace, D.M. (2005). It's not funny if they're laughing: Self-categorization, social influence, and responses to canned laughter. *Journal of Experimental Social Psychology*, Volume 41, Issue 5, 2005, Pages 542-550.

226   Platow, M.J. Haslam, S.A., Both, A., Chew, I. Cuddon, M. Goharpey, N., Maurer, J., Rosini, S., Tsekouras, A. & Grace, D.M. (2005). It's not funny if they're laughing: Self-categorization, social influence, and responses to canned laughter. *Journal of Experimental Social Psychology*, Volume 41, Issue 5, 2005, Pages 542-550.

227   Berger, J. (2020). *Removing barrier to change*. Wharton Business School of the Universit of Pennsylvania, Coursera.

228   Sivers, D. (2015). *How to start a movement*. TEDTalks.

229   Verplanken, B. & Orbell, S. (2003). Reflections on Past Behaviour: A Self-Report of Habit Strength. *Journal of Applied Social Psychology* 33, 6, pp. 1313-1330.

230   Rogers, T., Ternovski, J. & Yoel, E. (2016). Potential follow-up increases private contributions to public goods. *PNAS*, 113 (19).

231   Bursztyn, L. & Jensen, R. (2016). Social Image and Economic Behavior in the Field: Identifying, Understanding and Shaping Social Pressure. *Annual Review of Economics*, Vol. 9 (2017).

232   Funk, P. (2010). Social Incentives and Voter Turnout: Evidence from the Swiss Mail Ballot System. *Journal of the European Economic Association*, 2010,8(5), 1077–1103.

233   Kettle, S., Hernandez, M., Ruda, S. & Sanders, M. (2016). *Behavioral Interventions in Tax Compliance: Evidence from Guatemala*. The World Bank.

234   Rind, B. & Bordia, P. (1996). Effect on restaurant tipping of male and female servers drawing a happy, smiling face on the backs of customers' checks. *Journal of Applied Social Psychology*, 26, 218-225.

235   Lynn, M., Le, J. & Sherwyn, D S. (1998). Reach out and touch your customers. *Cornell Hotel and Restaurant Administration Quarterly*, 39 (3), 60-65.

236   Lynn, M., & Mynier, K. (1993). Effect of server posture on restaurant tipping. *Journal of Applied Social Psychology*, 23, 678-685.

237   Crusco, A.H., & Wetzel, C.G. (1984). The Midas touch: The effects of interpersonal touch on restaurant tipping. *Personality and Social Psychology Bulletin*, 10, 512-517.

238   https://unbounce.com/conversion-rate-optimization/design-call-to-action-buttons.

239   Mogollón, M., Ortega, D, & Scartascini, C. (2019). *Who's Calling?: The Effect of Phone Calls and Personal Interaction on Tax Compliance*. Inter-American Development Bank.

240   Doctor, J.N., Nguyen, A., Lev, R., Lucas, J., Knight, T., Zhao, H. &l Menchine, M. (2018). Opioid prescribing decreases after learning of a patient's fatal overdose. *Science*, 10 Aug 2018 : 588-590.

241   https://www.povertyactionlab.org/evaluation/assessing-effectiveness-alternative-text-messages-improve-collection-delinquent-fines

242   Ortega, D. & Scartascini, C. (2015). *Don't Blame the Messenger: A Field Experiment on Delivery Methods for Increasing Tax Compliance*. Inter-American Development Bank, IDB Working Paper Series ; 627.

243   Aggarwal, P. & McGill, A.L. (2007). Is that car smiling at me? Schema congruity as a basis for evaluating anthropomor-phized products. *Journal of Consumer Research*, 34, 468–479.

244   Ahn H-K., Kim H.J., Aggarwal, P. (2014) Helping Fellow Beings: Anthropomorphized Social Causes and the Role of Anticipatory Guilt. *Psychological Science.*

245   Ahn H-K, Kim HJ, Aggarwal P. (2014). Helping Fellow Beings: Anthropomorphized Social Causes and the Role of Anticipatory Guilt. *Psychological Science.* 25(1):224-229.

246   Morewedge, C.K., Preston, J., & Wegner, D.M. (2007). Timescale bias in the attribution of mind. *Journal of Personality and Social Psychology*, 93, 1–11.

247   The Behavioral Insights Team (2016). *Behavioral Insights for Cities.* Retrieved by: https://www.bi.team/wp-content/uploads/2016/10/Behavioral-Insights-for-Cities-2.pdf

248   Yeager, D.S., & Dweck, C.S. (2012). Mindsets that promote resilience: When students believe that personal characteristics can be developed. *Educational Psychologist*, 47(4), 302-314.

249   Tversky, A. & Kahneman, D. (1981). The Framing of decisions and the psychology of choice. *Science.* 211 (4481): 453–58.

250   Levin, I.P., & Gaeth, G.J. (1988). How consumers are affected by the framing of attribute information before and after consuming the product. *Journal of Consumer Research*, 15(3), 374-378.

251   Holzwarth, A. Berman, C.J., Schwartz, J., Schanbacher, A., Juarez, L., Mathera, R., Lindemans, J.W., Beasley, M. & Ariely, D. (2020). *Applying Behavioral Science to Health and Financial Decisions. Five Case Studies on the Impact of Framing on Real-World Decisions.* Center for Advanced Hindsight.

252   Brune, L., Giné, X., Goldberg, J., & Yang, D. (2011). *Commitments to save: A field experiment in rural Malawi.* The World Bank.

253   McCarthy, J. (2018, December 10). *Six in 10 Americans worry about higher healthcare premiums.* Retrieved from https://news.gallup.com/poll/245312/six-americans-worry-higher-healthcare-premiums.aspx. and Gallup (2019). *Honesty/ethics in professions.* Retrieved from https://news.gallup.com/poll/1654/honesty-ethics-professions.aspx.

254   Berman, C. J., O'Brien, J. D., Zenko, Z., & Ariely, D. (2019). The limits of cognitive reappraisal: Changing pain valence, but not persistence during a resistance exercise task. *International Journal of Environmental Research and Public Health*, 16(19), 3739.

255   Gross, J. J., & Thompson, R.A. (2007). Emotion regulation: Conceptual foundations. *In J.J. Gross (Ed.), Handbook of Emotion Regulation (pp. 3-24).* New York, NY: The Guilford Press.

256   Rhodes, R.E., & Kates, A. (2015). Can the affective response to exercise predict future motives and physical activity behavior? A systematic review of published evidence. *Annals of Behavioral Medicine,* 49(5), 715-731.

257   Nemeth, C., Personnaz, B., Personnaz, M, & Goncalo, J. (2004). The liberating role of conflict in group creativity: A study in two countries. *European Journal of Social Psychology*, 34. 365-374.

258   http://www.poverty-action.org/study/recruiting-and-motivating-community-health-workers-zambia

259 Kahneman, D. & Tversky, A. (1977). *Prospect Theory. An Analysis of Decision Making Under Risk*. doi:10.21236/ ada045771.

260 Thaler, R. H. (1999). Mental accounting matters. *Journal of Behavioral Decision Making*, 12, 183-206.

261 http://www.eief.it/butler/files/2009/11/thaler80.pdf

262 Kahneman, D. & Tversky, A. (1982). The psychology of preference. *Scientific American*, 246, 160-173.

263 Carmon, Z., Wertenbroch, K. & Zeelenberg, M. (2003). Option attachment: When deliberating makes choosing feel like losing. *Journal of Consumer Research*, Jun 2003; 30, 1; ABI/INFORM Global, page 15.

264 Tay, S.W., Ryan, P., Ryan, C.A. (2016-10-18). "Systems 1 and 2 thinking processes and cognitive reflection testing in medical students". *Canadian Medical Education Journal*. 7 (2): e97–e103.

265 Sumitava Mukherjee, Arvind Sahay, V. S. Chandrasekhar Pammi, Narayanan Srinivasan (2017). Is loss-aversion magnitude-dependent? Measuring prospective affective judgments regarding gains and losses. *Judgment and Decision Making*, Vol. 12, No. 1, January 2017, pp. 81-89.

266 Wang, M., Rieger, M.O., & Hens, T. (2016). The Impact of Culture on Loss aversion. *Journal of Behavioral Decision Making*, 30(2), 270-281.

267 Bontempo, R.N., Bottom, W. P., & Weber, E. U. (1997). Cross-cultural differences in risk perception: A model-based approach. *Risk Analysis*, 17(4), 479–488.

268 Fernández, C. R. (2019). *New Results Show GM Mosquitoes Keep Dengue and Zika at Bay in Brazil*. Retrieved from https://www.labiotech.eu/medical/oxitec-dengue-zika-brazil/

269 Fernández, C. R. (2019). *New Results Show GM Mosquitoes Keep Dengue and Zika at Bay in Brazil*. Retrieved from https://www.labiotech.eu/medical/oxitec-dengue-zika-brazil/

270 Inesi, M. (2010). Power and Loss aversion. *Organizational Behavior and Human Decision Processes*, 112, 58–69.

271 Tanaka, T., Camerer, C., and Nguyen, Q. (2010). Risk and time preferences: Linking experimental and household survey data from Vietnam. *American Economic Review*, 100 (1), 557–71.

272 The Behavioural Insights Team. *EAST. Four simple ways to apply behavioural insights*. Retrieved by: https:// www.behaviouralinsights.co.uk/wp-content/uploads/2015/07/BIT-Publication-EAST_FA_WEB.pdf.

273 Behavioural Insights Team (2012). *Applying Behavioural Insights to Reduce Fraud, Debt and Error*. Cabinet Office.

274 www.stickk.com. The program was founded by Dean Karlan, a Professor of Behavioral Economics at Yale University and Ian Ayres, a Professor at Yale Law School.

275 Banks, S.M., Salovey, P., Greener, S., Rothman, A J., Beauvais, J., & Epel, E. (1995). The effects of message framing on mammography utilization. *Health Psychology*, 14,178-184. Retrieved from: IDB Behavioral Economics for Better Public Policies, edition 2.

276 Banks, S.M., Salovey, P., Greener, S., Rothman, A.J., Beauvais, J., & Epel, E. (1995). The effects of message framing on mammography utilization. *Health Psychology*, 14,178-184. Retrieved from: http://ei.yale.edu/ wp-content/uploads/2014/03/The-effects-of-message-framing-on-mammography-utilization.pdf.

277   Novemsky N, Kahneman D. (2005). The Boundaries of Loss Aversion. *Journal of Marketing Research*. 2005;42(2):119-128.

278   Levin, I.P., Schneider, S.L., & Gaeth, G.J. (1998). All Frames Are Not Created Equal: A Typology and Critical Analysis of Framing Effects. *Organizational Behavior and Human Decision Processes*,76 (2), 149-188.

279   Homonoff, T.A. (2018). Can Small Incentives Have Large Effects? The Impact of Taxes versus Bonuses on Disposable Bag Use. *American Economic Journal: Economic Policy*, 10 (4): 177-210.

280   Taylor, R.L. & Villas-Boas, S.B. (2016). Bans vs. Fees: Disposable Carryout Bag Policies and Bag Usage. *Applied Economic Perspectives and Policy*, Volume 38, Issue 2, June 2016, Pages 351–372.

281   O'Donoghue, T. & Rabin, M. (1999). Doing it now or later. *American Economic Review*, 89(1), 103-124.

282   Bickel, W., Odum, A. & Madden, G. (1999). Impulsivity and cigarette smoking: Delay discounting in current, never, and ex-smokers. *Psychopharmacology*, 146(4),447-454.

283   Bickel, W.K., Odum, A.L., & Madden, G.J. (1999). Impulsivity and cigarette smoking: Delay discounting in current, never, and ex-smokers. *Psychopharmacology*,146(4), 447-454.

284   Prospect Theory and Loss Aversion: How Users Make Decisions. (n.d.). Retrieved July 11, 2020, from https://www.nngroup.com/articles/prospect-theory/

285   Sheffer, C.E., Mackillop, J., Fernandez, A., Christensen, D., Bickel, W.K., Johnson, M.W., ... & Mathew, M. (2016). Initial examination of priming tasks to decrease delay discounting. *Behavioural Processes*, 128, 144-152.

286   https://open.spotify.com/track/6WfL1pwMyFf3IvFWLnre4P?si=F9WwvOwCSmGNAV9fIJ2I2w

287   Sheffer, C.E., Mackillop, J., Fernandez, A., Christensen, D., Bickel, W.K., Johnson, M.W. & Mathew, M. (2016). Initial examination of priming tasks to decrease delay discounting. *Behavioural Processes*, 128, 144-152.

288   Loewenstein, G. & Thaler, R.H. (1989). Anomalies: Intertemporal Choice. *The Journal of Economic Perspectives*, vol. 3, no. 4, 1989, pp. 181–193. *JSTOR*, www.jstor.org/stable/1942918. Accessed 26 Nov. 2020.

289   https://www.kiva.org/borrow

290   https://www.justgiving.com/

291   Karlan, D. & List, J.A. (2007). Does Price Matter in Charitable Giving? Evidence from a Large-Scale Natural Field Experiment. *American Economic Review*, 97 (5): 1774-1793.

292   https://hbr.org/2002/12/the-competitive-advantage-of-corporate-philanthropy

293   Nunes, J.C. & Drèze, X. (2006). The Endowed Progress Effect: How Artificial Advancement Increases Effort. *Journal of Consumer Research*, Vol. 32, March 2006.

294   Retrieved from: https://zapier.com/blog/endowed-progress-effect/

295   Fielding, K., Russell, S, Spinks, A, Mccrea, R, Stewart, R, & Gardner, J. (2012). *Water End Use Feedback Produces Long-Term Reductions in Residential Water Demand.*

296   Hull, C.L. (1932). The goal-gradient hypothesis and maze learning. *Psychological Review*, 39(1), 25–43.

297   Tversky, A. & Kahneman, D. (1974). Judgment under Uncertainty: Heuristics and Biases. *Science*, 185 (4157), 1124-1131.

298   Ariely, D. (2009). *Predictably Irrational. The hidden forces that shape our decisions.* Harper.

299   Teach, E. (2004). Avoiding Decision Traps, *CFO,* 1 June 2004.

300   Furnham, A., & Boo, H. C. (2011). A literature review of the anchoring effect. *The Journal of Socio-Economics,* 40(1), 35-42.

301   Mussweiler, T. & Strack, F. (1999). Hypothesis-Consistent Testing and Semantic Priming in the Anchoring Paradigm: A Selective Accessibility Model. *Journal of Experimental Social Psychology.* 35 (2): 136–164.

302   Mussweiler, T. & Strack, F. *(1999).* Hypothesis-Consistent Testing and Semantic Priming in the Anchoring Paradigm: A Selective Accessibility Model. *Journal of Experimental Social Psychology, 35 (2): 136–164.*

303   Scott, P. J. & Lizieri, C. (2012). Consumer house price judgments: New evidence of anchoring and arbitrary coherence. *Journal of Property Research, 29,* 49-68.

304   Wansink, B., Kent, R.J., & Hoch, S.J. (1998). An anchoring and adjustment model of purchase quantity decisions. *Journal of Marketing Research, 35* (1), 71–81.

305   Englich, B. et al. (2006). Playing Dice With Criminal Sentences: The Influence of Irrelevant Anchors on Experts' Judicial Decision Making. *Personality and Social Psychology Bulletin, 32* (2006): 188 - 200.

306   Chapman, G.B., & Bornstein, B.H. (1996). The more you ask for, the more you get: Anchoring in personal injury verdicts. *Applied Cognitive Psychology,* 10 (6), 519-540.

307   Chapman, G.B., & Bornstein, B.H. (1996). The more you ask for, the more you get: Anchoring in personal injury verdicts. *Applied Cognitive Psychology,* 10 (6), 519-540.

308   Retrieved from: Poundstone, W. (2010). *Priceless. The Hidden Psychology of Value.* Oneworld Publications.

309   Englich, Bi., Mussweiler, T. & Strack, F (2006). Playing Dice With Criminal Sentences: The Influence of Irrelevant Anchors on Experts' Judicial Decision Making. *Personality & Social Psychology Bulletin,* 32, 188-200.

310   Ariely, D., Loewenstein, G., & Prelec, D. (2006). Tom Sawyer and the Construction of Value. *Journal of Economic Behavior and Organization,* Vol. 60: 1-10.

311   Ariely, D., Loewenstein, G., & Prelec, D. (2003). Coherent Arbitrariness: Stable Demand Curves without Stable Preferences. *Quarterly Journal of Economics,* Vol. 118, No. 1: 73105.

312   Dooley, R. (2008, July 18). Anchor Pricing Strategies. *Neuromarketing.* Retrieved November 11, 2013, from https://www.neurosciencemarketing.com

313   Barrio, P.J., Goldstein, D.G. & Hofman, J.M. (2015). *Improving the Comprehension of Numbers in the News.* Columbia.edu papers. Retrieved by: http://cj2015.brown.columbia.edu/papers/numbers-in-news.pdf

314   'Amazon Mechanical Turk is a crowdsourcing website for businesses (known as Requesters) to hire remotely located "crowd workers" to perform discrete on-demand tasks that computers are currently unable to do'. Retrieved by:

315   Barrio, P.J., Goldstein, D.G. & Hofman, J.M. (2015). *Improving the Comprehension of Numbers in the News.* Columbia.edu papers. Retrieved by: http://cj2015.brown.columbia.edu/papers/numbers-in-news.pdf

316   https://open.nytimes.com/we-built-a-plugin-but-its-not-a-secret

317 Mussweiler, T., Strack, F. & Pfeiffer, T. (2000). Overcoming the Inevitable Anchoring Effect: Considering the Opposite Compensates for Selective Accessibility. *Personality and Social Psychology Bulletin, 26*, 1142-1150.

318 Mussweiler, T., Strack, F. & Pfeiffer, T. (2000). Overcoming the Inevitable Anchoring Effect: Considering the Opposite Compensates for Selective Accessibility. *Personality and Social Psychology Bulletin*, 26. 1142-1150.

319 Koriat, A., Lichtenstein, S. & Fischhoff, B. (1980). Reasons for confidence. *Journal of Experimental Psychology: Human Learning and Memory*, 6, 107-118.

320 Davies, M.F. (1992). Field dependence and hindsight bias: Cognitive restructuring and the generation of reasons. *Journal of Research in Personality, 26*, 58-74.

321 https://en.wikipedia.org/wiki/Hindsight_bias

322 Chartrand, T.L., & Bargh, J.A. (1996). Automatic activation of impression formation and memorization goals: Nonconscious goal priming reproduces effects of explicit task instructions. *Journal of Personality and Social Psychology*, 71(3), 464–478.

323 Bargh, J.A., Chen, M. & Burrows, L. (1996). Automaticity of social behavior: Direct effects of trait construct and stereotype activation on action. *Journal of Personality and Social Psychology*, 71, 230-244.

324 Wryobeck, J. and Chen, Y. (2003), *Using Priming Techniques to Facilitate Health Behaviours.* Clinical Psychologist, 7: 105-108.

325 Friedman, R., & Elliot, A.J. (2008). Exploring the influence of sports drink exposure on physical endurance. *Psychology of Sport and Exercise*, 9(6), 749–759.

326 Bateson, M., Nettle, D., & Roberts, G. (2006). Cues of being watched enhance cooperation in a real-world setting. *Biology letters*, 2(3), 412–414.

327 Wansink, B. & Sobal, J. (2007). Mindless Eating: The 200 Daily Food Decisions We Overlook. *Environment and behaviour*, 39, page 106-123.

328 North, A.C., Hargreaves, D. J., & McKendrick, J. (1997). In-store music affects product choice. *Nature*, 390, 132.

329 Areni, C.S. & Kim, D. (1993). The influence of background music on shopping behavior: classical versus top-forty music in a wine store. *Advances in Consumer Research*, 20, 336-340.

330 North, A. Wine & Song. Retrieved by: https://www.wineanorak.com/musicandwine.pdf

331 Ariely, Dan (2009). *Predictably Irrational. The hidden forces that shape our decisions.* Harper.

332 Aarts, H., Custers, R. & Veltkamp, M. (2008). Goal Priming and the Affective-Motivational Route to Nonconscious Goal Pursuit. *Social Cognition.*

333 Ideas42 (2015). *Increasing FAFSA Applications: Making college more affordable.* December 2015.

334 Ideas42 (2015). *Increasing FAFSA Applications: Making college more affordable.* December 2015.

335 Ideas42 (2015). *Increasing FAFSA Applications: Making college more affordable.* December 2015.

336 Ideas42 (2015). *Increasing FAFSA Applications: Making college more affordable.* December 2015.

337 https://www.theguardian.com/money/2018/jul/02/norway-electric-cars-subsidies-fossil-fuel retrieved by: https://suebehaviouraldesign.com/how-norway-nudges-its-citizens-to-drive-electric/

338 Ries, E. (2011). *The Lean Startup. How Today's Entrepreneurs Use Continuous Innovation to Create Radically Successful Businesses.* Currency.

339 https://www.linkedin.com/pulse/arent-any-typos-essay-we-launched-too-late-reid-hoffman/

340 https://medium.theuxblog.com/11-best-prototyping-tools-for-ui-ux-designers-how-to-choose-the-right-one-c5dc69720c47

341 www.ideo.com

342 https://www.oxfordreference.com/

343 https://www.netflix.com/tudum/articles/jeen-yuhs-directors-coodie-and-chike-talk-documenting-ye

344 https://www.ted.com/

345 Chartrand, T.L. & Bargh, J.A. (1999). The chameleon effect: The perception–behavior link and social interaction. *Journal of Personality and Social Psychology.* 76 (6): 893–910.

346 Chartrand, T.L. & Bargh, J.A. (1999). The chameleon effect: The perception–behavior link and social interaction. *Journal of Personality and Social Psychology.* 76 (6): 893–910.

347 Chartrand, T.L. & Bargh, J.A. (1999). The chameleon effect: The perception–behavior link and social interaction. *Journal of Personality and Social Psychology.* 76 (6): 893–910.

348 Brewer, M.B. (1991). The social self: On being the same and different at the same time. *Personality and Social Psychology Bulletin*, 17, 475-482.

349 Ballew, C.C. 2nd. & Todorov, A. (2007). Predicting political elections from rapid and unreflective face judgments. *Proceedings of the National Academy of Sciences of the United States of America*, vol. 104,46 (2007): 17948-53.

350 https://www.bbc.com/future/article/20171018-the-hidden-ways-that-faces-shape-politics

351 https://www.nationalgeographic.com/science/phenomena/2015/06/09/george-washingtons-oh-so-mysterious-hair/

352 https://www.bbc.com/news/world-us-canada-43981366

353 Bohnet, I. (2016). *What Works. Gender equality by design.* Belknap Press.

354 Levy Paluck, E. & Green, D.P. (2009). *Prejudice Reduction: What Works? A Review and Assessment of Research and Practice.* Annual Review of Psychology, 2009. 60:339–67.

355 https://hbr.org/2016/07/why-diversity-programs-fail

356 Redelmeier, D.A.., Katz, J. & Kahneman, D. (2003). *Memories of colonoscopy: a randomized trial.* International Association for the Study of Pain. Published by Elsevier Science B.V.

357 Kahneman, D., Fredrickson, B.L., Schreiber, C.A. & Redelmeier, D.A. (1993). When More Pain Is Preferred to Less: Adding a Better End. *Psychological Science.* 4 (6): 401–405.

358 Bateson, M., Nettle, D. & Roberts, G. (2006). Cues of being watched enhance cooperation in a real-world setting. *Biology letters* 2.3.

359 https://www.inc.com/dave-kerpen/you-need-to-become-a-better-storyteller-heres-some-inspiration.
     html

360 Kagan, M. (2016). *How to Create an Awesome Elevator Pitch (in just 5 slides)*. Retrieved by: https://www.
     youtube.com/watch?v=o3Xs8rbwb9Y

361 Webb, C. (2016). *How to have a good day. Harness the power of behavioural science to transform your working life*.
     London: Pan Macmillan.

362 Inspired by: The Reflective Practitioner, Donald A. Schön, 1983

363 http://ethicskit.org/downloads/little-book-of-me.pdf

364 Luft, J. (1969). *Of Human Interaction*. Mayfield Publishing; Luft, J. (1969). *Group Processes. An introduction to
     group dynamics*. National Press Books.

365 Ethical toolkit.org and the BASIC toolkit have inspired our checklist and cards, but we have made them
     relevant for our way of working/company mission. Feel free to use them both and adjust them to your
     mission, as long as you design for good.

366 https://www.youtube.com/watch?v=RHmXPyX7czU&feature=emb_logo